MCSA Managing a Windows® 2000 Network Environment Lab Manual

Student Edition

MCSA Managing a Windows® 2000 Network Environment Lab Manual

Student Edition

Nick LaManna

McGraw-Hill/Osborne

New York Chicago San Francisco Lisbon London Madrid
Mexico City Milan New Delhi San Juan Seoul Singapore Sydney Toronto

McGraw-Hill/Osborne
2600 Tenth Street
Berkeley, California 94710
U.S.A.

To arrange bulk purchase discounts for sales promotions, premiums, or fund-raisers, please contact **McGraw-Hill/**Osborne at the above address. For information on translations or book distributors outside the U.S.A., please see the International Contact Information page immediately following the index of this book.

MCSA Managing a Windows® 2000 Network Environment Lab Manual, Student Edition

1234567890 FGR FGR 0198765432

ISBN 0-07-222479-7

Publisher Brandon A. Nordin	**Project Editor** Mark Karmendy	**Indexer** Jack Lewis
Vice President & **Associate Publisher** Scott Rogers	**Acquisitions Coordinator** Athena Honore	**Computer Designers** Lucie Ericksen, Jean Butterfield
Editorial Director Gareth Hancock	**Technical Editors** Chris Crane, Brian Carroll	**Illustrator** Lyssa Wald
Acquisitions Editor Chris Johnson	**Copy Editor** Dennis Weaver	**Series Design** Roberta Steele
	Proofreader Susie Elkind	

This book was published with Corel VENTURA™ Publisher.

Nicola (Nick) LaManna, M.Ed., is currently the Associate Department Chair for Information Technology and Assistant Professor at New England Institute for Technology, based in Warwick, R.I. He has worked in various positions in the computer-networking field for approximately 12 years. He completed training in Novell Netware Engineering and was employed as a network administrator at Johnson and Wales University in Providence, R.I.

After completing his Master of Education Degree in Information Technology from J & W, Nick began his teaching career as an Adjunct with the university. Several teaching assignments followed, and his present position is at N.E.I.T., where he currently focuses on networking.

Nick has worked on various texts for Osborne Press as a Technical Editor and reviewer. His first publication, *MCSE Windows 2000 Network Administration Lab Manual* was published in early 2002. He continues to keep current with industry changes and standards, including Microsoft's Windows 2000 and Novell's NetWare 5.1 Certification courses.

Nick lives in Warwick, R.I., with his lovely wife of 23 years, Jane, daughter Amanda, and faithful dog, Gremlin. He enjoys hiking in the mountains, cycling, and travel.

I want to thank my wonderful wife Jane, and daughter Amanda, who have again provided support and understanding over the course of this project.

La mama, che dà di sé e non chiede niente in ritorno ma il nostro amore.

ACKNOWLEDGMENTS

I would like express my appreciation to the following people for all their hard work on this project:

- The wonderful hard-working team at McGraw-Hill/Osborne, especially Chris Johnson, Acquisitions Editor, and Athena Honore, Acquisitions Coordinator, for their patience and encouragement.

- Mark Karmendy, Executive Project Editor, and Dennis Weaver, Copy Editor, for putting "polish" on the manuscript.

- The production team, for their 'rapid fire' assemblage of the final chapters.

- Chris Crane and Brian Carroll, for their technical editing expertise and for catching those overlooked mistakes.

CONTENTS

About the Author . . . . *v*
Acknowledgments . . . . *vii*
Introduction . . . . *xvii*

1 Configuring and Troubleshooting TCP/IP 1

Configuring TCP/IP on Servers and Clients 2
Creating Custom Subnet Masks 4
Configuring Routes 6
Troubleshooting TCP/IP and Routing 8
    LAB ANALYSIS TEST 11
    KEY TERM QUIZ 12
    LAB SOLUTIONS FOR CHAPTER 1 13
    ANSWERS TO LAB ANALYSIS 24
    ANSWERS TO KEY TERM QUIZ 24

2 Implementing and Troubleshooting Name Resolution 25

Understanding Name Resolution 26
Configuring NetBIOS Name Resolution 28
Implementing and Configuring WINS 29
Troubleshooting WINS Settings on a Client Computer 31
    LAB ANALYSIS TEST 34
    KEY TERM QUIZ 35
    LAB SOLUTIONS FOR CHAPTER 2 36
    ANSWERS TO LAB ANALYSIS TEST 48
    ANSWERS TO KEY TERM QUIZ 48

**3 Configuring, Managing, and Troubleshooting
Domain Name System (DNS)** 49

Creating an Active Directory–Integrated Zone 50
Managing DNS Database Records 53

Configuring Dynamic DNS 55

Configuring Client Computer Name Resolution 56

Troubleshooting DNS Name Resolution 58

      LAB ANALYSIS TEST 60

      KEY TERM QUIZ 61

      LAB SOLUTIONS FOR CHAPTER 3 62

      ANSWERS TO LAB ANALYSIS 75

      ANSWERS TO KEY TERM QUIZ 76

4   Configuring and Troubleshooting DHCP **77**

Installing and Authorizing DHCP Servers 78

Configuring DHCP Scopes 81

Configuring DHCP Servers for DNS Integration 83

Configuring DHCP Clients 84

Troubleshooting DHCP 86

      LAB ANALYSIS TEST 88

      KEY TERM QUIZ 89

      LAB SOLUTIONS FOR CHAPTER 4 90

      ANSWERS TO LAB ANALYSIS 102

      ANSWERS TO KEY TERM QUIZ 102

5   Active Directory Users and Groups **103**

Creating and Configuring Domain User Accounts 104

Creating a Default User Profile 107

Creating and Administering a Global Group 109

Creating and Managing Organizational Units 111

Delegating Administrative Control 113

      LAB ANALYSIS TEST 115

      KEY TERM QUIZ 116

      LAB SOLUTIONS FOR CHAPTER 5 117

      ANSWERS TO LAB ANALYSIS 133

      ANSWERS TO KEY TERM QUIZ 133

6   Implementing Security Policies **135**

Using Group Policies to Apply Security Settings 137

Using Group Policy to Configure an Audit Policy 139

Delegating Group Policy Authority 142

Troubleshooting Group Policy 144
    LAB ANALYSIS TEST 146
    KEY TERM QUIZ 147
    LAB SOLUTIONS FOR CHAPTER 6 148
    ANSWERS TO LAB ANALYSIS 158
    ANSWERS TO KEY TERM QUIZ 159

7 Publishing Resources in Active Directory **161**
Publishing Shared Folders 162
Publishing Shared Printers 164
Publishing Network Services 165
    LAB ANALYSIS TEST 168
    KEY TERM QUIZ 169
    LAB SOLUTIONS FOR CHAPTER 7 170
    ANSWERS TO LAB ANALYSIS 177
    ANSWERS TO KEY TERM QUIZ 178

8 Deploying Software with Group Policies **179**
Using Group Policies to Deploy Software 181
Using Group Policies to Set Up Application Categories 184
Using Group Policies to Remove Software 186
    LAB ANALYSIS TEST 188
    KEY TERM QUIZ 189
    LAB SOLUTIONS FOR CHAPTER 8 190
    ANSWERS TO LAB ANALYSIS 198
    ANSWERS TO KEY TERM QUIZ 198

9 Managing and Troubleshooting Active Directory **199**
Managing Active Directory Objects 200
Configuring a Global Catalog Server 203
Troubleshooting Active Directory Replication 204
    LAB ANALYSIS TEST 207
    KEY TERM QUIZ 208
    LAB SOLUTIONS FOR CHAPTER 9 209
    ANSWERS TO LAB ANALYSIS 215
    ANSWERS TO KEY TERM QUIZ 216

10 Managing Data Storage **217**

Configuring Disks and Volumes 218

Configuring and Enforcing Disk Quotas 220

Implementing Encrypting File System (EFS) 222

Implementing and Managing a Distributed File System (Dfs) 223

        LAB ANALYSIS TEST 225

        KEY TERM QUIZ 226

        LAB SOLUTIONS FOR CHAPTER 10 227

        ANSWERS TO LAB ANALYSIS 237

        ANSWERS TO KEY TERM QUIZ 237

11 Configuring Internet Information Services (IIS) **239**

Creating Web Sites 240

Creating FTP Sites 242

Securing Web and FTP Sites 244

IIS Maintenance and Troubleshooting 245

        LAB ANALYSIS TEST 247

        KEY TERM QUIZ 248

        LAB SOLUTIONS FOR CHAPTER 11 249

        ANSWERS TO LAB ANALYSIS 257

        ANSWERS TO KEY TERM QUIZ 257

12 Implementing and Analyzing Security **259**

Configuring and Auditing Security 260

Administering Security Templates 262

Analyzing Security Settings 264

        LAB ANALYSIS TEST 267

        KEY TERM QUIZ 268

        LAB SOLUTIONS FOR CHAPTER 12 269

        ANSWERS TO LAB ANALYSIS 276

        ANSWERS TO KEY TERM QUIZ 276

13 Configuring Remote Access and VPN Connections . . . **277**

Configuring a Routing and Remote Access Service (RRAS)
    Virtual Private Network (VPN) Server 278

Configuring a Remote Access Policy 280

Configuring a Virtual Private Network (VPN) Using
    a PPTP Connection 282

Managing Existing Server-to-Server PPTP Connections
Using Remote Access Security 283
Configuring and Verifying the Security of a VPN Connection 285
LAB ANALYSIS TEST 287
KEY TERM QUIZ 288
LAB SOLUTIONS FOR CHAPTER 13 289
ANSWERS TO LAB ANALYSIS 298
ANSWERS TO KEY TERM QUIZ 298

14 Implementing Security Policies **299**
Configuring Remote Access Service (RAS) to Use
Internet Authentication Service (IAS) 301
Configuring Authentication and Encryption Protocol
for Demand-Dial Routers 303
Troubleshooting a Remote Access Policy 306
LAB ANALYSIS TEST 308
KEY TERM QUIZ 309
LAB SOLUTIONS FOR CHAPTER 14 310
ANSWERS TO LAB ANALYSIS 320
ANSWERS TO KEY TERM QUIZ 320

15 Implementing Terminal Services for Remote Access .. **321**
Configuring Terminal Services for Remote Administration 323
Configuring Terminal Services Licensing Server 324
Configuring Remote Access Security 326
LAB ANALYSIS TEST 329
KEY TERM QUIZ 330
LAB SOLUTIONS FOR CHAPTER 15 331
ANSWERS TO LAB ANALYSIS 339
ANSWERS TO KEY TERM QUIZ 340

**16 Configuring Network Address Translation (NAT) and
Internet Connection Sharing** **341**
Installing and Configuring Internet Connection Sharing 342
Troubleshooting Internet Connection Sharing Problems 344
Configuring Routing and Remote Access to Perform NAT 345
LAB ANALYSIS TEST 347
KEY TERM QUIZ 348

LAB SOLUTIONS FOR CHAPTER 16 349
ANSWERS TO LAB ANALYSIS 355
ANSWERS TO KEY TERM QUIZ 355

**17 Installing and Configuring Server
and Client Hardware** **357**
Verifying Hardware Compatibility 358
Configuring Driver Signing Options 359
Verifying Digital Signatures 360
Configuring Operating System Support for Legacy
Hardware Devices 361
LAB ANALYSIS TEST 363
KEY TERM QUIZ 364
LAB SOLUTIONS FOR CHAPTER 17 365
ANSWERS TO LAB ANALYSIS 372
ANSWERS TO KEY TERM QUIZ 372

18 Troubleshooting Startup Problems **373**
Create and Interpret a Startup Log File 374
Repair an Operating System by Using Various Startup Options 376
Repair an Operating System by Using the Recovery Console 377
Recover Data from a Hard Disk in the Event that
the Operating System Will Not Start 378
Restore an Operating System and Data from Backup 380
LAB ANALYSIS TEST 382
KEY TERM QUIZ 383
LAB SOLUTIONS FOR CHAPTER 18 384
ANSWERS TO LAB ANALYSIS 394
ANSWERS TO KEY TERM QUIZ 394

**19 Monitoring and Troubleshooting Server Health
and Performance** **395**
Monitoring and Interpreting Real-Time Performance
by Using System Monitor 396
Configuring System Monitor Alerts and Logging 398
Diagnosing Server Health Problems with Event Viewer 399
Identifying and Disabling Unnecessary Services 401

LAB ANALYSIS TEST 402

KEY TERM QUIZ 403

LAB SOLUTIONS FOR CHAPTER 19 404

ANSWERS TO LAB ANALYSIS 412

ANSWERS TO KEY TERM QUIZ 412

20 Installing and Managing Software Updates **413**

Using Slipstreaming to Update an Installation Source 414

Applying and Verifying a Service Pack Installation 416

Applying and Verifying a Hotfix Installation 418

Uninstalling a Hotfix and a Service Pack 420

LAB ANALYSIS TEST 422

KEY TERM QUIZ 423

LAB SOLUTIONS FOR CHAPTER 20 424

ANSWERS TO LAB ANALYSIS 430

ANSWERS TO KEY TERM QUIZ 430

Index **431**

INTRODUCTION

Welcome to *Managing a Windows® 2000 Network Environment Lab Manual, Student Edition.* This lab manual is meant to complement the *MCSA Managing a Windows® 2000 Network Environment Study Guide (Exam 70-218).* Skills needed to manage and employ Windows 2000 networking components are reinforced with real-world lab exercises for each of the certification objectives. A prerequisite to successfully accomplishing the intended learning outcomes of this lab manual is an understanding of the Windows 2000 Professional and Windows 2000 Server architecture.

In This Lab Manual

This lab manual provides the necessary exposure and training to install, configure, manage, monitor, and troubleshoot a Windows 2000 network. Topics that are covered include the use and manipulation of standard networking components and Windows 2000 Server services:

- Publishing Resources in Active Directory
- Managing Data Storage
- Creating Share Resources Within a Network and the Internet
- Configuring and Troubleshooting Internet Information Services (IIS)
- Monitoring and Managing Network Security
- Configuring and Troubleshooting TCP/IP
- Configuring and Administering DHCP
- Configuring and Administering DNS
- Installing and Updating Windows 2000 Updates

Each chapter includes a lab analysis test and a key term quiz. Solutions for each chapter are also provided for comparison. At the completion of this lab manual, you will gain a better understanding of a Windows 2000 networking infrastructure and be capable of managing its daily operation.

Lab Exercises

Understanding the theory behind networking and Windows 2000 Server principles is important for a network administrator. The question is, "Can you transfer this knowledge to a system situation?" Each exercise allows you to apply and practice a particular concept or skill in a real-world scenario.

Case Studies   Each certification objective is presented as a case study. Each case study provides a conceptual opportunity to apply your newly developed knowledge.

Learning Objectives   As you work hand in hand with the study guide, your primary objective is to pass the certification exam. The second objective is to develop your critical thinking. In networking, not all installations, re-installations, or network and system problems present themselves in the same fashion each time. To this end you need to be able to analyze a situation, consider your options and the result of each option, and select and implement that option. If it works, great; if it doesn't, you start over again.

Lab Materials and Setup   To fully accomplish each lab, it is necessary that the hardware and software requirements listed here be met. If this is not possible, then read through the steps and become familiar with the procedures as best you can.

The following hardware requirements are necessary for the hands-on lab scenarios:

- Pentium II 200 MHz or higher
- 128MB of RAM
- VGA monitor or better
- Mouse or other pointing device
- 12X CD-ROM or faster
- One or more hard drives with a minimum of 4GB free space
- Network card with either a cat5 connection or a dial-up or LAN connection

Getting Down-to-Business   The hands-on portion of each lab is step by step, not click by click. Step-by-step instructions provide necessary practice, walking you through each task relevant to the certification exam.

Lab Analysis Test

These are short-to-medium–answer questions to quickly assess your comprehension of what you've learned in the study guide and each lab in the chapter. The answers should be in your own words. This shows that you've synthesized the information and you have a comprehensive understanding of the key concepts.

Key Term Quiz

The key term quizzes focus on technical words that you should recognize and whose definitions and purpose should be familiar to you. The quizzes will help you with the exam and on the job.

Solutions

Each chapter also provides solutions for the lab exercises, the lab analysis test, and the key term quiz. These solutions are provided for you to compare your lab procedures, answer, or definition to the correct lab procedure, answer, or definition. Individuals who are familiar with Windows 2000 may find that in certain parts of the lab exercises there will be more than one way to accomplish a step. Both the end result and the understanding of the process to reach that end result are the main objectives.

MCSA™
MICROSOFT CERTIFIED SYSTEMS ASSOCIATE

1

Configuring and Troubleshooting TCP/IP

LAB EXERCISES

1.01   Configuring TCP/IP on Servers
       and Clients

1.02   Creating Custom Subnet Masks

1.03   Configuring Routes

1.04   Troubleshooting TCP/IP
       and Routing

■   Lab Analysis Test

■   Key Term Quiz

■   Lab Solutions

W hen people communicate, they do so through an agreed upon set of language standards that determine the sentence structure—how to form sentences, placement of nouns, verbs, adjectives, etc. There is also the particular language used to communicate—English, French, Italian, Japanese, etc. The same principles are applied to computers and computer components before they can communicate and understand the signals that are transmitted.

This first lab chapter will focus on the industry-standard suite of protocols designed for large networks: Transmission Control Protocol/Internet Protocol (TCP/IP). Originally developed by the government for use by the Department of Defense (DoD) in 1973, it was to be used to allow the government's mainframes and servers to communicate on a local and distant level in case of a disaster. The beauty of TCP/IP is in its simple, fault-tolerant, routable, and vendor-neutral design.

cross
Reference

For additional information, refer to the beginning pages of Chapter 1 of "Managing a Microsoft Windows 2000 Network Environment Study Guide."

CERTIFICATION OBJECTIVE 1.01

Configuring TCP/IP on Servers and Clients   10 Minutes

A new computer lab has been added to the BitByte College, in which you are one of three junior network administrators. One of your coworkers, Jim, has already installed the nineteen workstations and one server in the room. Your task today is to finish the project by configuring TCP/IP on the server and the last workstation, which Jim didn't get to.

Learning Objectives

In order to start using TCP/IP on any network, it's necessary to have an available valid IP addresses, the IP address of your router (gateway), and the subnet mask for your network. TCP/IP is installed by default when building Windows 2000 Professional or Windows 2000 Server on a computer. The procedure for configuring TCP/IP on either a member server or client is the same. A DHCP server can be used to assign IP addresses automatically. Labs for this topic will be covered in Chapter 4.

In this lab exercise, you have two tasks to perform: set a static IP address on a member server and a client PC in a newly installed computer lab.

By the end of this lab, you'll be able to

■ Configure TCP/IP with a static IP address, subnet mask, and default gateway.

Lab Materials and Setup

For this lab exercise, you'll need

■ A working computer

■ Installed network card (NIC)

■ Windows 2000 Professional software (installed), or

■ Windows 2000 Server software (installed)

lab
Hint
You may want to have the corresponding software CDs handy in case you need to extract files not found on the hard drive. A live connection is not required to perform this lab. Since TCP/IP configuration is the same for the server or workstation, you may perform either the server or workstation portion of this lab if you only have access to one of the software products.

Getting Down to Business

The labs in the college have static IP addresses in order to further distinguish the location of a computer by using the third octet set. This particular lab uses its room number of 142 to help identify the computers on the network. The IP addressing parameters are as follows:

■ IP address for the server is 192.128.142.1.

■ IP address for the workstation is 192.128.142.19.

■ The subnet mask is 255.255.0.0.

■ The gateway IP address is 192.128.100.1.

■ No DNS and DHCP servers are being used.

Step 1. First, you need to configure the IP address on the server. Access the Network and Dial-up Connections window and launch the Local Area Connection

Properties dialog box. This dialog box displays the system's installed adaptors, services, and protocols.

Step 2. Next, locate and select the TCP/IP protocol component in the Connection window. This activates the Properties button below the window. Click the Properties button to display the Internet Protocol (TCP/IP) Properties dialog box.

Step 3. Choose the manual method of assigning an IP address to the server. (If we were using a DHCP server to assign IP addresses, we would select the Obtain an IP Address Automatically radio button.)

Step 4. Enter the information provided in the appropriate fields. Once the information has been entered, click OK to accept the entries. Click OK again to exit the Local Area Connections Properties window. Repeat the steps above to configure the IP address on the workstation.

CERTIFICATION OBJECTIVE 1.02

Creating Custom Subnet Masks

15 Minutes

Paul from Juniper Industries calls you for some help. He's trying to find the subnet of a particular computer that is having problems. He also wants to know the range of assignable IP addresses on this same subnet, because it will be expanding to another floor in the same building.

He's at a complete loss as to how to figure it out. Because he took over the administrator's position three months ago, he can't find any documentation from the previous administrator on the six subnets within the company. Paul is asking for your help to solve this problem. You agree to sit down with him and help calculate which subnet the host is on, and determine the IP address range.

Learning Objectives

Subnetting allows an administrator to further divide the host portion of the address into additional subnets. This is accomplished by modifying the default subnet mask. And, a part of the host address is reserved to identify the particular subnet.

This lab exercise consists of two tasks. First, you need to figure out which subnet the host is on; secondly, you will calculate the IP address range for that subnet. Knowing the range of IP addresses will give you the number of computers (hosts) that can be connected to that subnet. By the end of this lab, you will know how to

- Convert the IP address to binary.
- Determine the subnet address.
- Determine the range of assignable IP addresses on that subnet.

Lab Materials and Setup

This lab requires a pencil, paper, and maybe a calculator.

Getting Down to Business

Paul has given you the following information from which to determine the subnet address of the host and the range of available IP addresses for that subnet.

- IP address: 186.60.50.2
- Subnet mask: 255.255.224.0

Step 1.   You need to determine the subnet. To help accomplish this, we need to convert the third octet of the IP address and the subnet mask into binary.

Compare the two binary numbers by placing them one on top of the other and eliminate all except the positions where there is a number 1.

Example:

	128	64	32	16	8	4	2	1
50 =	0	0	1	1	0	0	1	0
224 =	1	1	1	0	0	0	0	0

Step 2. Next, you need to find the range of IP addresses by taking the result of the above calculation and comparing it with the subnet mask.

For additional help with subnetting, refer to the section on creating custom subnet masks in Chapter 1 of "Managing a Microsoft Windows 2000 Network Environment Study Guide."

CERTIFICATION OBJECTIVE 1.03

Configuring Routes

10 Minutes

Barbara is the network administrator of a medium network. She is using a Windows 2000 server to connect the network, which spans several floors. Two routers connect each segment. Because her network is divided into three segments, she needs to configure routing using static routes. Each segment is configured with a Class C address. Barbara needs to add a route to allow the workstation with address 192.168.2.2 on segment 192.168.2.0 to communicate with network 192.168.24.0. What steps would she perform to accomplish this using the ROUTE command?

Learning Objectives

A router is a computer that functions at the network layer of the OSI model and acts as a device that directs information packets between networks based on the IP addresses entered in the routing table. LANs and WANs attain connectivity by the use of this system. It can also link different network topologies, such as Ethernet and token ring.

In this lab, you will use the ROUTE command to add an entry to the routing table. By the end of this lab, you will be able to

- Update a Windows 2000 routing table.
- Use the ROUTE command to add a static route.

Lab Materials and Setup

For this lab exercise, you will need

- A working computer
- Installed network card
- Routing and Remote Access (installed)
- Windows 2000 Server software (installed)

cross
Reference

For more information on installing Routing and Remote Access, refer to the section on Routing and Remote Access in Chapter 13 of "Managing a Microsoft Windows 2000 Network Environment Study Guide."

Getting Down to Business

Let's first gather the necessary information about Barbara's network. This is what we know:

- Her network segments are Class C (this determines the subnet mask).
- 192.168.2.2 on segment 192.168.2.0 needs to communicate with network 192.168.24.0.

To update a routing table, perform the following steps:

Step 1. Open a Command Prompt window.

lab
Hint

Using the Run option from the Start menu would not maintain an open command prompt session. The command will execute, but the window will disappear—leaving you uncertain whether the static route was applied.

Step 2.   Within the Command Prompt window, type the appropriate ROUTE command using the following syntax:

route add [destination] [mask subnetmask] [gateway] [metric m]

A successful syntax entry will result in a return to the command prompt, with no error message.

Step 3.   To display the new route information, type **route print** and press ENTER.

Step 4.   Close the command prompt session.

For more information on the ROUTE command, refer to the section on configuring routing tables in Chapter 1 of "Managing a Microsoft Windows 2000 Network Environment Study Guide."

CERTIFICATION OBJECTIVE 1.04

Troubleshooting TCP/IP and Routing

15 Minutes

James and Sam, junior network administrators, are discussing the command-line utilities and how these utilities are used to test and troubleshoot TCP/IP. Being new to these utilities, they are not quite sure if they understand when, and how, to use them. As their "guru," they look to you for help to set them straight. Explain and demonstrate the three popular and common testing utilities for James and Sam.

Learning Objectives

Whenever TCP/IP configuration is involved, it is always wise to verify and test that configuration to confirm that your computer can connect to other TCP/IP hosts and networks. Basic TCP/IP configuration testing can be performed using IPconfig, PING, and TRACERT utilities. Each of these utilities has switches that control their function.

In this lab, you will become familiar with these three testing tools and understand what purpose each serves. By the end of this lab, you will be able to

- Identify common TCP/IP utilities.
- Explain IPconfig, PING, and TRACERT.
- Demonstrate their purpose and function.

cross
Reference   *For help in completing this lab exercise, refer to the section on troubleshooting TCP/IP and routing in Chapter I of "Managing a Microsoft Windows 2000 Network Environment Study Guide."*

Lab Materials and Setup

For this lab exercise, you will need

- A working computer
- Installed network card
- Windows 2000 Professional software (installed), or
- Windows 2000 Server software (installed)
- A live Internet connection

Getting Down to Business

There are two steps to your discussion with James and Sam. The first thing is to explain what each utility does; the second is to give a demonstration of each.

Step 1.   Identify and explain the function of IPconfig.

_____

_____

Step 2.   Demonstrate the IPconfig utility using the Command Prompt window and Microsoft's support site (support.microsoft.com). What information does it provide?

Step 3.   Identify and explain the function of PING.

_____

_____

Step 4.   Demonstrate the PING utility using the Command Prompt window and Microsoft's support site (support.microsoft.com). What information does it provide?

Step 5.   Identify and explain the function of TRACERT.

_____

_____

Step 6.   Demonstrate the TRACERT utility using the Command Prompt window and Microsoft's support site (support.microsoft.com). What information does it provide?

LAB ANALYSIS TEST

1. What is the purpose of a subnet mask?

   _____

   _____

2. How would you define a network protocol?

   _____

   _____

3. How did the TCP/IP protocol suite come to be developed?

   _____

   _____

4. List and define the three TCP/IP utilities you would use to help troubleshoot a
   TCP/IP network?

   _____

   _____

5. What is the purpose of the ROUTE function?

   _____

   _____

KEY TERM QUIZ

Use the following vocabulary terms to complete the sentences below. Not all of the terms will be used. Definitions for these terms can be found in "Managing a Microsoft Windows 2000 Network Environment Study Guide."

TCP/IP

Subnet

Subnet mask

Router

Gateway

Static address

PING

Protocol

IPconfig

IP addressing

1. The term used to identify a router as the exit point of one network to another is named

 _____.

2. A _____ is a 32-bit number used to determine the portion of an IP address that represents the network ID and the host ID.

3. _____ is the 32-bit number address used to identify a host on a TCP/IP network.

4. A _____ is a set of rules or parameters that define how computers will communicate with each other.

5. A segment of a network that shares a network address with other segments of the network is named _____.

LAB SOLUTIONS FOR CHAPTER 1

In this section, you'll find solutions to the Lab Exercises, Lab Analysis Test, and Key Term Quiz.

Lab Solution 1.01

In this lab exercise, your task was to configure IP addressing for a member server and a workstation in a new computer lab.

You were given the following information: All the computer labs in the college have static IP addresses in order to distinguish the location of a computer by using the third octet set. This particular lab uses its room number of 142 to help identify the computers on the network in that room. The IP addressing parameters are

- The IP address for the server is 192.128.142.1.
- The IP address for the workstation is 192.128.142.19.
- The subnet mask is 255.255.0.0.
- The gateway IP address is 192.128.100.1
- No DNS and DHCP servers are being used.

To begin the configuration process, perform the following steps:

Step 1.   First, you need to configure the IP address on the server. Access the Network and Dial-up Connections window by right-clicking My Network Places on your desktop. Select Properties from the context menu. This opens the Network and Dial-up Connections window, as seen in Figure 1-1.

Step 2.   Right-click the Local Area Connection icon and select Properties. This opens the dialog box displaying the system's installed adaptors, services, and protocols.

Step 3.   Next, using the scroll bar, locate and select the TCP/IP protocol component in the Connection window. This activates the Properties button below the window. Click the Properties button to display the Internet Protocol (TCP/IP) Properties dialog box, as seen in Figure 1-2.

FIGURE 1-1

View your
Network
and Dial-up
Connection
window.

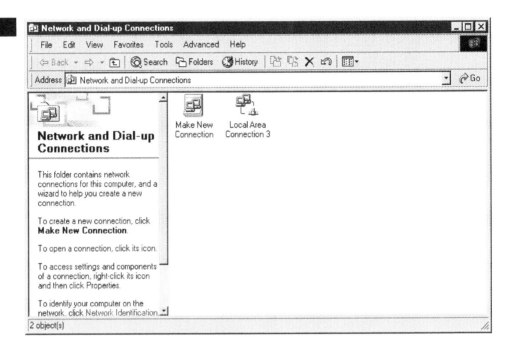

FIGURE 1-2

Click the
Properties button
for your TCP/IP
protocol.

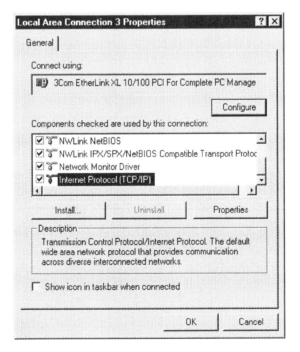

Step 4. This dialog box provides two different methods of configuring an IP address, as seen in Figure 1-3. If your network uses a DHCP server to assign IP addresses, you would activate the Obtain an IP Address Automatically radio button. If you opt to manually assign an IP address, you would activate the Use the Following IP Address radio button. In our case, we will be assigning an IP address manually.

Step 5. Enter the information provided in the appropriate fields, as seen in Figure 1-4.

- IP address: 192.128.142.1
- Subnet mask: 255.255.0.0
- Default gateway: 192.128.100.1

Since we are not using a DNS server, be sure that the Obtain DNS Server Address Automatically radio button is selected.

FIGURE 1-3

Choose to set your IP address settings manually.

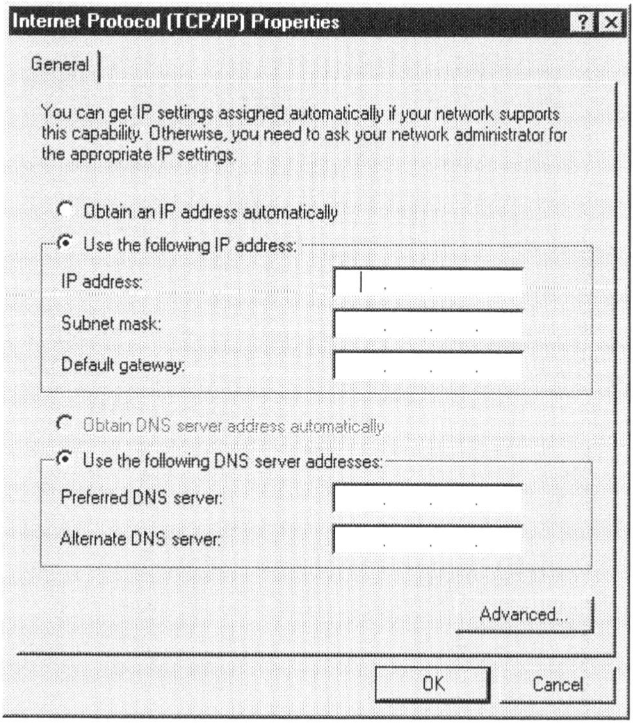

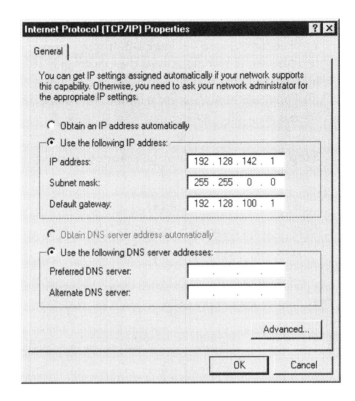

Enter your
IP address, subnet
mask, and default
gateway in the
appropriate fields.

Once the information has been entered, click OK to accept it. This brings you back to the Local Area Connections Properties window. Click OK again to exit. You may now also exit the Network Connections window.

lab
⓵int *The same sequence of steps is used to configure TCP/IP on the client computer as well.*

Lab Solution 1.02

This lab exercise can be a challenge for any network administrator. It's definitely not for the faint of heart. Yet, it's something that needs to be learned.

In this lab exercise, your task was to figure out which subnet the host is on, calculate the IP address range for that subnet, and use binary numbers to solve it. Knowing the range of IP addresses will give you the number of computers (hosts) that can be connected to that subnet. By the end of the lab, you will know how to

■ Convert the IP address to binary.

■ Determine the subnet address.

■ Determine the range of assignable IP addresses on that subnet.

James has given you the following information from which to determine the subnet address of the host and the range of available IP addresses for that subnet:

■ IP address: 186.60.50.2

■ Subnet mask: 255.255.224.0

Before we perform any calculations, we need to convert the third octet into binary.

cross
Reference

For additional help with subnetting, refer to the section on creating custom subnet masks in Chapter 1 of "Managing a Microsoft Windows 2000 Network Environment Study Guide."

Step 1.   You need to determine the subnet.

	128	64	32	16	8	4	2	1
50 =	0	0	1	1	0	0	1	0
224 =	1	1	1	0	0	0	0	0

We compare the two binary numbers and eliminate all except the positions where there is a 1. This happens to be position 32. Therefore, the value is 32. The subnet that the host resides on is 186.60.32.0. Based on the class of the IP address, there was no need to address the first two octets (186.60) because they represent the network ID.

Step 2.   Next, you need to find the range of IP addresses.
We again compare the results of the above calculation with the subnet mask that will give us the end of the subnet range.

	128	64	32	16	8	4	2	1
32 =	0	0	1	0	0	0	0	0
224 =	1	1	1	0	0	0	0	0

As we look at the binary number, the bits that are converted by the mask will be left alone. The rest of the bits, we will convert to 1's. This results in the following:

128	64	32	16	8	4	2	1
0	0	1	1	1	1	1	1 = 63

Thus, the range for assignable IP addresses on the subnet 186.60.32.0 is 186.60.32.1 to 186.60.63.254. Remember, we figured out that the subnet is 32, and then figured out the end of the subnet range, 63. The third octet number of the mask, 224, allows us to have the subnet range.

cross
Reference

For more information, refer to the section on creating custom subnet masks in Chapter 1 of "Managing a Microsoft Windows 2000 Network Environment Study Guide."

Lab Solution 1.03

Static routing is a function of Internet Protocol (IP) that lets you manually build and update routing tables on a network.

In this lab, you used the ROUTE command to add an entry to the routing table. By the end of this lab, you were able to

- Update a Windows 2000 routing table.

- Use the ROUTE command to add a static route.

We gathered the following information about Barbara's network:

- Her network segments are Class C.

This translates into a subnet mask equal to 255.255.255.0.

- 192.168.2.2 on segment 192.168.2.0 needs to communicate with network 192.168.24.0.

This tells us that 192.168.24.0 is the destination network, and 192.168.2.0 is the gateway for the host address of 192.168.2.2.

The ROUTE command syntax, therefore, will be

route 192.168.24.0 mask 255.255.255.0 192.168.2.0

To update a routing table, perform the following steps:

Step 1.   On the Windows 2000 server, open a Command Prompt window by clicking Start | Programs | Accessories and selecting Command Prompt from the list. This will open a DOS session.

lab
Hint

Using the Run option from the Start menu would not maintain an open command prompt session. The command will execute, but the window will disappear—leaving you uncertain whether the static route was applied.

Step 2.   Within the Command Prompt window, type the appropriate ROUTE command, as shown in Figure 1-5, using the following syntax:

route add [destination] [mask subnetmask] [gateway] [metric m]
route add 192.168.24.0 mask 255.255.255.0 192.168.2.0

A successful syntax entry will result in a return to the command prompt, with no error message. Metric is used when designating the number of hops a packet takes to reach its destination. This is used when you want Windows 2000 to select the route with the least amount of hops it takes to reach a destination when there are multiple routes available.

Step 3.   If all went well, to display the new route information, type **route print** and press ENTER. This will show you the new ROUTE table, as shown in Figure 1-6.

Step 4.   Type **exit** at the prompt to close the session.

cross
Reference

For more information on the ROUTE command, refer to the section on configuring routing tables in Chapter 1 of "Managing a Microsoft Windows 2000 Network Environment Study Guide."

FIGURE 1-5

Type the ROUTE command to add a new host to your ROUTE table.

```
Command Prompt                                                        _ □ ✕

C:\>route print
===================================================================================
Interface List
0x1 ............................ MS TCP Loopback interface
0x1000003 ...00 01 02 69 2c ff ...... 3Com EtherLink PCI
===================================================================================
===================================================================================
Active Routes:
Network Destination        Netmask          Gateway        Interface  Metric
          0.0.0.0          0.0.0.0     192.168.100.1    192.168.142.1       1
        127.0.0.0        255.0.0.0         127.0.0.1        127.0.0.1       1
      192.168.0.0      255.255.0.0     192.168.142.1    192.168.142.1       1
    192.168.142.1  255.255.255.255         127.0.0.1        127.0.0.1       1
  192.168.142.255  255.255.255.255     192.168.142.1    192.168.142.1       1
        224.0.0.0        224.0.0.0     192.168.142.1    192.168.142.1       1
  255.255.255.255  255.255.255.255     192.168.142.1    192.168.142.1       1
Default Gateway:       192.168.100.1
===================================================================================
Persistent Routes:
  None

C:\>route add 192.168.24.0 mask 255.255.255.0 192.168.2.0

C:\>_
```

Lab Solution 1.04

Whenever TCP/IP configuration is involved, it is always wise to verify and test that configuration to confirm that your computer can connect to other TCP/IP hosts and networks. Basic TCP/IP configuration testing can be performed using the IPconfig, PING, and TRACERT utilities. These command-line utilities may have gone the way of the "manual transmission" for end users, but are still components of an administrator's "toolkit" for troubleshooting networks.

FIGURE 1-6

The screen shows the new addition on fourth line of the screen.

```
Command Prompt                                                        _ □ ✕
C:\>route add 192.168.24.0 mask 255.255.255.0 192.168.2.0

C:\>route print
===================================================================================
Interface List
0x1 ............................ MS TCP Loopback interface
0x1000003 ...00 01 02 69 2c ff ...... 3Com EtherLink PCI
===================================================================================
===================================================================================
Active Routes:
Network Destination        Netmask          Gateway        Interface  Metric
          0.0.0.0          0.0.0.0     192.168.100.1    192.168.142.1       1
        127.0.0.0        255.0.0.0         127.0.0.1        127.0.0.1       1
      192.168.0.0      255.255.0.0     192.168.142.1    192.168.142.1       1
     192.168.24.0    255.255.255.0       192.168.2.0    192.168.142.1       1
    192.168.142.1  255.255.255.255         127.0.0.1        127.0.0.1       1
  192.168.142.255  255.255.255.255     192.168.142.1    192.168.142.1       1
        224.0.0.0        224.0.0.0     192.168.142.1    192.168.142.1       1
  255.255.255.255  255.255.255.255     192.168.142.1    192.168.142.1       1
Default Gateway:       192.168.100.1
===================================================================================
Persistent Routes:
  None

C:\>
```

As universal commands, the same syntax is used for various operating systems. In this lab, your task was to explain and demonstrate to James and Sam the three testing tools used to troubleshoot a TCP/IP network. By the end of this lab, you were able to

■ Identify common TCP/IP utilities.

■ Explain IPconfig, PING, and TRACERT.

■ Demonstrate their purpose and function.

There are two steps to your discussion with James and Sam. The first thing is to explain what each utility does, and the second is to give a demonstration of each.

Step 1.   IPconfig is a command that tells the system to show what the configuration parameters are for a computer connected to the network using IP addressing. Adding the /all switch will verify that the computer has the correct IP address, subnet mask, and default gateway information. The correct command syntax is ipconfig /all, or ipconfig.exe /all.

Step 2.   To demonstrate the IPconfig utility, open a Command Prompt window by clicking Start | Programs | Accessories and selecting Command Prompt from the list. This will open a DOS session.

lab
ⓗint

Another way to open a DOS session is to use the Run option from the Start menu. You can type either cmd *or* command.

Step 3.   At the command prompt, type **ipconfig /all**, as shown in Figure 1-7. Information will appear relative to your system. The screen shows two segments of information: a Windows 2000 IP Configuration segment and an Ethernet adaptor segment.

The important fields to review are the IP address, subnet mask, default gateway, DHCP server (if the DHCP server is enabled), DNS server, and WINS server. You can then match the field values with your network configuration. This information can assist you in troubleshooting any computer that has problems communicating on the network.

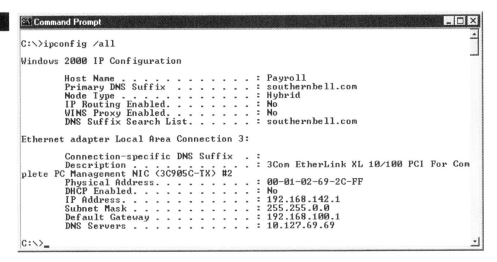

The command produces results for the Windows 2000 IP configuration as well as the network card configuration.

```
C:\>ipconfig /all

Windows 2000 IP Configuration

        Host Name . . . . . . . . . . . . : Payroll
        Primary DNS Suffix  . . . . . . . : southernbell.com
        Node Type . . . . . . . . . . . . : Hybrid
        IP Routing Enabled. . . . . . . . : No
        WINS Proxy Enabled. . . . . . . . : No
        DNS Suffix Search List. . . . . . : southernbell.com

Ethernet adapter Local Area Connection 3:

        Connection-specific DNS Suffix  . :
        Description . . . . . . . . . . . : 3Com EtherLink XL 10/100 PCI For Com
plete PC Management NIC (3C905C-TX) #2
        Physical Address. . . . . . . . . : 00-01-02-69-2C-FF
        DHCP Enabled. . . . . . . . . . . : No
        IP Address. . . . . . . . . . . . : 192.168.142.1
        Subnet Mask . . . . . . . . . . . : 255.255.0.0
        Default Gateway . . . . . . . . . : 192.168.100.1
        DNS Servers . . . . . . . . . . . : 10.127.69.69

C:\>_
```

Step 4.   Other IPconfig switches can help you reset these values. They are

■ **/release**   This command switch will release the IP address for the network adaptor.

■ **/renew**   This command switch will refresh the IP address for the network adaptor.

lab
ⓗ**int**

These two switches are normally used together. You especially would not want to use ipconfig /release *without invoking* ipconfig /renew.

Step 5.   PING is another basic TCP/IP utility. Just about every TCP/IP network includes some version of it. As a command-line utility, it's used to verify that the TCP/IP protocol on another system is functioning properly. The way PING works is that it sends out an Echo Request message using ICMP (Internet Control Message Protocol), which targets packets containing control and information messages. This is a way of asking the target system to identify itself to you. The syntax is PING *target*, where *target* is either the IP address (207.46.196.102) or the URL (support.microsoft.com).

Step 6.   To demonstrate the PING utility, open a Command Prompt window by clicking Start | Programs | Accessories and selecting Command Prompt from the list. This will open a DOS session.

Step 7.   At the command prompt, type **ping support.microsoft.com**. The PING request generates a reply message, as seen in Figure 1-8. The information that is

FIGURE 1-8

Notice the four echo requests as a result of the PING command.

```
Command Prompt                                                    _ □ ×

C:\>ping support.microsoft.com

Pinging support.microsoft.com [207.46.196.102] with 32 bytes of data:

Reply from 207.46.196.102: bytes=32 time=99ms TTL=47
Reply from 207.46.196.102: bytes=32 time=109ms TTL=47
Reply from 207.46.196.102: bytes=32 time=98ms TTL=47
Reply from 207.46.196.102: bytes=32 time=95ms TTL=47

Ping statistics for 207.46.196.102:
    Packets: Sent = 4, Received = 4, Lost = 0 (0% loss),
Approximate round trip times in milli-seconds:
    Minimum = 95ms, Maximum = 109ms, Average = 100ms

C:\>_
```

echoed back from the address shows the IP address of the computer, the number of bytes of that data, the time between the sending of the request and the reply receipt, and, lastly, the value of the Time To Live (TTL) field in the packet header. The TTL field in the Internet Protocol (IP) specifies the limitations the packet has, which are measured in hops. So if a TTL value is equal to 100, it means that the packet can make 100 more hops before it is discarded.

Step 8. A variation of the PING utility is the TRACERT utility. TRACERT displays the paths packets take to reach their destination. This display shows a list of routers that are forwarding packets to their destinations. This is the same principle that the airline industry uses. If you're traveling on a particular airline from the Midwest to Florida, the airline has the plane pass through a central exchange airport (hub) on the East Coast. Depending on the airline, the hub could be LaGuardia, Baltimore, or Atlanta before you can continue on to your Florida destination.

The syntax for TRACERT is tracert *target name*, where *target name* is either the IP address (207.46.196.102) or the URL (support.microsoft.com).

Step 9. To demonstrate the TRACERT utility, open a Command Prompt window by clicking Start | Programs | Accessories and selecting Command Prompt from the list. This will open a DOS session.

Step 10. At the command prompt, type **tracert support.microsoft.com**. The TRACERT request generates a reply message from each router as the request travels towards its destination. The information that is echoed back from each router is the time between the sending and receiving of three sets of echo requests. The further the hops from the sending system, the greater the elapsed time between sending and receiving.

TRACERT is a low-cost handy troubleshooting tool to isolate a router that may be causing either a roadblock or a bottlenecking of packets as they travel throughout the Internet. It shows you how far a packet is going before it runs into a problem.

ANSWERS TO LAB ANALYSIS

1. A subnet mask is used to camouflage the beginning portion of an IP address in order to distinguish the network ID from the host ID.

2. A network protocol is an agreed-upon language used between two computers that communicate on a network. The protocol defines how that information is transmitted, and how it is fragmented into small packets for transport over the network.

3. TCP/IP was the birth child of the U.S. Defense Advanced Research Projects Agency (DARPA) in 1973 to investigate techniques and technologies for interlinking packet networks of various kinds. They needed a way to let networked computers communicate transparently. Its intended purpose was to provide government installations with a communications vehicle that would survive in case of a nuclear disaster.

4. IPconfig grabs TCP/IP configuration information on a computer.

   TRACERT traces the path a packet takes, from the source to its destination.

   PING helps confirm connectivity on a network.

5. Routing is the function of moving packets of information across connected networks from a source to a destination.

ANSWERS TO KEY TERM QUIZ

1. Gateway

2. Subnet mask

3. IP addressing

4. Protocol

5. Subnet

2

Implementing and Troubleshooting Name Resolution

LAB EXERCISES

2.01 Understanding Name Resolution with NetBIOS over TCP/IP Node Types

2.02 Configuring NetBIOS Name Resolution Using an LMHOSTS File

2.03 Implementing and Configuring WINS

2.04 Troubleshooting WINS Settings on a Client Computer

■ Analysis Test

■ Term Quiz

■ Lab Solutions

I n the beginning days of networking, a computer was only recognized on the network by an encoded address number. This MAC (media access control) address (still used today, and also considered the computer's unique hardware number) is alphanumeric. This made it difficult to keep track (and know the physical location) of each computer on the network. The Windows operating system has simplified computer identification by using a standard naming convention, which is associated with the IP address required for TCP/IP communication. Although during setup the program refers to it as a computer name, it is really a Network Basic Input/Output System (NetBIOS) name. A mechanism associated with NetBIOS translates this NetBIOS name into the Internet Protocol (IP) address needed for TCP/IP communication. Microsoft has enhanced the NetBIOS process by implementing a Windows Internet Naming Service (WINS). This service registers NetBIOS computer names, resolves them with their IP address, and creates a dynamic database that maps the computer name to the IP address. When a client's NetBIOS name-to-IP-address registration occurs, the WINS server returns a message indicating the amount of time the NetBIOS name is associated with the client—specified as the Time To Live (TTL).

In this lab chapter, we will look at becoming familiar with name resolution and how it functions, and how to resolve NetBIOS name-to-IP-address problems through the use of HOST and LMHOST files. We'll also look at how to implement and configure WINS for networks running earlier versions of Windows—what the purpose and function of WINS is and how it provides name registration.

CERTIFICATION OBJECTIVE 2.01

Understanding Name Resolution

20 Minutes

You're the network administrator of ITs-NET-FOR-US Enterprise's Windows 2000 server. You are considering setting up a Windows Internet Network Service (WINS), which includes the use of NetBIOS name resolution. Because it's been several years since your CIO, Perry Natale, has configured NetBIOS name resolution, he would like a better understanding of how it works and how the different node types work (he does remember that there are types). Describe the four NetBIOS node types, and how they function in a Windows 2000 WINS environment.

Learning Objectives

NetBIOS naming support was, and still is, required on all MS-DOS and Windows-based operating systems prior to Windows 2000. With Windows 2000, support for NetBIOS is no longer required in order to network computers. This is accomplished through TCP/IP. Windows 2000 still supports NetBIOS for those legacy systems that require its use. The proper method by which NetBIOS names are resolved to IP addresses depends on the NetBIOS node type that is configured for the node.

In this lab, your task is to identify the four node types and explain their function. By the end of this lab, you'll be able to

- List the four NetBIOS over TCP/IP node types.
- Explain their main function.
- Explain which method each uses for name resolution.

Lab Materials and Setup

For this lab exercise, you'll need

- A working computer
- Windows 2000 Server software (installed), or
- Windows 2000 Professional software (installed)

cross
Reference

For information about the different NetBIOS over TCP/IP node types, refer to the NetBIOS Name Resolution sections of Chapter 2 of "Managing a Microsoft Windows 2000 Network Environment Study Guide."

lab
Hint

Additional information may be acquired from sources on the Internet, such as www.webopedia.com.

Getting Down to Business

Put together the necessary information to explain NetBIOS name resolution to your CIO by following these steps.

Step I. To put together information for your informal presentation, first list the four NetBIOS node types in the space below.

_____

_____

Step 2. Next, in the space below, you'll need to describe how each node type handles the name resolution process.

_____

_____

Step 3. Finally, you'll need to include any advantage or disadvantage each node type may exhibit. List any of these elements below.

_____

_____

CERTIFICATION OBJECTIVE 2.02

Configuring NetBIOS Name Resolution

15 Minutes

Arthur is the system administrator for the Cycle-Delic Cycle shops in Spokane, Washington. After installing WINS services on the Windows 2000 server at one of the shops, a Windows NT Workstation presents an error message stating _No domain controller found_ when the user tries to log on to the network. The domain controller is on the same network segment as the workstation, but the workstation can't find it. How would you solve this?

Learning Objectives

In this lab, you will use an LMHOSTS file to map a hostname to its IP address. The LMHOSTS file is found in the systems32\drivers\etc of your system root directory. The root directory is usually indicated by using %systemroot% followed by the remainder of the subdirectories. By the end of this lab, you will be able to

■ Create an entry in a computer's LMHOSTS file.

■ Resolve a NetBIOS name-to-IP-address error.

Lab Materials and Setup

For this lab exercise, you will need

■ A working computer

■ Windows 2000 Professional software (installed)

Getting Down to Business

To resolve the error and create an LMHOSTS, file perform the following steps:

Step 1.   First, we need to know the IP address and NetBIOS name of the domain controller. It is 192.168.0.15, named *dealership1*. Now we need to create an LMHOSTS file, using a text editor, and enter the information.

lab
Hint

Be sure that you are in the appropriate subdirectory when creating this file. Also, because we want this entry to be permanent, you'll need to add #PRE in the entry.

cross
Reference

For additional information, refer to the LMHOSTS section in Chapter 2 of "Managing a Microsoft Windows 2000 Network Environment Study Guide."

Step 2.   Save the LMHOSTS file in the same directory and ensure it does *not* have an extension in the filename. The user will now have access to the domain resources.

CERTIFICATION OBJECTIVE 2.03

Implementing and Configuring WINS

20 Minutes

The Lambda family car dealership has just added a third location to their franchise. As the network administrator, you are responsible for the network system connecting the three sites. With this new site, you have decided to migrate from a Windows NT 4 workgroup environment to a Windows 2000 network. A frame relay connection and a bridge connect the sites. As part of the migration, you wish to implement WINS for the Windows 98 and Windows NT Workstation computers. This is just a temporary service for the migration only. What steps are required to install and configure WINS on your system?

Learning Objectives

You have two goals in this lab exercise: to install and configure WINS on a Windows 2000 server, and to configure a legacy client to use WINS. By the end of this lab, you'll be able to

■ Install WINS on a Windows 2000 server.

■ Configure WINS on a Windows 2000 server.

■ Configure a WINS 2000 client.

Lab Materials and Setup

For this lab exercise, you will need

■ A working computer (two computers preferred)

■ Windows 2000 Server software (installed), or

■ Windows 2000 Professional software (installed)

lab
ⓗint
It is possible to perform this lab with one computer that has Windows 2000 Professional or Windows NT Workstation, and Windows 2000 Server installed as a multiboot system.

Getting Down to Business

To install the Windows 2000 WINS service, perform the following steps:

Step 1.   Access the Windows Optional Networking Components Wizard via the My Network Places icon.

lab
ⓗint
WINS can also be installed using the Add/Remove Programs utility in the Control Panel folder.

Step 2.   Install WINS using the Networking Services dialog box.

Step 3.   Continue and complete the installation using the Windows Components Wizard. Now that you've installed the WINS server, you need to configure the server as a WINS client. This allows it to access resources on the network running earlier versions of Windows. In this case, we need to access resources on the Windows NT 4 server.

Step 4.   If your Network and Dial-up Connections window is still open, access the Properties dialog box of your Local Area Connection icon.

Step 5.   Access the Advanced TCP/IP settings via the TCP/IP Properties dialog box. Verify that the IP address, subnet mask, and default gateway have been assigned to your server.

Step 6.   Additionally, be sure that LMHOSTS lookup and NetBIOS over TCP/IP is enabled. Click the OK buttons to close out of your nested dialog boxes.

Step 7.   Your last task is to ensure that your Windows clients obtain their NetBIOS-to-IP-address resolution through the WINS server.
   Log on to each workstation and configure the appropriate TCP/IP settings.

lab
⬇️int   *The easiest way to configure a client for WINS is to set DHCP as your IP address provider.*

CERTIFICATION OBJECTIVE 2.04

Troubleshooting WINS Settings on a Client Computer

15 Minutes

Staying with the same case study as Lab Exercise 2.03, you receive a call from a user at dealership site 2 a few days after implementing the temporary WINS solution during the Windows 2000 migration. He claims that he is having a problem obtaining access to resources from the dealership's headquarters. Since you will be heading to that site later in the afternoon, you tell him that you will stop by and address his problem.

Learning Objectives

You know that you configured each client workstation to use the DHCP and WINS server for their IP address. By what the user told you, you'll need to test the settings on your client workstation and possibly renew the correct information assigned to the workstation via the DHCP and WINS server.

IPconfig is a utility that provides a user with diagnostic information related to TCP/IP network configuration. IPconfig also accepts various Dynamic Host Configuration Protocol (DHCP) commands, allowing a system to update or release its TCP/IP network configuration.

In this lab, you will use the IPconfig utility with various switches to release and renew your client workstation settings. By the end of this lab, you'll be able to

■ Release and renew a client computer's DHCP lease information.

Lab Materials and Setup

For this lab exercise, you will need

■ A working computer
■ Windows 2000 Professional software (installed)

Getting Down to Business

Before we test the setting, we can rule out the wrong setting for the TCP/IP properties. The DHCP service has been set to provide the IP addressing on this client computer.

To reconfigure the settings on the client computer, perform the following steps:

Step 1. Open a command prompt on the client computer. (For those of you that thought the DOS environment was long gone…welcome back!)

Step 2. Type the IPCONFIG command with the appropriate switch to shed the assigned IP parameters. Make note of the results.

Step 3. Type the IPCONFIG command with the appropriate switch to obtain new IP configuration settings. Make note of the results.

Step 4. Type the IPCONFIG command with the appropriate switch to review the new IP configuration settings. Make note of the adaptor settings for the connection. What is the Node Type field set to?

LAB ANALYSIS TEST

1. You are the administrator of the A. Noyance Direct Marketing Company. Your network contains two segments, each with a server, and a Windows 2000 server is used to route between the two segments. It also contains a mix of two DOS computers, six Windows 98 computers, and three Windows NT computers. You've installed WINS on the Windows 2000 server, and your DOS client computers cannot see the servers on the other side of the router. What do you think is the reason?

   _____

   _____

2. You've been working for Party Treats, a novelty manufacturing company, as a junior network administrator now for almost four months. You are still discovering, and organizing, all the components and services on your network. There are 26 Windows NT workstations connected to a Windows 2000 server. One of your goals is to become familiar with how WINS works. You ask the systems engineer if she would explain it to you. By default, you want to know which WINS server a client computer will use for name resolution.

   _____

   _____

3. You are still looking for more information about the process of NetBIOS names-to-IP-address resolution. Specifically, you want to know what the difference is between the HOSTS file and the LMHOSTS file, and if either one is still necessary?

   _____

   _____

4. You are the network administrator for a popular snack food company. You've configured a Windows client to use a WINS server. Which node type is used for its name resolution?

   _____

   _____

5. You have successfully implemented WINS on your network. Your users have no problem browsing the network. How does the WINS database obtain its information about other computers to make this possible?

   _____

   _____

KEY TERM QUIZ

Use the following vocabulary terms to complete the sentences below. Not all of the terms will be used. Definitions for these terms can be found in "MCSE Windows 2000 Network Administration Study Guide."

> LAN Manager HOSTS (LMHOSTS)
>
> B-node
>
> H-node
>
> M-node
>
> NetBIOS
>
> TCP/IP
>
> WINS
>
> Broadcasts
>
> IPconfig
>
> LOCALHOST

1. This node type, _____, relies completely on broadcast messages to resolve name requests.

2. _____ is a Windows 2000 service that provides NetBIOS name resolution.

3. The NetBIOS node type that uses broadcasts first and then looks to a WINS server to resolve NetBIOS names to IP addresses is named _____.

4. You can use _____ to release and renew DHCP-assigned TCP/IP configuration parameters.

5. _____ provides a static NetBIOS name-to-IP-address resolution in a Windows environment.

LAB SOLUTIONS FOR CHAPTER 2

In this section, you'll find solutions to the lab exercises, Lab Analysis Test, and Key Term Quiz.

Lab Solution 2.01

NetBIOS naming support was, and still is, required on all MS-DOS and Windows-based operating systems prior to Windows 2000. With Windows 2000, support for NetBIOS is no longer necessary to network computers. This is accomplished through TCP/IP. Windows 2000 still supports NetBIOS for those legacy systems that still require its use. The proper method by which NetBIOS names are resolved to IP addresses depends on the NetBIOS node type that is configured for the node.

In this lab, your task was to identify the four node types and explain their function. By the end of this lab, you were able to

- List the four NetBIOS over TCP/IP node types.
- Explain their main function.
- Explain which method each uses for name resolution.

cross Reference

For information about the different NetBIOS over TCP/IP node types, refer to the NetBIOS name resolution sections of Chapter 2 of "Managing a Microsoft Windows 2000 Network Environment Study Guide."

lab Hint

Additional information may be acquired from sources on the Internet, such as www. webopedia.com.

Step 1. First, let's list the four NetBIOS node types. They are

- B-node (broadcast node)
- P-node (point-to-point node)
- M-node (modified node)
- H-node (hybrid node)

Step 2.   Next, we'll need to describe how each node type handles the name resolution process.

- **B-node (broadcast node)**   This type relies completely on broadcast messages to resolve name requests. This is also the oldest NetBIOS name resolution mode. A host asking to have the address associated with a hostname sends out the broadcast message.

- **P-node (point-to-point node)**   P-node relies on a WINS server for name resolution. As each client computer comes on the network, the WINS server registers it. The WINS server then handles name-to-IP-address resolution requests.

- **M-node (modified node)**   An M-node is a hybrid form that first looks to the B-node method to resolve a name, and if that fails will request the name resolution using the P-mode.

- **H-node (hybrid node)**   The H-node is also a hybrid form that is the reverse of the M-node. It favors the use of WINS for its name resolutions through the P-node method. If this fails, it will resort to the B-node, or broadcast, method of resolving a name-to-IP-address name resolution.

Step 3.   Finally, you'll need to include any advantage or disadvantage each node type may exhibit. List any of these elements:

- **B-node (broadcast node)**   Broadcasting consumes a considerable amount of bandwidth, and TCP/IP routers cannot forward broadcast messages, which limits this method for use in a single network.

- **P-node (point-to-point node)**   Because WINS servers use direct messages, and can cross TCP/IP routers, this method can be used on interconnected networks. Because P-node relies on WINS, the downside is that if the WINS server is unavailable, this method fails.

- **M-node (modified node)**   This method was the first to be put into operation. The downside is that because it favors the broadcast mode, it consumes considerable bandwidth.

- **H-node (hybrid node)**   This method results in the most efficient network utilization. Hence, it is the method of choice for TCP/IP-configured systems.

Lab Solution 2.02

Arthur is trying to resolve an error message that one of the users is getting at one of the shops. The error message states there is *No domain controller found* when the user tries to log on to the network. We know that the domain controller is on the same network segment as the workstation, but the workstation can't find it.

In this lab, you will use an LMHOSTS file to map a hostname to its IP address. The LMHOSTS file is found in the systems32\drivers\etc of your system root directory. By the end of this lab, you were able to

- Create an entry in a computer's LMHOSTS file.
- Resolve a NetBIOS name-to-IP-address error.

Step 1. First, we need to know the IP address and NetBIOS name of the domain controller. The IP address is 192.168.0.15 and the domain controller's name is *dealership1*. With this information, we can create an LMHOSTS file, using a text editor, and enter the information.

lab
Hint

Be sure that you are in the appropriate subdirectory when creating this file. Also, because we want this entry to be permanent, you'll need to add #PRE in the entry.

cross
Reference

For additional information, refer to the LMHOSTS entries section in Chapter 2 of "Managing a Microsoft Windows 2000 Network Environment Study Guide."

Step 2. Click Start | Run, and in the dialog box type

  notepad %systemroot%\system32\drivers\etc\lmhosts.sam

if you want to use the existing file, or

  notepad %systemroot%\system32\drivers\etc\lmhosts

if you want to create a new file. Click OK. If Notepad asks to create a new file, click YES.

Be sure to type the "." at the end of the file name; otherwise, it will save the file as a test file.

Add the following entry to the LMHOSTS file, as shown in Figure 2-1:

192.168.0.15   dealership1   #PRE

Step 3.   Save the file in the same subdirectory. Click File | Save if you've created a new LMHOSTS file, or Click File | Save As if you're using the existing LMHOSTS file. The filename is LMHOSTS, with no extension. If you are using Notepad, it may append *.txt* automatically. If it does this, you will need to rename the file using no extension at a command prompt. Then, exit the text editor.

To avoid having notepad append the .txt extension, place the filename in double quotes.

Step 4.   You will have to reboot the computer before Windows can begin to use this file you created.

FIGURE 2-1

The #PRE
indicates that
this IP address
will be preloaded
at bootup.

```
# This file contains the mappings of IP addresses to host names. Each
# entry should be kept on an individual line. The IP address should
# be placed in the first column followed by the corresponding host name.
# The IP address and the host name should be separated by at least one
# space.
#
# Additionally, comments (such as these) may be inserted on individual
# lines or following the machine name denoted by a '#' symbol.
#
# For example:
#
#      102.54.94.97     rhino.acme.com          # source server
#       38.25.63.10     x.acme.com              # x client host

127.0.0.1       localhost
192.168.0.15    dealership1        #PRE
```

Lab Solution 2.03

Although WINS is supplied with Windows 2000 Server, it is not installed by default. The options are to install it during the initial server build, or install it later using either the Add/Remove Program utility in the Control Panel or using the Windows Optional Networking Components Wizard via the My Network Places icon. Lastly, the server needs to be configured with a static IP address, subnet mask, and default gateway, rather than obtaining them using a Dynamic Host Configuration Protocol (DHCP) server.

In this lab exercise, your task is to install WINS on the server and then configure the server as a WINS client. Then, you need to configure your legacy clients to obtain NetBIOS-to-IP-address name resolution from the WINS server. By the end of this lab, you were able to

- Install WINS on a Windows 2000 server.
- Configure WINS on a Windows 2000 server.
- Configure a WINS 2000 client.

lab
ⓗint
It is possible to perform this lab with one computer that has Windows 2000 Professional or Windows NT Workstation, and Windows 2000 Server installed as a multiboot system.

Perform the following steps to install the Windows 2000 WINS service:

Step 1. Right-click the My Network Places icon on the desktop and select Properties. This will open the Network and Dial-up Connections window.

lab
ⓗint
WINS can also be installed using the Add/Remove Programs utility in the Control Panel folder.

Step 2. In the lower-left corner of the window, click Add Network Components. This hyperlink opens the Windows Components dialog box of the Windows Optional Networking Components Wizard, as seen in Figure 2-2. You will notice in this window that the Networking Services option has a check mark in the box. The box has a gray fill in it to indicate that not all of the Network Services have been installed.

Specific
network-related
services and
protocols are
contained in
the Networking
Services
component.

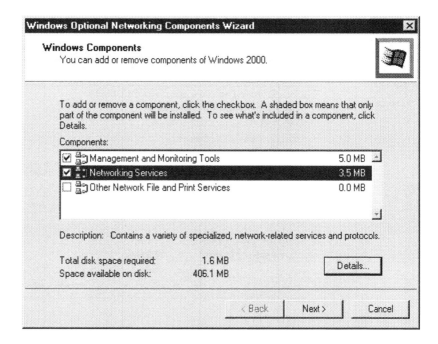

Step 3. Select the Network Services component and then click the Details button. The Networking Services window opens, revealing the optional components. Select Windows Internet Name Service (WINS), as shown in Figure 2-3, and click OK. This brings you back to the Optional Windows Networking Components Wizard dialog box.

Step 4. Complete the installation by clicking the Next button. This process will also make the WINS console available under the Administrative Tools category in the Start menu.

Now that you've installed the WINS server, you need to configure the server as a WINS client. This allows it to access resources on the network running earlier versions of Windows. In this case, we need to access resources on the Windows NT 4 server.

lab
ⓗint

Have your Windows 2000 Server CD available in case the installation process needs to copy files not found on your server.

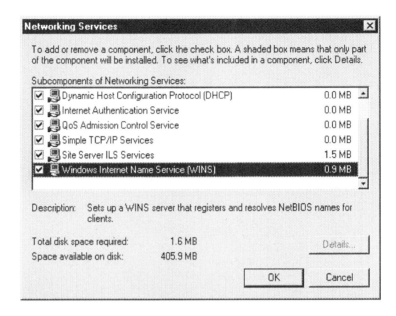

Step 5. Even though WINS is not needed by Windows 2000 to access other Windows 2000 resources, it does require WINS to access resources running earlier versions of Windows. Therefore, you need to configure your WINS server to also be a WINS client.

If your Network and Dial-up Connections window is still open, access the Properties dialog box of your Local Area Connection icon, as shown here:

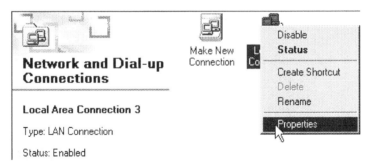

Step 6. In the Local Area Connection Properties window, select Internet Protocol (TCP/IP) and click Properties. This will display the Internet Protocol (TCP/IP) Properties dialog box, as shown in Figure 2-4. Verify that the IP address, subnet mask, and default gateway have been assigned to your server. If the Obtain

FIGURE 2-4

It is recommended
that WINS
servers have an
assigned static IP
address, a subnet
mask, and default
gateway.

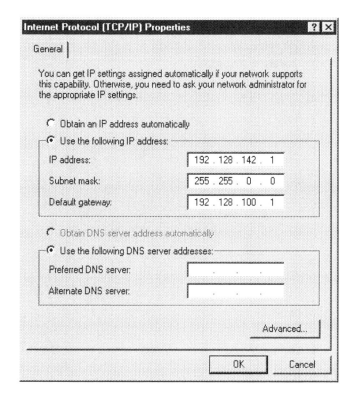

an IP Address Automatically radio button is on, you need to select the Use the
Following IP Address radio button and input that information.

Step 7.   Click the Advanced button to open the Advanced TCP/IP Settings
dialog box. There are four tabs at the top of the window—select the WINS tab.
Click Add to display the TCP/IP WINS Server dialog box. Enter the IP address
of the WINS server in the WINS Server text box, as shown here,

and click the Add button. The WINS address window now displays the primary WINS server. If you had additional WINS servers, you would be able to add them by repeating the steps.

Step 8.   Additionally, be sure that LMHOSTS lookup and NetBIOS over TCP/IP are enabled, as shown here:

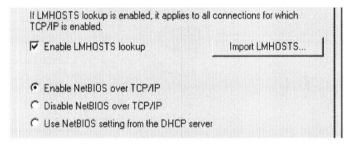

Click OK (not shown here) to close out of the Advanced TCP/IP Settings dialog box.

Step 9.   Click the OK buttons to exit the Internet Protocol (TCP/IP) Properties dialog box and the Local Area Connection Properties dialog box.

Step 10.   Your last task is to ensure that your Windows clients obtain their NetBIOS-to-IP-address resolution through the WINS server. Log on to a workstation with administrative rights.

lab
ⓗint   *The easiest way to configure a client for WINS is to set DHCP as your IP address provider.*

Step 11.   In the Local Area Connection Properties window, select Internet Protocol (TCP/IP) and click Properties. This will display the Internet Protocol (TCP/IP) Properties dialog box, as shown in Figure 2-5. Verify that the Obtain an IP Address Automatically radio button is on. If the Use the Following IP Address radio button is on, then you'll need to select Obtain an IP address automatically.

Step 12.   Click the Advanced button to open the Advanced TCP/IP Settings dialog box. There are four tabs at the top of the window—select the WINS tab.

FIGURE 2-5

This setting provides for dynamic distribution of IP addresses from the DHCP server.

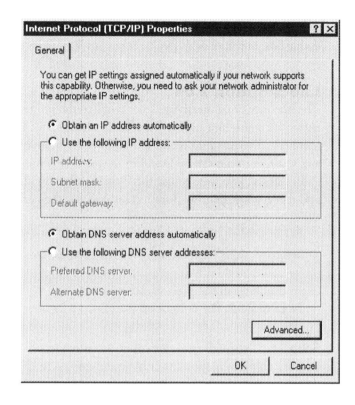

Delete any WINS address that shows in the window. A DHCP-enabled client guarantees the receipt of the WINS server's IP address and the correct node type of the NetBIOS name resolution.

The Use NetBIOS Setting from the DHCP Server radio button also needs to be selected, as shown here:

Step 13. Click the OK buttons to exit the Internet Protocol (TCP/IP) Properties dialog box and the Local Area Connection Properties dialog box.

Lab Solution 2.04

The majority of connectivity issues relate to the proper configuration of the network's communication protocol—in our case, TCP/IP. The inclusion of WINS and DHCP servers makes configuration issues more complex. Fortunately, solutions and testing utilities can be found in simple DOS commands.

In this lab, you were to use the IPconfig utility with various switches to release and renew your client workstation settings. By the end of this lab, you were able to

■ Release and renew a client computer DHCP lease information.

Before we tested the settings, we knew that we could rule out the wrong TCP/IP properties. The DHCP service had been set to provide the IP addressing on this client computer in the previous lab exercise.

To reconfigure the settings on the client computer, perform the following steps:

Step 1. The quickest way to open a command prompt on a client computer (if you don't have a shortcut on your desktop) is to click Start | Run and then type the command in the dialog box. A longer way would be to search for it in the programs list.

Step 2. The command with the appropriate switch to shed the assigned IP parameters is **ipconfig /release**. Type this command at the command prompt. The result of this command is a message stating that the IP address has been successfully released, as shown next. The configuration list will also appear with all the settings at zero.

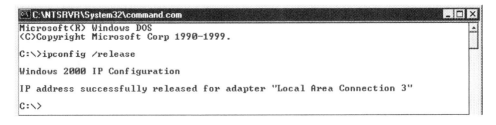

```
C:\NTSRVR\System32\command.com                              _ □ X
Microsoft(R) Windows DOS
(C)Copyright Microsoft Corp 1990-1999.

C:\>ipconfig /release

Windows 2000 IP Configuration

IP address successfully released for adapter "Local Area Connection 3"

C:\>
```

Step 3. The command with the appropriate switch to obtain a new IP configuration setting is **ipconfig /renew**. Type this command at the command prompt. The result of this command is a display of renewed adapter settings obtained from the DHCP server, as shown next. This only shows the IP address, subnet mask, and the default gateway of the adaptor.

```
C:\NTSRVR\System32\command.com                                    _ □ ×

C:\>ipconfig /renew

Windows 2000 IP Configuration

Ethernet adapter Local Area Connection 3:

        Connection-specific DNS Suffix  . : neit.edu
        IP Address. . . . . . . . . . . : 10.127.50.136
        Subnet Mask . . . . . . . . . . : 255.255.0.0
        Default Gateway . . . . . . . . : 10.127.100.1

C:\>_
```

Step 4. The command with the appropriate switch to show all the settings, including the DNS server, DHCP server, the node type and lease expiration is **ipconfig /all|more**. Type this command at the command prompt, the results of which are shown in Figure 2-6. The addition of the dos option **|more** prevents the information from scrolling by. What is the node type set to? The popular setting is the Hybrid, or H-node, setting.

FIGURE 2-6

Notice in particular the physical address, node type, DHCP, and DNS servers.

```
C:\NTSRVR\System32\command.com                                    _ □ ×

C:\>ipconfig /renew

Windows 2000 IP Configuration

Ethernet adapter Local Area Connection 3:

        Connection-specific DNS Suffix  . : neit.edu
        IP Address. . . . . . . . . . . : 10.127.50.136
        Subnet Mask . . . . . . . . . . : 255.255.0.0
        Default Gateway . . . . . . . . : 10.127.100.1

C:\>_
```

ANSWERS TO LAB ANALYSIS TEST

1. If we review the four methods of name resolutions—B-node, P-node, M-node, and H-node—we know that DOS cannot use WINS. This is because DOS can only use the B-node method, and the B-node method broadcasts messages to resolve NetBIOS names. B-node cannot cross the router. Therefore, it cannot communicate with the other segments of the network.

2. Since there is no designated WINS server, the client computer will use whichever WINS server is assigned from the DHCP server or configured in TCP/IP properties. Once the client computer goes onto the network, it registers with that WINS server—which will then respond to all its name resolution messages.

3. A HOSTS file is a text file used in the early days of networking when the TCP/IP protocol was being used. It provides a simple lookup table that contains a list of hostnames (computer names) and the equivalent IP addresses. An LMHOSTS file is built on the same concept except that it can resolve NetBIOS name-to-IP addresses anywhere on an interconnected network—the Internet.

4. Once a Windows client is configured for WINS, it defaults to H-node for its name resolution. This method results in the most efficient network utilization.

5. The WINS client computer populates the WINS database. When a client logs onto the network, it automatically registers its name and address with the WINS server. Once the client computer is registered, it receives a Time To Live (TTL) setting. This setting determines how long the registered information is valid before the WINS server rechecks the information of the client computer to update its database.

ANSWERS TO KEY TERM QUIZ

1. B-node

2. WINS

3. M-node

4. IPconfig

5. LAN Manager HOSTS (LMHOSTS)

MICROSOFT CERTIFIED SYSTEMS ASSOCIATE

3

Configuring, Managing, and Troubleshooting Domain Name System (DNS)

LAB EXERCISES

3.01   Creating an Active Directory–Integrated Zone

3.02   Managing DNS Database Records

3.03   Configuring Dynamic DNS

3.04   Configuring Client Computer Name Resolution

3.05   Troubleshooting DNS Name Resolution

■   Lab Analysis Test

■   Key Term Quiz

■   Lab Solutions

Consider DNS to be an electronic version of your yellow pages. The yellow pages are categorized by business types—Automotive, Charities, Dentists, etc. So, too, the Domain Name system is categorized by type—com (commercial), edu (education), mil (military), org (non-profit organization), etc. Each category, then, lists each individual business (web site) along with a corresponding telephone number (IP address).

DNS is user friendly in the sense that it uses "common names" that are easier to remember. These are the names of companies and organizations that we wish to access on the Web. For example, if we're looking for the Microsoft site, all you need to do is use its common name (Microsoft) in the URL field and the web site will appear. If you're looking for the *Newsweek* magazine web site, all you need to do is use its common name (Newsweek) in the URL field and the web site will appear. Hostnames hardly ever change. Even if the IP address changes, the hostname will be the same.

In this chapter, we'll look at DNS zones and how to create and configure the three different types. We'll look at managing the different resource records that are stored in the database file: Start of Authority (SOA), Host (A), and Pointer (PTR). We'll configure a dynamic DNS and a DNS client. And lastly, we'll review some of the problems you may encounter relative to DNS and Active Directory, and how to resolve them.

CERTIFICATION OBJECTIVE 3.01

25 Minutes

Creating an Active Directory–Integrated Zone

You are the network administrator for the Stuff-It Sausage Packing Company. This is a pure Windows 2000 network with six servers spanning one production location and three distribution locations. You have been asked to implement DNS Server services on the system, taking advantage of the security and database replication benefits of Windows 2000. How would you go about implementing this service?

Learning Objectives

DNS lets you divide the DNS namespace into zones storing information about each DNS domain. DNS zones are portions of the DNS namespace that can be administered as a single unit. DNS Server service has also been carefully integrated into the design and implementation of Active Directory. The zone uses the Active Directory database to store and replicate the zone files. By directory integrating your zones, you can take advantage of additional Windows 2000 DNS features such as secure dynamic updates and record aging/scavenging features.

In this lab, you'll perform the needed steps to install and configure DNS. By the end of this lab, you'll be able to

- Install DNS services.

- Create an Active Directory–integrated zone.

- Configure an Active Directory–integrated zone.

- Install a reverse lookup zone.

Lab Materials and Setup

For this lab exercise, you'll need

- A working computer

- Installed network card (NIC)

- Windows 2000 Server software (installed)

- TCP/IP installed

- Active Directory (AD) installed

Getting Down to Business

First, you need to gather information about your network. You have been given the following information:

IP address of server	192.168.2.1
Subnet mask	255.255.255.0

DNS server	192.168.2.1
Gateway	192.168.2.10
Name of registered domain	southernbell.com

To install the Windows 2000 DNS Server, and then create and configure your first zone, perform the following steps:

Step 1. Access the Windows Optional Networking Components Wizard via the My Network Places icon.

lab **Hint**

DNS server can also be installed using the Add/Remove Programs utility in the Control Panel folder.

Step 2. Install the DNS server using the Networking Services dialog box in the Windows Optional Networking Components Wizard. Use the Add Network Components hyperlink in the Network and Dial-up Connections window.

Step 3. Continue and complete the installation using the Windows Components Wizard. Now that you've installed the DNS server, you need to configure the DNS server with an Active Directory–integrated standard primary zone.

lab **Hint**

You may want to have the corresponding software CD handy in case you need to extract files not found on the hard drive.

Step 4. Open the DNS console from the Administrative Tools program group. Launch the Configure DNS Server Wizard by right-clicking your New Server icon.

Step 5. Create a new zone using the New Zone Wizard. This new zone will be an Active Directory–integrated zone.

Step 6. During the wizard process, also install a reverse lookup zone. Complete the configuration process by entering the "network ID" listed earlier.

lab
Warning
It is recommended that you configure the computer running the Windows 2000 DNS server with a static IP address and not one assigned by a DHCP server—because client computers use the IP address to access the DNS server, you can't have it potentially changing its address. It would be like trying to hit a moving target. Also, when configuring the DNS server's TCP/IP properties for DNS, you should use its own IP settings.

CERTIFICATION OBJECTIVE 3.02

Managing DNS Database Records

20 Minutes

Your company, Big-bITe Consultants, has sent you to San Antonio, Texas to help South-of-the-Border Importers set up their DNS. The company, which imports food products from Mexico and South America, employs 1,500 employees in three buildings. They use their intranet to give their employees access to personal payroll information, check stub information, yearly deductions and earnings, benefits status, sick time and vacation time balances, medical insurance information, and so on.

You've installed the DNS component of Windows 2000 and set up a primary DNS zone for the company's headquarters building based on the information shown here:

IP address of server	192.168.2.01
Subnet mask	255.255.255.0
DNS server	192.168.2.01
Gateway	192.168.2.10
Name of registered domain	Southernbell.com

You've also been asked to go one step further and implement an additional resource record on the primary DNS server—an alias (CNAME) record. FTP.southernbell.com represents an alternate name for the computer domain, but is associated with the same IP address. What procedures might you perform in order to accomplish these tasks?

Learning Objectives

Resource records define data types in the Domain Name System (DNS). There are several record types for data in the DNS. The most common record types are

- Mail exchangers (MX records). These are the machines that normally handle mail sent to this domain.
- DNS Name Server (NS) contains the list of name servers assigned to a domain.
- Aliases that specify alternative names for the host (CNAME records).
- A Host (A) provides name-to-IP-address mappings for a forward lookup zone.
- A Pointer (PTR) is a host record that is used in a reverse zone file to enable IP address-to-name resolution.

In this lab, you'll continue with our previous scenario and create one more record type. By the end of this lab, you'll be able to

- Create and configure an alias (CNAME) record.

Lab Materials and Setup

For this lab exercise, you will need

- A working computer
- Installed network card (NIC)
- Windows 2000 Server software (installed)
- TCP/IP installed
- Active Directory (AD) installed
- Active Directory–integrated zone installed

Getting Down to Business

To create and configure a CNAME record, perform the following steps:

Step 1.   Open the DNS console from the Administrative Tools program group. Expand the tree by clicking the Plus symbol next to the server name.

Step 2. Right-click your forward zone, and click New Record. Select CNAME Record from the Record Type list box in the New Resource Record dialog box.

Step 3. Enter the alternate name for access to this computer. Enter the original hostname in For Host DNS Name. Click OK. Now when Jerry's users make a query for either of these hostnames, the DNS server will return the same IP address.

lab
ⓗint *It is important to use the fully qualified domain name (FQDN) for the originating host DNS name.*

CERTIFICATION OBJECTIVE 3.03

Configuring Dynamic DNS

15 Minutes

You are the system administrator for a regional chain named Phil-er-UP convenience store and gas station. As part of the network, you have recently installed a DNS on a Windows 2000 server configured for Active Directory. You wish to configure the server to receive dynamic DNS updates. What are the necessary steps to activate this feature?

Learning Objectives

The DNS service includes the capability to dynamically update name-to-IP-address data. This dynamic DNS update integrates DNS with DHCP. The two protocols are complementary: DHCP centralizes and automates IP address allocation; a dynamic DNS update automatically records the association between assigned addresses and hostnames.

When you use DHCP and dynamic DNS update, this configures a host automatically for network access whenever it attaches to the IP network. You can locate and reach the host using its permanent, unique DNS hostname. Mobile hosts, for example, can thereby move freely on a network without user or administrator intervention.

In this lab, you'll configure a zone to maintain synchronized name-to-IP-address mappings for a network host. By the end of this lab, you'll be able to

■ Configure a zone for Dynamic Domain Name System (DDNS) service.

Lab Materials and Setup

For this lab exercise, you will need

- A working computer
- Installed network card (NIC)
- Windows 2000 Server software (installed)
- TCP/IP installed
- Active Directory (AD) installed
- Active Directory–integrated zone installed

Getting Down to Business

Step 1.   Open the DNS console from the Administrative Tools program group. Expand the tree by clicking the Plus symbol next to the server name.

Step 2.   Select the zone you wish to configure to receive dynamic updates. Open the Properties dialog box for the zone.

Step 3.   Allow for dynamic updates by selecting Yes in the appropriate selection box. Click OK to complete the process. The zone has been configured to accept dynamic updates.

CERTIFICATION OBJECTIVE 3.04

15 Minutes

Configuring Client Computer Name Resolution

You've just replaced Roberto's workstation at the Ring-A-Dingy Telephone Company. The workstation is installed with Windows 2000 Professional software. On your network is a single DNS server that resolves names for your intranet. This workstation will also have Internet access. It's necessary to configure DNS on this workstation in order to resolve Internet addresses. What is the procedure to do that?

Learning Objectives

Once DNS services have been installed and configured on a Windows 2000 server, we need to look at installing DNS on a Windows 2000 client computer. This gives the client computer access to the DNS server to resolve name-to-IP-address queries.

In this lab, you'll configure a new client computer, which has been added to the network, to access the DNS server. By the end of this lab, you'll be able to

■ Configure a DNS client computer to request an IP address and DNS options from a DHCP.

Lab Materials and Setup

For this lab exercise, you will need

■ A working computer

■ Installed network card (NIC)

■ Windows 2000 Professional software (installed)

■ TCP/IP installed

lab
Warning *It's necessary that the client computer is a member of a domain. This procedure was covered in the Windows 2000 Server exam.*

Getting Down to Business

Begin to configure DNS on a client computer by performing the following steps:

Step 1. Open the TCP/IP properties window of your Local Area Connection. This is accessed through the Network and Dial-up Connections window.

Step 2. Within the Properties window, enter the preferred DNS server address.

Step 3. Click OK to apply your settings.

CERTIFICATION OBJECTIVE 3.05

Troubleshooting DNS Name Resolution   10 Minutes

You've just finished configuring your newly installed DNS server at the Phil-er-UP convenience store and gas station from a previous scenario. You wish to perform a quick test to make sure that it can handle client queries. Which tool would you use to go about performing this test?

Learning Objectives

There are many utilities that Windows 2000 provides that can help you diagnose and solve problems with DNS. The more popular utilities are

- **Nslookup** Used to perform DNS queries and to examine the contents of zone files on local and remote servers. The syntax is nslookup <dnsname><dnsserver>.

- **IPconfig** Used to view DNS client settings, display and flush the resolver cache, and force a dynamic update client to register its DNS records.

- **NetDiag** A utility included with the Support Tools on the Windows 2000 Setup CD that helps isolate networking and connectivity problems by performing a series of tests to determine the state of your network client.

- **DNS monitoring snap-in tool** Lets you monitor DNS server services. It is a quick way to identify potential problems by performing either a simple query or a recursive query on the server.

In this lab, you'll use the monitoring tool to perform a test on your DNS server. By the end of this lab, you'll be able to

- Access the DNS monitoring tool.
- Perform a simple query on the DNS server.

Lab Materials and Setup

For this lab exercise, you will need

- A working computer
- Installed network card (NIC)
- Windows 2000 Server software (installed)
- TCP/IP installed
- DNS Server installed

Getting Down to Business

To test a simple query on your DNS server, perform the following steps:

Step 1. Open your DNS console. Access the Properties windows of your DNS server.

Step 2. Select the Monitoring tab and perform a simple query on the DNS server. Results of the query test appear in the Test Results window.

LAB ANALYSIS TEST

1. Jeff, one of your student interns, is a little confused about what a forward lookup query does and what a reverse lookup query does. Explain to him the purpose of each function.

    _____

    _____

2. Melissa, another student intern, saw you install a DNS server and create an Active Directory–integrated zone. Now she wants to know what the advantage is of using an Active Directory–integrated zone. Explain the advantage.

    _____

    _____

3. How does DDNS improve the efficiency of a DNS server?

    _____

    _____

4. If you have a single DNS server resolving names for an internal domain that is connected to the Internet, how would you configure DNS on the client computers to resolve Internet addresses?

    _____

    _____

5. List the three common command-line utilities and explain the function of each?

    _____

    _____

KEY TERM QUIZ

Use the following vocabulary terms to complete the sentences below. Not all of the terms will be used. Definitions for these terms can be found in "MCSE Windows 2000 Network Administration Study Guide."

Forward lookup

Reverse lookup

Start of Authority (SOA)

Dynamic DNS

Nslookup

Active directory

Zone

Resource records

Namespace

Hostname

1. A _____ is a portion of the DNS namespace that can be administered as a single unit.

2. A query process where the IP address of a host computer is searched in order to find its DNS domain name is called _____.

3. A command-line utility, _____, is used to test and troubleshoot a DNS installation.

4. In a DNS zone file, _____ is used to zone parameters to all installed DNS servers in that zone.

5. A computer's name that is recognized by a TCP/IP network is called a _____.

LAB SOLUTIONS FOR CHAPTER 3

In this section, you'll find solutions to the lab exercises, Lab Analysis Test, and Key Term Quiz.

Lab Solution 3.01

The need for security and database replication is important.

DNS takes advantage of Active Directory's multimaster replication engine. Network managers can centralize and simplify system administration and overall system management by not having to maintain a separate replication topology for DNS, which also provides greater reliability.

In this lab, you performed the necessary steps to install and configure DNS. By the end of this lab, you were able to

- ▓ Install DNS services.

- ▓ Create an Active Directory–integrated zone.

- ▓ Configure an Active Directory–integrated zone.

- ▓ Configure a Reverse Lookup zone.

lab

⚠ Warning *Prior to installing DNS, it is strongly recommended that you configure the computer running the Windows 2000 DNS server with a static IP address— not one assigned by a DHCP server. Also, when configuring the DNS server's TCP/IP properties for DNS, you should use its own IP settings.*

You know the following about your network:

IP address of server	192.168.2.1
Subnet mask	255.255.255.0
DNS server	192.168.2.1
Gateway	192.168.2.10
Name of registered domain	Southernbell.com

To install the Windows 2000 DNS server, create and configure your first zone by performing the following steps:

Step 1. Right-click the My Network Places icon on the desktop and select Properties. This will open the Network and Dial-up Connections window.

lab
Hint

DNS server can also be installed using the Add/Remove Programs utility in the Control Panel folder.

Step 2. In the lower-left corner of the window, click Add Network Components. This hyperlink opens the Windows Components dialog box of the Windows Optional Networking Components Wizard, as seen in Figure 3-1. You will notice in this window that the Networking Services option has a check mark in the box. The box has a gray-fill in it to indicate that not all of the Network Services have been installed.

Step 3. Select the Network Services component and then click the Details button. The Networking Services window opens, revealing the optional components. Select Domain Name System (DNS), as shown in Figure 3-2, and click OK. This brings you back to the Optional Windows Networking Components Wizard dialog box.

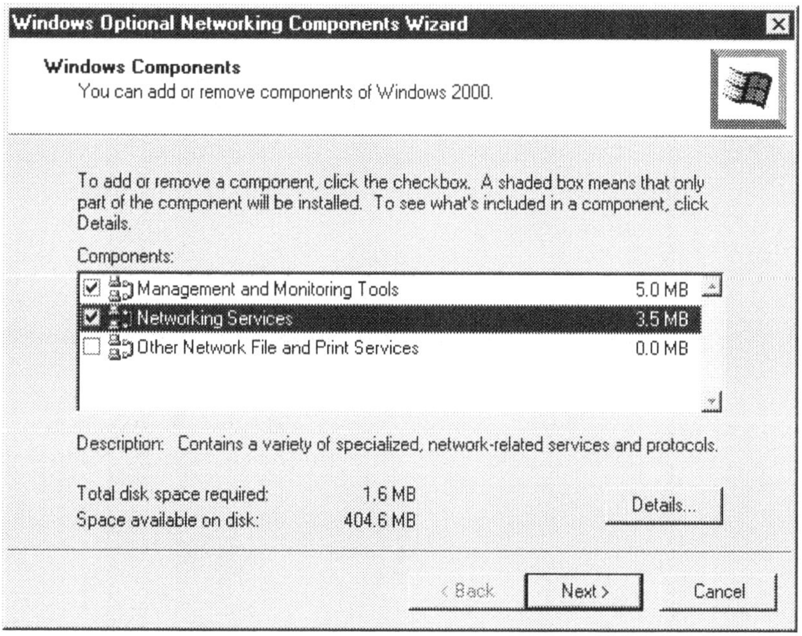

FIGURE 3-1

Adding and removing window components is accomplished through this wizard.

FIGURE 3-2

Adding and
deleting
subcomponents
of network
services is
accomplished
through this
window.

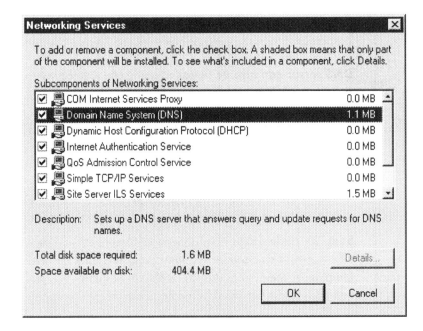

Step 4. Continue the installation by clicking the Next button. This process will also make the DNS console available under the Administrative Tools category in the Start menu. Continue and complete the installation using the Windows Components Wizard. Now that you've installed the DNS server, you need to configure the DNS server with an Active Directory–integrated zone.

lab
Hint
You may want to have the corresponding Windows 2000 Server CD handy in case you need to extract files not found on the hard drive.

Step 5. Click Start | Programs | Administrative Tools | DNS to open the DNS console. Expand the tree by clicking the Plus symbol next to the server name.

Step 6.   Launch the Configure DNS Server Wizard by right-clicking your New Server icon. Select Configure the Server, as shown here:

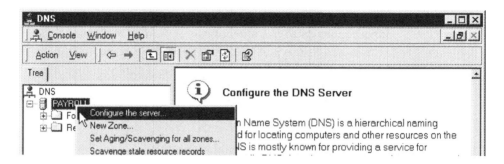

Step 7.   Click Next to open the Forward Lookup Zone window. This forward lookup zone is a database that contains domain namespaces associated with their corresponding IP addresses. This database will assist a computer with converting a domain namespace into an IP address.

Step 8.   Click the Yes, Create a Forward Lookup Zone radio button to create your first zone, as shown here:

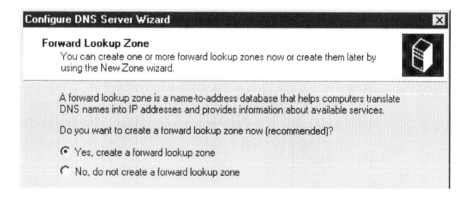

Click Next (not shown). This will open the Zone Type dialog box where you will select the type of zone. Notice that there are three different variations, as shown in Figure 3-3. We will select the Active Directory–integrated type. This process will create a master copy of a new zone. As mentioned above, Active Directory provides zone data replication as part of domain replication. The other two options are Standard Primary and Standard Secondary. Standard Primary provides zone information in a text file, usually stored on a non-Windows 2000 DNS server. The Standard Secondary creates a read-only copy of the zone information used for redundancy or load balancing of DNS on a network.

Step 9. Click Next to open the Zone Name dialog box. Here, we will type the name of the domain (southernbell.com) that we will be resolving for, as shown next. On a network connected to the Internet, this would need to be a valid registered domain name.

Step 10. Click Next to open the Reverse Lookup Zone window. In this configuration, we will be creating a reverse lookup zone. A reverse lookup zone is the opposite of the forward lookup zone process. Troubleshooting tools, such as the Nslookup command-line utility, use this reverse lookup process to echo back a hostname.

FIGURE 3-3

You select the
type of zone to
install through
this window.
The types are
explained in
the lab text.

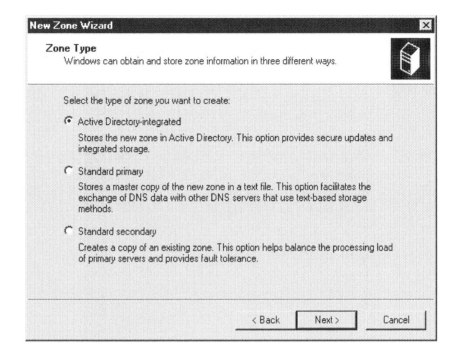

Step 11.   To create a reverse lookup zone, select the Yes, Create a Reverse
Lookup Zone radio button, as shown here:

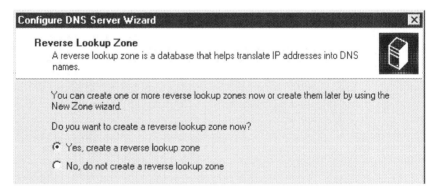

Click Next to open the New Zone Wizard window to select the zone type.

Step 12. We will again choose the Active Directory–integrated zone type for the most secure implementation. Click Next to open the Reverse Lookup Zone dialog box. Enter the Network ID (192.168.2) to identify the domain name by using the network identifier IP address, as shown in Figure 3-4. This wizard actually reverses the order of the bytes from 192.168.2 to 2.168.192. In addition, it will add the Internet IP-to-domain resolution domain, in-addr.arpa.

Step 13. Click Next to open the final window, which summarizes and lets you review the applied settings you selected. Here, you have the option of going back to correct any errors in those settings. Click Finish to complete the configuration process.

Lab Solution 3.02

You've installed the DNS component of Windows 2000 and set up a primary DNS zone for the company's headquarters building based on the information shown here:

IP address of server	192.168.2.01
Subnet mask	255.255.255.0
DNS server	192.168.2.01
Gateway	192.168.2.10
Name of registered domain	southernbell.com

You have also been asked to go one step further and implement an additional resource record on the primary DNS server—an alias (CNAME) record. FTP.southernbell.com represents an alternate name for the computer domain, but is associated with the same IP address. What procedures might you perform in order to accomplish these tasks?

In this lab, we continued with our previous scenario and created two more record types. By the end of this lab, you were able to

■ Create and configure an alias (CNAME) record.

To create and configure a CNAME record, perform the following steps:

FIGURE 3-4

A reverse lookup
zone provides an
IP-address-to-
name resolution
service.

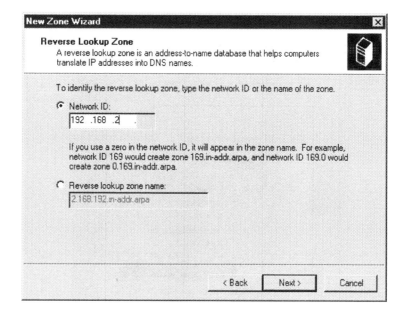

Step 1.   Click Start | Programs | Administrative Tools | DNS to open the DNS console. Expand the tree by clicking the Plus symbol next to the server name.

Step 2.   Click the Forward Lookup Zones folder on the left side of the window to display the zones on the server. These zones will be displayed on the right side of the window, as shown here:

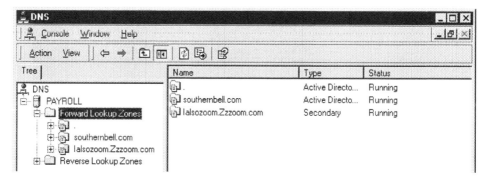

Step 3. Right-click your forward zone and click Other New Record, as shown next. A new pop-up menu screen opens to reveal optional resource record types that can be created. Select Alias from the Record Type list box. Click Create Record.

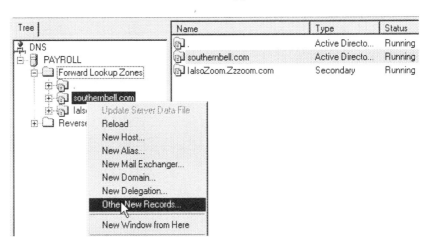

Step 4. In the New Resource Record dialog box, enter the alternate name for access to this computer—**ftp**. Enter the original hostname in the Fully Qualified Name for Target Host field—**southernbell.com**, as shown here:

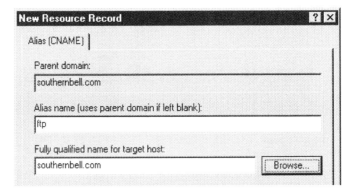

Click OK. This brings you back to the Resource window. Click Done. Now when Jerry's users make a query for either of these hostnames (southernbell.com or ftp.southernbell.com), the DNS server will return the same IP address.

lab
ⓗint

It is important to use the fully qualified domain name (FQDN) for the originating host DNS name.

Lab Solution 3.03

Your task is to configure your DNS server to receive dynamic DNS updates. This allows the server to dynamically update name-to-IP address data. This Dynamic DNS update integrates DNS with DHCP.

In this lab, you configured a zone to maintain synchronized name-to-IP-address mappings for a network host. By the end of this lab, you were able to

■ Configure a zone for Dynamic Domain Name System (DDNS) service.

To configure a zone for DDNS, perform the following steps:

Step 1. Click Start | Programs | Administrative Tools | DNS to open the DNS console. Expand the tree by clicking the Plus symbol next to the server name.

Step 2. Select the zone you wish to configure to receive dynamic updates. From the context menu, select Properties. This opens the Properties dialog box for the zone, as shown in Figure 3-5.

FIGURE 3-5

The Zone Properties window enables you to configure the DNS server to accept dynamic updates.

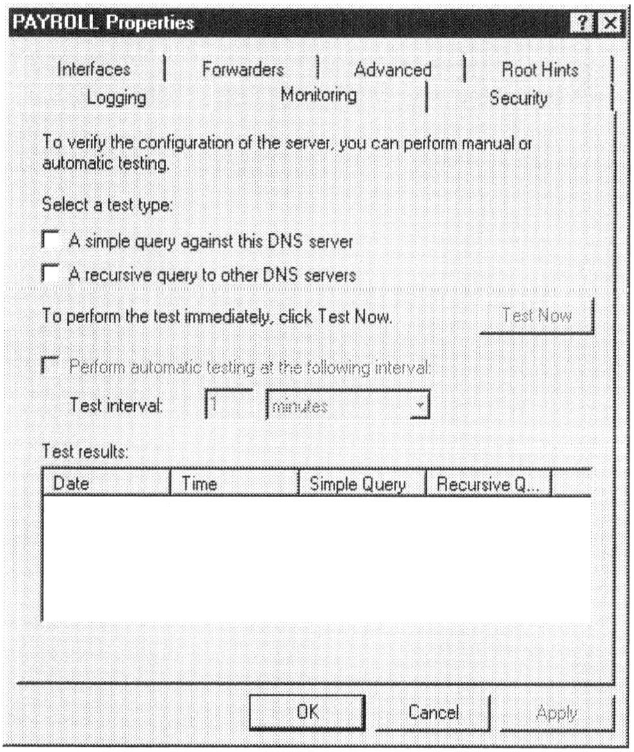

Step 3.   The Zone Properties window displays information for configuring various options. In the General tab dialog box, set the Allow Dynamic Updates pull-down menu to Only Secure Updates. The available selections listed provide the following options:

- **No**   Does not allow for dynamic updates.
- **Yes**   Allows all DDNS update requests.
- **Only Secure Updates**   Allows only DDNS updates that use secure DNS for this zone. This option is preferred. Also, this option only appears if the zone is an Active Directory–integrated zone. By making this selection, an update in the zone database goes through an approval process before it is accepted.

Click OK to complete the process. The zone has been configured to accept dynamic updates.

Lab Solution 3.04

Installing DNS on a Windows 2000 client computer gives it access to the DNS server to resolve name-to-IP-address queries. You configure DNS clients with a preferred DNS name server address that will resolve name-to-IP-address queries.

In this lab, you configured a new client computer, which has been added to the network, to access the DNS server. By the end of this lab, you were able to

- Configure a DNS client computer by manually entering an IP address for the preferred DNS.

lab
Warning   *It's necessary that the client computer be a member of a domain. This procedure was covered in the Windows 2000 Server exam.*

Begin to configure DNS on a client computer by performing the following steps:

Step 1.   Right-click My Network Places and select Properties from the context menu. The Network and Dial-up Connections window opens. Here, you will right-click the Local Area Connection icon and select Properties from the context menu.

Step 2.   In the Local Area Connection Properties window, locate and select Internet Protocol (TCP/IP), then click Properties. This will display the Internet Protocol

(TCP/IP) Properties dialog box, as shown in Figure 3-6. Getting to the TCP/IP properties box can also be accomplished by double clicking the TCP/IP entry.

Step 3. In the DNS section of the dialog box, enter a static DNS server address. Click OK to apply your setting. The client computer will automatically register itself with the DNS server.

Lab Solution 3.05

Now you wish to perform a quick test to make sure that it can handle client queries. What tool would you use to go about performing this test?

There are many utilities that Windows 2000 provides that can help you diagnose and solve problems with DNS in this lab exercise. The more popular utilities are Nslookup, IPconfig, NetDiag, and the DNS monitoring snap-in tool.

FIGURE 3-6

Enter the preferred DNS server address in this dialog box.

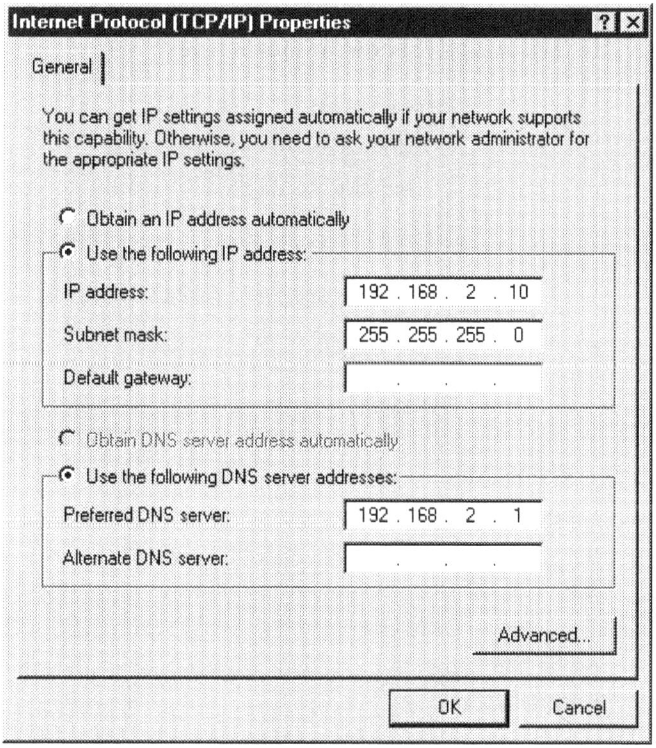

In this lab, you used the monitoring tool to perform a test on your DNS server. By the end of this lab, you were able to

▧   Access the DNS monitoring tool.

▧   Perform a simple query on the DNS server.

To test a simple query on your DNS server, perform the following steps:

Step 1.   Click Start | Programs | Administrative Tools | DNS to open the DNS console. To access the Properties windows of your DNS server, right-click the DNS server in the console tree.

Step 2.   Click the Monitoring tab and perform a simple query on the DNS server by selecting the checkbox for A Simple Query Against this DNS Server.

Step 3.   Click Test Now to process the query. Results of the query test appear in the Test results window, as shown here:

DNS queries resolve in several ways. A client can answer a query locally using cached information obtained from a previous query. The DNS server can use its own cache of resource record information to answer a query. And, a DNS server can also query or contact other DNS servers on behalf of the requesting client to fully resolve the name, then send an answer back to the client. This process is known as *recursive query.*

ANSWERS TO LAB ANALYSIS

1. A forward lookup query resolves a hostname to its IP address, and a reverse lookup query resolves an IP address to its hostname.

2. DNS takes advantage of Active Directory's multimaster replication engine. A network manager can centralize and simplify system administration and overall system management by not having to maintain a separate replication topology for DNS. It also provides greater reliability and improved network administration.

3. Automatic updates to resource records in the DNS database occur when using DDNS. Whenever an IP address is assigned to a computer by a DHCP server, the DDNS process updates that entry in the DNS table.

4. The client computers need to be configured to use the existing DNS server for name resolution. Within the TCP/IP properties windows there is an option to designate a DNS server for that purpose.

5. The three utilities, and the purpose for each, are

- **Nslookup** This utility queries a DNS domain name server to look up and find IP address information of a computer on a network or the Internet. The syntax for the utility is **nslookup** *name* (where *name* is the domain name) or **nslookup** *ipaddress* (this performs a reverse lookup and gives you the domain name).

- **IPconfig** By using this utility with the /displaydns switch, it will list a client computer's local resolver cache for name resolution and look to see if there are any bad mappings. This would be used if a client computer cannot resolve domain name queries. The syntax is **ipconfig /displaydns**.

- **NetDiag** This command-line diagnostic tool helps to isolate networking and connectivity problems by performing a series of tests to determine the state of your network client, and whether it is functional. The syntax is **netdiag**.

ANSWERS TO KEY TERM QUIZ

1. Zone

2. Reverse lookup

3. Nslookup

4. Start of Authority (SOA)

5. Hostname

4

Configuring and Troubleshooting DHCP

LAB EXERCISES

4.01   Installing and Authorizing DHCP Servers

4.02   Configuring DHCP Scopes

4.03   Configuring DHCP Servers for DNS Integration

4.04   Configuring DHCP Clients

4.05   Troubleshooting DHCP

■   Lab Analysis Test

■   Key Term Quiz

■   Lab Solutions

D ynamic Host Configuration Protocol (DHCP) was introduced in 1993 as a means to dynamically (this really means without any human intervention) assign an IP address (an identifier/pass/key) to a computer, allowing it permission to send information on a network. Dynamic addressing simplifies network administration because the software keeps track of IP addresses rather than requiring an administrator to manage the task. This means that a new computer can be added to a network without the hassle of manually assigning it a unique IP address.

The way it works is that a DHCP-enabled client obtains a lease for an IP address from a DHCP server. Without DHCP, any change to a computer's IP address would have to be changed anytime the computer changed subnets or you had to rearrange your IP address strategy. Because each computer's IP address is set as static, you or the user would have to physically go into the TCP/IP network properties and change the address. If this involves one or maybe two machines once in a blue moon, no big deal. In a large-scale environment, however, it would be a major undertaking. As an extreme analogy, let's say that when you get your driver's license, the number for that state is etched on the windshield of your car. Now, if you move from one state to live in another state, your license number and car registration are no longer valid in the new state. You need another license number that conforms to that state's system and you need to register your car. Replacing the license ID is easy, but now you have to take your car into the Department of Motor Vehicles and have the old number etched out and the new one etched in, in order to register your car.

In this chapter, we'll work with Dynamic Host Configuration Protocol (DHCP), from installing the service to configuring a DHCP scope. We'll configure a client computer to use a DHCP server for IP address assignment, and lastly, we'll look at how to troubleshoot DHCP problems.

CERTIFICATION OBJECTIVE 4.01

Installing and Authorizing DHCP Servers

20 Minutes

You are the network administrator for the Kent County Sheriff's Department. The department relies on you to ensure that the sheriffs are able to connect to the database on the network while on patrol. As the department has grown, the system has kept pace. Today, your job is to proceed with phase one of configuring a DHCP server that will dynamically assign IP addresses to the sheriffs, installing the service on a server. What steps are taken to implement a DHCP server?

Learning Objectives

The Dynamic Host Configuration Protocol (DHCP) provides configuration parameters to Internet hosts in a client/server model. DHCP server hosts allocate network addresses and deliver configuration parameters to other (client) hosts. It consists of two components: a protocol for delivering host-specific configuration parameters from a server to a host, and a mechanism for allocating network addresses to hosts. The following are three mechanisms that DHCP supports for IP address allocation:

- **Automatic allocation**   A permanent IP address is assigned to the client.
- **Dynamic allocation**   An address is assigned/leased for a limited period of time.
- **Manual allocation**   An address is assigned manually.

The client sends a message to request configuration parameters and the server responds with a message carrying the desired parameters back to the client. Some of the benefits of DHCP are as follows:

- **Safe and reliable configuration**   DHCP minimizes configuration errors caused by manual IP address configuration—syntax errors as well as duplicate IP addresses, to name two.
- **Reduced network administration**   TCP/IP configuration is centralized and automated. Global and subnet-specific TCP/IP configurations can be defined from a central location.

In this lab, you will implement a DHCP server working along with Active Directory to assign IP addresses to client computers. By the end of this lab, you'll be able to

- Install the DHCP Server services.
- Authorize the DHCP server.

Lab Materials and Setup

For this lab exercise, you'll need

- A working computer
- Installed network card (NIC)
- Windows 2000 Server software (installed)
- TCP/IP installed
- Domain Name System (DNS) installed
- Active Directory (AD) installed

Getting Down to Business

To begin installing and then authorize DHCP, perform the following steps:

Step 1.   Access the Windows Optional Networking Components Wizard via the My Network Places icon. You can use the Add Network Components hyperlink in the Network and Dial-up Connections window.

lab
Hint   *DHCP can also be installed using the Add/Remove Programs utility in the Control Panel folder.*

Step 2.   Install the DHCP server using the Networking Services dialog box in the Windows Optional Networking Components Wizard.

Step 3.   Continue and complete the installation using the Windows Components Wizard. Now that you've installed the DHCP Server, you need to authorize it in Active Directory.

lab
Hint   *The following steps are necessary because this server is using Active Directory. Active Directory is not necessary for DHCP to function.*

Step 4.   Open the DHCP console window. Select the DHCP server and select the Authorize action from the Action menu.

Step 5.   This will start the authorization processes, which takes a few minutes to complete. When the process is done, the DHCP server is ready to issue addresses.

CERTIFICATION OBJECTIVE 4.02

Configuring DHCP Scopes

15 Minutes

In the second part of the installation process at the Kent County Sheriff's Department, you now need to configure a scope, or pool, of dynamically assigned IP addresses. There are 75 sheriffs working three shifts, each shift sharing 25 squad cars with computers, plus six administration people on each shift. You need to enter the following information during configuration:

■ DHCP scope name: DHCP SCOPE

■ SCOPE description: Pool of available IP addresses

■ IP address range: 192.168.32.5–192.168.32.200

■ Excluded IP address: 192.168.32.40

■ Lease duration time: 21 days

■ Subnet mask: 255.255.255.0

Learning Objectives

Once DHCP is installed, you need to make available a range of IP addresses that can be dynamically assigned to a host on a given subnet. In this lab, you will configure a scope for your DHCP server. By the end of this lab, you'll be able to

■ Create a DHCP scope.

■ Name a DHCP scope.

■ Enter a range of IP addresses.

■ Set the lease duration on the IP addresses.

■ Assign the subnet mask for the IP addresses.

- Activate the scope.
- Exclude reserved IP addresses from a DHCP scope.

Lab Materials and Setup

For this lab exercise, you will need

- A working computer
- Installed network card (NIC)
- Windows 2000 Server software (installed)
- TCP/IP installed
- Domain Name System (DNS) installed
- Active Directory (AD) installed

Getting Down to Business

To begin configuring DHCP, perform the following steps:

Step 1. Open the DHCP Console Manager. Select the DHCP server and right-click on the DHCP server. Select New Scope.

Step 2. This begins the Create Scope Wizard. You first need to enter information in the Scope Name window provided in lab scenario 4.01 described earlier.

Step 3. The next window requires that you enter the IP address range along with the subnet. In the Add Exclusions window, enter excluded range of IP addresses.

Step 4. In the Lease Duration window, enter a lease time and then complete the process by activating the scope.

CERTIFICATION OBJECTIVE 4.03

Configuring DHCP Servers for DNS Integration

15 Minutes

As a member of the Network Administration team at the Phillips, Phlat, and Allen-Wrench Tool Company, you are responsible for the Windows 2000 DHCP servers. The network is a pure Windows 2000 network environment and you need to ensure that the client computers are registered properly in DNS for Active Directory Integration. How should you configure this DNS integration?

Learning Objectives

The combination of DHCP and DNS results in DDNS. DHCP is responsible for dynamic updates, and hence you will find the DHCP service running on every Windows 2000 computer whether it is a DHCP client or not. By default, DHCP clients will attempt to register their A records, while the DHCP server will take care of registering the PTR records. This process requires the use of an additional DHCP option, the client FQDN option (option 81). This option permits the client to provide its fully qualified domain name (FQDN) as well as instructions to the DHCP server on how it would like the server to process DNS dynamic updates (if any) on its behalf.

In this lab, you'll configure DHCP for DNS integration. By the end of this lab, you'll be able to

- Integrate DHCP and DNS.
- Understand how dynamic DNS updates work.

Lab Materials and Setup

For this lab exercise, you will need

- A working computer

- Installed network card (NIC)
- Windows 2000 Server software (installed)
- TCP/IP installed
- Domain Name System (DNS) installed
- Active Directory (AD) installed

Getting Down to Business

To configure this capability, perform the following steps:

Step 1. Open the DHCP console, select the DHCP server to configure DNS integration.

Step 2. In the General Tab section of the Properties window, enable the DHCP audit logging.

Step 3. In the DNS Tab section of the Properties window, allow for automatic update of DHCP client information in DNS only if requested by a DHCP client. And when an IP address lease expires, discard name-to-IP-address requests.

CERTIFICATION OBJECTIVE 4.04

Configuring DHCP Clients

15 Minutes

You are the network administrator of Eyemakid Toy Company. You have just upgraded your network to a Windows 2000 system and also added DHCP and DNS servers to automatically assign IP addresses to the client computers, and to automatically broadcast the DNS server that will resolve your client's request for name-to-IP-address resolutions. Now you need to configure the 25 client computers to connect to these services. What needs to be done to these computers to complete the process?

Learning Objectives

DHCP clients use two different processes to communicate with DHCP servers and obtain a configuration: the initialization process, which occurs when a client computer first starts and attempts to join the network; and the renewal process, which occurs after a client has a lease but needs to renew that lease with the server.

The first time a DHCP-enabled client starts, it automatically follows an initialization process to obtain a lease from a DHCP server.

In this lab, you'll configure a client computer to use DHCP. By the end of this lab, you'll be able to

- Configure the client computer to automatically receive an IP address.
- Configure the client computer to automatically obtain the DNS server address for name resolution.

Lab Materials and Setup

For this lab exercise, you will need

- A working computer
- Installed network card (NIC)
- Windows 2000 Professional software (installed)
- TCP/IP installed

Getting Down to Business

To configure a client computer for DHCP, perform the following steps:

Step 1.   Access the Network and Dial-up Connections window and launch the Local Area Connections Properties dialog box. This dialog box displays the system's installed adaptors, services, and protocols.

Step 2.   Next, locate and select the TCP/IP protocol component in the Connection window. This activates the Properties button below the window. Click the Properties button to display the Internet Protocol (TCP/IP) Properties dialog box.

Step 3. Activate the Obtain an IP Address Automatically option and the Obtain DNS Server Addresses option.

Step 4. Access the WINS tab through the Advanced button and activate the Use NetBIOS Setting from the DHCP Server option. Complete and apply your settings.

CERTIFICATION OBJECTIVE 4.05

Troubleshooting DHCP

15 Minutes

You are a network administrator for a national cosmetic company. You have a 150-host network and are running a Windows 2000 DHCP server. Part of your responsibilities as a network administrator is to ensure that all services on the network are running at peak performance. Today, on your checklist of DHCP performance duties is to look at the DHCP database. Your job is to compact the database to remove any obsolete and deleted DHCP client entries and recover the unused space. You notice that the database, DHCP.MDB, has increased in size since it was last compacted, a year ago. What are the steps and the utility needed to perform this task?

Learning Objectives

DHCP Server stores the information about its IP address leases in an access database named DHCP.MDB. There is no built-in limit to the number of records that a DHCP server can store. The size of the database is dependent upon the number of DHCP clients on the network. The DHCP database grows over time as a result of clients starting and stopping on the network. The size of the DHCP database is not directly proportional to the number of active client lease entries. Over time, as some DHCP client entries become obsolete and are deleted, there remains some unused space.

To recover the unused space, the DHCP database must be compacted. Starting with the Windows NT Server 4.0 up to the present Windows 2000 Server, dynamic database compaction occurs on DHCP servers as an automatic background process during idle time after a database update.

Compacting the DHCP database with the jetpack program is a fairly uncommon but necessary administrative task. You use the jetpack.exe utility (syntax: jetpack <database name> <temp database name>) included with Windows 2000 to compact the database. Jetpack compresses the DHCP database, which is found in the %SystemRoot%\system32\dhcp folder, to a temporary file (TEMP.MDB). Once the process is complete, the program deletes the TEMP.MDB file. You finish up by restarting the DHCP Server service.

In this lab, you'll use the jetpack program to compact the DHCP database. By the end of this lab, you'll be able to

- Stop the DHCP server.
- Compact the DHCP database using the jetpack program.
- Start the DHCP server.

Lab Materials and Setup

For this lab exercise, you will need

- A working computer
- Installed network card (NIC)
- Windows 2000 Server software (installed)
- TCP/IP installed
- Domain Name System (DNS) installed
- Active Directory (AD) installed

Getting Down to Business

To compact the DHCP database, perform the following steps:

Step 1. Begin by first stopping the DHCP Server service.

Step 2. Next, access the \%SystemRoot%\system32\dhcp folder within a Command Prompt window and enter **jetpack dhcp.mdb temp.mdb**.

Step 3. Once completed, restart the DHCP Server service.

LAB ANALYSIS TEST

1. You are the systems administrator of the new Two-Foot Sports Department Store in Stamping Ground, Kentucky. You're responsible for configuring the DHCP server added to the network that services your store. The address of the router port is 192.168.25.1, and is subnetted with a Class C subnet mask. You have 40 IP addresses you need to provide, starting with 192.168.25.20. What steps must you take to configure the server?

   _____

   _____

2. You are the Windows 2000 administrator for Wing-and-a-Prayer Travel Agency. When checking on your DHCP server, you notice that DHCP requests are much higher than the number of users on the network. Where is the first place to look to help troubleshoot this situation?

   _____

   _____

3. Which two advantages are derived through the use of a DHCP server on a network?

   _____

   _____

4. What are the two different processes the DHCP client uses to communicate with DHCP servers and to obtain a configuration?

   _____

   _____

5. What utility is used—and briefly explain the process—to compact the DHCP database?

   _____

   _____

KEY TERM QUIZ

Use the following vocabulary terms to complete the sentences below. Not all of the terms will be used. Definitions for these terms can be found in "Managing a Microsoft Windows 2000 Network Environment Study Guide."

> Domain Name System (DNS)
>
> Dynamic Host Configuration Protocol (DHCP)
>
> Lease
>
> Subnet mask
>
> Bootstrap Protocol (BOOTP)
>
> Scope
>
> Exclusion
>
> Proxy
>
> DHCP client
>
> DHCP server

1. Any computer that has a DHCP setting enabled to request an IP address assignment is named a (an) _____.

2. A _____ is the length of time that an IP address is assigned to a client computer.

3. _____ is an Internet protocol enabling a diskless workstation to discover its IP address from a network server.

4. The range of possible IP addresses for a network is named a (an) _____.

5. A (an) _____ indicates the process where IP addresses or a range of IP addresses are removed from a DHCP scope.

LAB SOLUTIONS FOR CHAPTER 4

In this section, you'll find solutions to the lab exercises, Lab Analysis Test, and Key Term Quiz.

Lab Solution 4.01

Your job today was to proceed with phase one of configuring a DHCP server so the server could dynamically assign IP addresses to the mobile sheriffs. What steps were taken to implement a DHCP server?

In this lab, you implement a DHCP Server working along with Active Directory to assign IP addresses to client computers. By the end of this lab, you were able to

- Install the DHCP Server services.
- Authorize the DHCP server.

To begin installing and then authorize DHCP, perform the following steps:

Step 1. Right-click the My Network Places icon on the desktop and select Properties. This will open the Network and Dial-up Connections window.

lab
◔int
DHCP can also be installed using the Add/Remove Programs utility in the Control Panel folder.

Step 2. In the lower-left corner of the window, click Add Network Components. This hyperlink, shown in Figure 4-1, opens the Windows Components dialog box of the Windows Optional Networking Components Wizard. You will notice in this window, Figure 4-2, that the Networking Services option has a check mark in the box. The box has a gray-fill in it to indicate that not all of the Network Services have been installed. Install the DHCP server using the Networking Services dialog box in the Windows Optional Networking Components Wizard.

Step 3. Select the Network Services component and then click the Details button. The Networking Services window opens revealing the optional components. Select Dynamic Host Configuration Protocol (DHCP), as shown in Figure 4-3, and click OK. This brings you back to the Optional Windows Networking Components Wizard dialog box.

FIGURE 4-1

This hyperlink gets you into the Optional Networking Components Wizard.

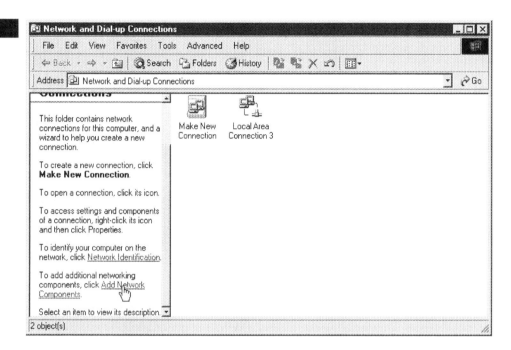

FIGURE 4-2

Component groups are shown in this window. Here we select the Networking Services group.

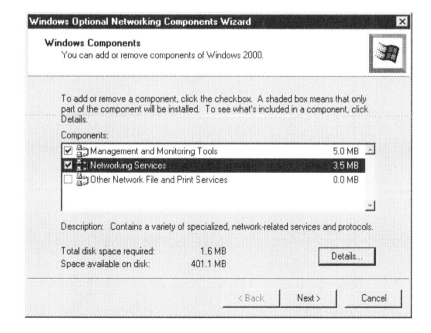

FIGURE 4-3

Select the DHCP subcomponent that will automatically assign IP addresses to client computers.

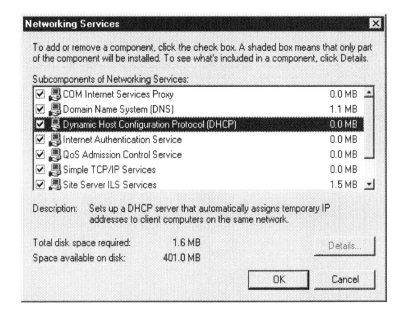

Step 4. Complete the installation by clicking the Next button. This process will also make the DHCP console available under the Administrative Tools category in the Start menu.

Step 5. Now that you've installed the DHCP server, you need to authorize a DHCP server in the Active Directory. Click Start | Programs | Administrative Tools and select DHCP. This opens the DHCP Console window.

Step 6. Select the DHCP Server and select the Authorize action from the Action menu, as shown in Figure 4-4. This will start the authorization processes, which takes a few minutes to complete. When the process is done, the DHCP Server will exhibit an Active status, signaling that your DHCP server is ready to issue addresses.

Lab Solution 4.02

Your task was to configure a scope, or pool, of dynamically assigned IP addresses for 25 shared squad cars with computers, plus six administration people on each shift. You needed to enter the following information during configuration:

- DHCP scope name: DHCP SCOPE

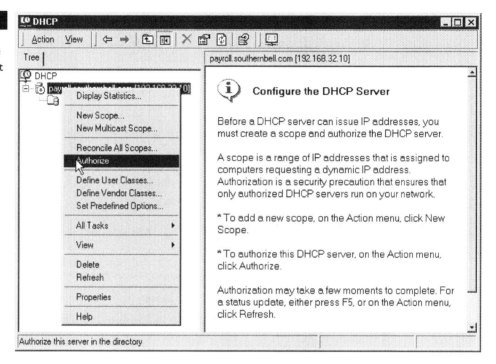

FIGURE 4-4

Select Authorize from the context menu to give the DHCP server authority to assign IP addresses.

- SCOPE description: Pool of available IP addresses
- IP address range: 192.168.32.5–192.168.32.200
- Excluded IP address: 192.168.32.10
- Lease duration time: 21 days
- Subnet mask: 255.255.255.0

Once DHCP is installed, you need to make available a range of IP addresses that can be dynamically assigned to a host on a given subnet. This range of IP addresses is called a scope (pool). A scope may also include values that provide configuration parameters to the client computer.

In this lab, you configured a scope for your DHCP server. By the end of this lab, you were able to

- Create, name, and activate a DHCP scope.
- Enter a range of IP addresses.

■ Set the lease duration on the IP addresses.

■ Assign the subnet mask for the IP addresses.

Exclude reserved IP addresses from a DHCP scope.
To begin configuring DHCP, perform the following steps:

Step 1.   Click Start | Programs | Administrative Tools | DHCP. This opens the
DHCP Console Manager. Select and right-click on the DHCP server in the console
tree. Select New Scope from the options menu, as shown next. This option is also
available from the Action menu.

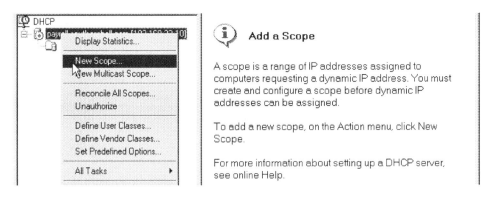

Step 2.   This begins the Create Scope Wizard. Click Next to bypass the Welcome
window. In the Scope Name window, type the name and description of the new
scope, as shown here:

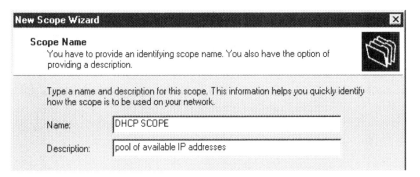

Click Next (not shown) to proceed to the IP Address Range page.

Step 3.   In the Start IP Address and End IP Address text boxes, enter the range of addresses, as shown here:

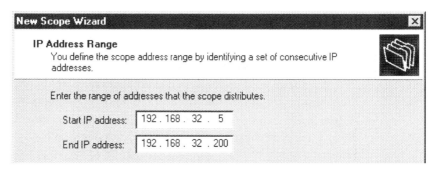

These will indicate the address range that the scope will assign to DHCP clients.

lab
①int

Generally, the scope doesn't include the x.x.x.0 and x.x.x.255 addresses—
these are reserved for network addresses and broadcast messages,
respectively. You would normally use a range of 192.168.32.1 to
192.168.32.254 rather than 192.168.32.0 to 192.168.32.255.

Step 4.   Next, verify that the subnet mask that will be used with the IP addresses is correct in the Subnet Mask field. When you enter an IP address range, the bit length and subnet mask are filled in for you automatically. Unless you use subnets, you should use the default values.

Step 5.   Click Next to proceed to the Add Exclusions window. Use the exclusion range fields (Start IP Address and End IP Address) to define IP address ranges that are to be excluded from the scope. Since we are excluding only one IP address, 192.168.32.10, enter the IP address in both the Start IP Address and End IP Address text boxes. Click Add to place this IP address into the Excluded Address Range window, as shown here:

These IP addresses are typically assigned to application servers, routers, printers, or other internal equipment that require a static address. It is possible to have multiple excluded IP addresses or ranges for each scope.

Click Next (not shown) to open the Lease Duration window.

Step 6. In the Lease Duration window, enter a lease time—this is the length of time that the IP address is assigned to a client computer by the server. This lease time is set in days, hours, and minutes. Once the lease time has expired, the IP address is automatically returned to the DHCP pool. A short lease duration is used if IP addresses are in short supply; a long lease duration is used to minimize the amount of network traffic generated by the DHCP server. Enter a lease time of 21 days, 0 hours, 0 minutes, as shown here:

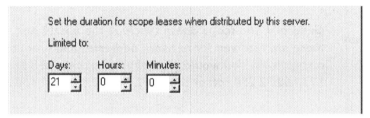

Click Next (not shown) to proceed to the Configure DHC Options window.

lab
Hint

The default lease time given to an IP address by DHCP is eight days. For most networks, this is sufficient.

Step 7. We shall opt out of this screen and select No, I Will Configure These Options Later. Click Next to open the Activate Scope window. The default selection in this window is Yes, I Want to Activate this Scope Now. Click Next to open the Completion window, and click Finish to create and activate the scope.

lab
Hint

Choosing Yes, I Want To Configure These Options Now in the Activate Scope window will cause the wizard to display four additional pages, which will allow you to configure a router, domain name, DNS server, and WINS server options, in addition to activating the scope. Since these options are addressed in other lab chapters, we have chosen not to configure these options at this time.

Lab Solution 4.03

In large companies like this, responsibilities are divided among a team of network administrators. You're responsible for several Windows 2000 DHCP servers in a pure Windows 2000 network environment. DHCP and DNS integration is common. What are the configuration steps to make this happen?

In this lab, you configured a DHCP for DNS integration. By the end of this lab, you were able to

- Integrate DHCP and DNS.

- Understand how dynamic DNS updates work.

To configure this capability, perform the following steps:

Step 1. Click Start | Programs | Administrative Tools | DHCP. This opens the DHCP Console Manager. Right-click on the DHCP server to configure DNS integration in the console tree.

Step 2. From the Options menu, select Properties. This opens the properties window of the DHCP server. It opens to the General Tab section. Verify that there is a check mark in the Enable DHCP Audit Logging option.

Step 3. Click the DNS Tab section of the Properties window. Verify the following three items are active: Automatically Update DHCP Client Information in DNS, Update DNS Only if DHCP Client Requests, and Discard Forward (Name-to-IP-Address) Lookups when Lease Expires, as shown here:

That's all there is to the mechanics of integrating DHCP in a DNS environment.

Lab Solution 4.04

You've upgraded your network to a Windows 2000 system and also added DHCP and DNS servers. Now you need to configure the 25 client computers to connect to these services. (In this lab scenario, the process is a manual one. It's necessary to configure each client computer one at a time.) What needs to be done to these computers to complete the process?

In this lab, you configured a client computer to use DHCP. By the end of this lab, you were able to

- Configure the client computer to automatically receive an IP address.
- Configure the client computer to automatically obtain the DNS server address for name resolution.

To configure a client computer for DHCP, perform the following steps:

Step 1.   Right-click My Network Places on your desktop. Select Properties from the context menu. This will open the Network and Dial-up Connections window.

Step 2.   Right-click the Local Area Connection icon and select Properties from the context menu. This opens the Properties dialog box, which displays the system's installed adaptors, services, and protocols, as shown in Figure 4-5.

Step 3.   Next, using the scroll bar, locate and select the TCP/IP protocol component in the connection window. This activates the Properties button below the window. Click the Properties button to display the Internet Protocol (TCP/IP) Properties dialog box.

Step 4.   This dialog box provides two different methods of configuring an IP address. If you opt to manually assign an IP address, you would activate the Use the Following IP Address radio button. If your network uses a DHCP server to assign IP addresses, you would activate the Obtain an IP Address Automatically radio button. In our case, we will be using the DHCP server to assign IP addresses to client computers. Click the radio button next to this option, as shown in Figure 4-6.

Select the TCP/IP
component to
configure its
settings.

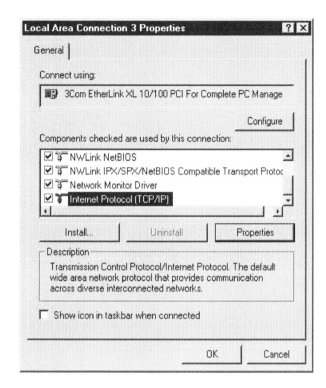

Step 5. Since we are also automatically broadcasting the DNS server address to resolve name-to-IP-address queries, we need to activate this option. Click the radio button next to the Obtain DNS Server Address Automatically option, also shown in Figure 4-6.

Step 6. Our last step is to allow for down-level clients to receive the IP address assignment from the DHCP server. Click the Advanced button.

Step 7. In this dialog box, click the WINS tab. Click the radio button next to Use NetBIOS Setting from DHCP Server to activate this option, as shown in Figure 4-7. Click OK through the various screens to apply your settings. You will be asked to reboot your system.

FIGURE 4-6

Choose to obtain
IP addresses and
DNS server
addresses
automatically.

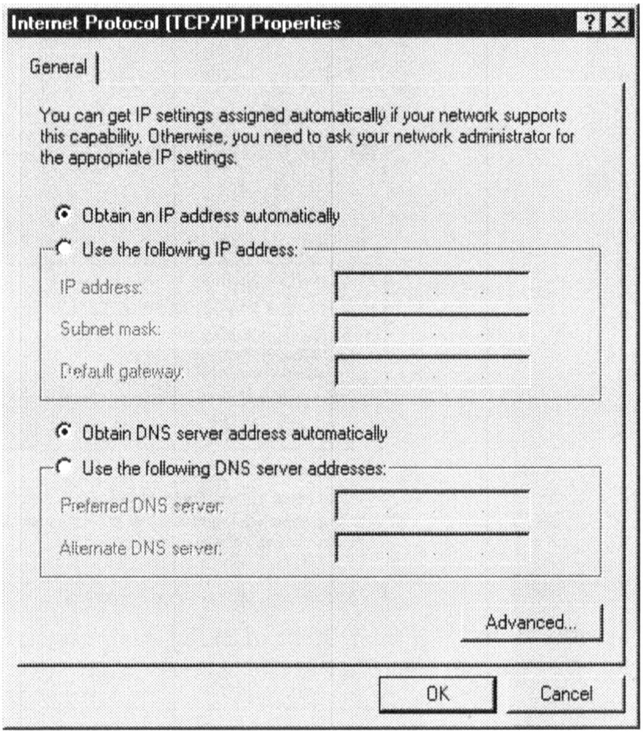

Lab Solution 4.05

Today's checklist includes the compacting of the DHCP database to remove any obsolete and deleted DHCP client entries and recover the unused space. You've noticed that the database, DHCP.MDB, has increased in size since it was last compacted a year ago. What are the steps and the utility needed to perform this task?

In this lab, you'll use the jetpack program to compact the DHCP database. By the end of this lab, you'll be able to

- Stop the DHCP Server.
- Compact the DHCP database using the jetpack program.
- Start the DHCP Server.

To compact the DHCP database using the command prompt, perform the following steps:

Step 1.   Begin by first stopping the DHCP Server service. Open a Command Prompt window by clicking Start | Program | Accessories and selecting Command Prompt from the list. This will open a DOS session.

FIGURE 4-7

Choose the
NetBIOS resolver
service to query
WINS servers.

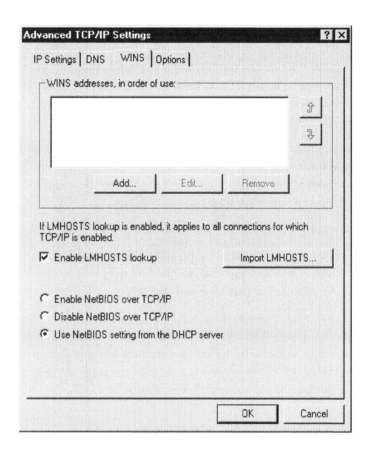

lab
Hint   *Using the Run option from the start menu, you can type* cmd, *or command,*
to open a DOS session.

Step 2.   At the command prompt, type **net stop dhcpserver**. This will take the
DHCP server offline.

Step 3.   Next, access the %SystemRoot%\system32\dhcp folder within the
Command Prompt window and enter **jetpack dhcp.mdb temp.mdb**. The second
database name can be anything—it does not have to be named temp.

Step 4.   Once completed, restart the DHCP Server service by typing **net start**
dhcpserver at the command prompt.

lab
Warning   *If an error message is displayed when you engage the jetpack function,*
don't be alarmed. It just means that there are no entries in the database.

ANSWERS TO LAB ANALYSIS

1. A single DHCP server can serve multiple segments, therefore eliminating the need for an additional server. The router's address, 192.168.25.1, is outside of the starting point of the assignable addresses. Since we're looking to assign 40 addresses and the beginning address is 192.168.25.20, the last assignable address is 192.168.25.59.

2. IP address requests from the DHCP can be affected by the ratio of available IP addresses to the number of hosts requesting those addresses. If the lease has been set for a short period of time, client computers will need to request addresses more frequently. Check the length of the DHCP lease and adjust the lease time accordingly.

3. Safe and reliable configuration. Reduced network administration.

4. The processes are the initialization process, which occurs when a client computer first starts and attempts to join the network, and the renewal process, which occurs after a client has a lease but needs to renew that lease with the server.

5. In order to manually compact a DHCP server, it must first be stopped. You use the jetpack.exe utility included with Windows 2000 to compact the database. Jetpack compresses the DHCP database, which is found in the %SystemRoot%\system32\dhcp folder, to a temporary file (TEMP.MDB). Once the process is complete, the program deletes the TEMP.MDB file. You finish up by restarting the DHCP server service.

ANSWERS TO KEY TERM QUIZ

1. DHCP client

2. Lease

3. BOOTP

4. Scope

5. Exclusion

MICROSOFT CERTIFIED SYSTEMS ASSOCIATE

5

Active Directory Users and Groups

LAB EXERCISES

5.01   Creating and Configuring Domain
        User Accounts

5.02   Creating a Default User Profile

5.03   Creating and Administering
        a Global Group

5.04   Creating and Managing
        Organizational Units

5.05   Delegating Administrative Control

■   Lab Analysis Test

■   Key Term Quiz

■   Lab Solutions

Active Directory is an integral part of the Windows 2000 architecture; a centralized and standardized system that automates network management of user data, security, and distributed resources, and enables interoperation with other directories. Active Directory contains and maintains every component that is part of the network with the use of objects. Objects contain properties that identify aspects, or parameters, of the objects. Each property associated with the object contains a value. This value provides information about that property. Think of Active Directory as a Rolodex. The Rolodex contains file cards—objects. Each object has lines (fields) of information: last name, first name, address, company, department, phone number properties. Each field contains information relative to that field—a value, information that is unique to that object.

Active Directory provides a single point of access for system administration (management of user accounts, clients, servers, and applications, for example) to reduce redundancy and errors, an object-oriented storage organization allowing for easier access to information, and support for the Lightweight Directory Access Protocol (LDAP) to enable integrated directory functionality, and it provides for both backward and forward compatibility.

In this lab chapter, we'll look at some new—as well as not so new—concepts relating to Active Directory: how to create and configure user accounts within a domain, the process of planning new group accounts, creating and moving Active Directory objects, and delegating administrative control of objects to individuals using the Delegation of Control Wizard.

CERTIFICATION OBJECTIVE 5.01

20 Minutes

Creating and Configuring Domain User Accounts

You are the network administrator of the tax accounting firm of Weezal, Cheetem, and Howe. During this time of year, the tax return season, temporary workers are hired to help with the influx of clients. Today is Friday, and before they start work on Monday you need to create accounts for each of the individuals in the following table, which was given to you by the personnel department:

Last Name	First Name	User Name	Password	Change Password
Reeves	Allen	Areeves	Flowers	Must
Campbell	Harold	Hcampbell	(blank)	Must
DiMiele	Susan	Sdimiele	(blank)	Must
Sposo	Ellen	Esposo	Floppy	Must

Learning Objectives

The purpose behind a user account is to provide that user access to the resources on that network. This includes not only access to information and resources on their local computer, but also access to shared information and resources on the network: files, databases, printers, applications, and web access.

In this lab you'll create and configure accounts for domain users. By the end of this lab, you'll be able to

- Create a domain user account and configure its properties.
- Rename, disable, and delete an account.

Lab Materials and Setup

For this lab exercise, you'll need

- A working computer
- Installed network card (NIC)
- Windows 2000 Server software (installed)
- TCP/IP installed
- Domain Name System (DNS) installed
- Active Directory (AD) installed

Getting Down to Business

The lab will be performed in three different stages. First, we'll create several domain user accounts. Second, we'll configure the associated account properties. And third, we'll disable and delete an account. To begin creating accounts, perform the following steps:

Step 1. Log on to your domain server with your Administrator account. Access the Active Directory Users and Computers console.

Step 2. Click the Users folder in the domain. This folder contains the default user accounts created during the Windows 2000 Server build.

Step 3. Right-click the Users folder to create the new users listed above. When creating an Active Directory user account, you enter the user's first name, last name, and middle initial. The Full Name field is automatically filled in. Lastly, enter the user's login name.

lab
ⓘint

User accounts can also be created using the New | User option in the Action menu.

Step 4. Enter the information in the New User Account Parameters window; this includes their password and password options. Complete the process new user process.

Step 5. Repeat steps 3 and 4 for each of the remaining users.

Step 6. Come Monday, there is an e-mail from personnel regarding the new hires. There are some changes that need to be made to three of them. The first deals with Allen Reeves. His start date will be delayed two weeks, so you need to disable the account for the time being.

Step 7. Be sure that you are logged on with your Administrator account. Open the Active Directory Users and Computers console. Expand the Active Directory Users and Computers tree, if necessary.

Step 8. Select Allen Reeves, which you created in the previous steps, and disable the account. A message will notify you that the account has been disabled. Close out of the message box. Using the details pane of the console, how can you tell that the user account has been disabled?

Step 9. Log off as Administrator and attempt to log on as Allen Reeves to confirm that the account is disabled.

Step 10. Ellen Sposo has gotten married since she applied for the temporary job. You need to change her now maiden name to her new married name, Esposato.

Step 11. Be sure you're logged on to your domain with your Administrator account. Access her domain user account and make the necessary last name change.

Step 12. The last change is for Harold Campbell's user account. The e-mail states that he is not going to be working here after all. You need to delete the account.

lab
ⓘint *If you've created a user account with special access parameters to fit a particular job function and you delete that account, you will have to re-create that account along with its attributes once a new worker is hired. An easier way of administrating this scenario is to disable the account instead. It will keep the account and its attributes intact, and when the new person is hired all you need to do is change the user's first name, last name, and logon name.*

CERTIFICATION OBJECTIVE 5.02

Creating a Default User Profile

25 Minutes

Some new network standards are being implemented at the Money-Pit Bank. The CIO is requiring all Windows 2000 Professional users to have the same desktop settings and there needs to be an icon on the desktop that opens an interest rate monitor program. As a member of the network administration team, your job is to create a default template with those settings and test it out on a domain user account.

The template information is as follows: First Name - Profile, Last Name - Template, Logon Name - ptemplate, Password - (blank), Desktop Settings - Slate.

The test user will be as follows: First Name - William, Last Name - Giubotto, Logon Name - wgiubotto, Password - Spring, Password Change - Cannot.

Learning Objectives

On computers running Windows 2000, user profiles automatically create and maintain the desktop settings for each user's work environment on the local computer. A user profile is created for each user when he or she logs on to a computer for the first time. There are three types of user profiles. A *local user profile, roaming user profile,* and a *mandatory user profile.*

In this lab, you'll create a default user profile. The property values entered in the user template for that container are copied into the New User object as it is created. By the end of this lab, you'll be able to

- Understand the difference between a local user profile, a roaming (default) user profile, and a mandatory user profile.
- Create a default user profile.

Lab Materials and Setup

For this lab exercise, you will need

- A working computer
- Installed network card (NIC)
- Windows 2000 Server software (installed)
- TCP/IP installed
- Domain Name System (DNS) installed
- Active Directory (AD) installed

Getting Down to Business

To create a default user profile, perform the following steps:

Step 1. Log on with the Administrator account. Create a new object named Template and make it a member of the Proofing Dept.

Step 2. Log off as Administrator. Log on as the template user. Change the Display Properties Appearance option to a different scheme—Slate. Add shortcuts to the desktop. Again, the purpose for this is to make a template by which all user object accounts associated will this template will receive their logon settings.

Step 3. Log off as the template account. Log on with the Administrator account. Access the System Properties window through the Control Panel.

Step 4. Through the Users Profiles tab, click the template account and copy it to the William Giubotto user account.

Step 5. It's also necessary to change the account permissions. Copy those permissions to the William Giubotto user account. Complete the copy process.

CERTIFICATION OBJECTIVE 5.03

Creating and Administering a Global Group

20 Minutes

You are a network consultant for the Eye-to-Eye Ophthalmology practice. The office consists of 11 networked Windows 2000 Professional client computers and a Windows 2000 Server running Active Directory services. There are ten optometrists, two nurse professionals, and three ophthalmologists. You need to provide a higher level of access to the three ophthalmologists and at the same time simplify your administration time by creating a global group for the three ophthalmologists. How would you create and add the ophthalmologists listed in the following table to this group?

Last Name	First Name	User Name	Password	Change Password
Righter	Simon	Srighter	Iris	Must
Stigmah	Haye	Hstigmah	Cornea	Must
Dialatter	Herbert	Hdialatter	Eyedrop	Must

Learning Objectives

Planning group strategies is an essential part of preparing to deploy Active Directory. Group management saves administration time by eliminating the repetitive steps necessary in managing user and resources on an individual basis.

For additional information, refer to the group types section of Chapter 5 in "Managing a Microsoft Windows 2000 Network Environment Study Guide."

In this lab, you'll create a group object and populate it with members. By the end of this lab, you'll be able to

- Create a Global Group.
- Add members to the Global Group.

Lab Materials and Setup

For this lab exercise, you will need

- A working computer
- Installed network card (NIC)
- Windows 2000 Server software (installed)
- TCP/IP installed
- Domain Name System (DNS) installed
- Active Directory (AD) installed

Getting Down to Business

Before beginning the Global Group process, we need to create the users listed in the lab scenario. By this point, you can perform the steps without any assistance.

To create a Global Group and add users to the group, perform the following steps:

Step 1.   Access the Active Directory Users and Computers console. Expand your domain to view the list of current objects.

Step 2. Create a new group named *Administration*, using the Users container icon. Be sure to select Global in the Global Scope box. Select Security in the Global Type box.

Step 3. Click OK to apply your Global Group. The Global Group icon will appear in the right pane of the window.

Step 4. Now you need to add the members in the list you created (see the previous lab hint). Access the Active Directory Users and Computers console. Expand your domain to view the list of current objects.

Step 5. Access the Properties window of the newly created Administration Global Group. Select and add the members using the Select Users, Contacts, or Computers dialog box within the Members tab window.

Step 6. Once the users have been added, click OK and complete the process.

CERTIFICATION OBJECTIVE 5.04

20 Minutes

Creating and Managing Organizational Units

In part two of the previous lab scenario, we need to take the two nurse professionals listed in the following table and place them in their own organizational unit (container) named Nurse Managers, and place them in the (container name) container.

Last Name	First Name	User Name	Password	Change Password
Nearse	Ivy	Inearse	Stick	Must
Fleat	AnnaMay	Afleat	flush	Must

Learning Objectives

Active Directory objects such as domains, computers, users, groups, folders, and organizational units have security permissions associated with them. In controlling access to Active Directory objects, there are two things to consider: the permissions that you are allowed to attach to the object, and the ways in which you can attach these permissions in order to delegate administrative responsibility for Active Directory objects.

In this lab you'll create a container object and move it within a domain. By the end of this lab, you'll be able to

- Know the difference between standard permissions and special permissions.
- Understand permission inheritance.
- Create an organizational unit (OU) with two user accounts.
- Move an object within a domain.

Lab Materials and Setup

For this lab exercise, you will need

- A working computer
- Installed network card (NIC)
- Windows 2000 Server software (installed)
- TCP/IP installed
- Domain Name System (DNS) installed
- Active Directory (AD) installed

Getting Down to Business

First, we'll create an OU, add two users, and look at the default security settings, and then move the object (the OU) within a domain. To make this happen, perform the following steps.

Step 1.   Access the Active Directory Users and Computers console. Expand your domain to view the list of current objects. Select your domain menu.

Step 2.   In the Name text box, type **Nurse Managers** and click OK. In the Managers OU, create the two nurse users listed in the previous table with the designated information.

Step 3.   Grant both users membership in the Administration group with the logon rights to the domain controller. View the default permissions for the newly created OU—administration.

Step 4.   Choose Advance Features from the View menu. Choose the Properties from the Nurse Managers object. Click the Security tab.

Step 5.   Select the Domain Admins group and list the assigned permissions for the OU.

_____

_____

Step 6.   Now we need to move the object within the domain. Right-click the OU and open the Move dialog box. Select the OU or container to which you wish to move the object.

Step 7.   Click OK to complete the move process.

CERTIFICATION OBJECTIVE 5.05

Delegating Administrative Control

10 Minutes

Now that we have created an OU named Nurse Managers and populated it with the two nurse professionals, we need to assign one of the ophthalmologists as the administrator of the group. What steps do we take to give Hebert Dialatter control of the OU?

Learning Objectives

In Windows 2000 Server, other objects can manage objects such as users, groups, folders, and organizational units. Administrative control can be granted to a user or group by using the Delegation of Control Wizard. It allows you to select the user or group to which you want to delegate control, the organizational units and objects you want to grant those users the right to control, and the permissions to access and modify objects.

In this lab, you'll learn how to use the Delegation of Control Wizard. By the end of this lab, you'll be able to

■ Delegate administrative control of objects and OUs.

Lab Materials and Setup

For this lab exercise, you will need

■ A working computer

■ Installed network card (NIC)

■ Windows 2000 Server software (installed)

■ TCP/IP installed

■ Domain Name System (DNS) installed

■ Active Directory (AD) installed

Getting Down to Business

To delegate control of the Nurse Managers OU, perform the following steps:

Step 1.   Access the Active Directory Users and Computers console. Right-click the Nurse Managers OU. Activate the Delegation of Control Wizard.

Step 2.   Click Add within the Users or Groups window. Select hdialatter to give him control of the Nurse Managers OU.

Step 3.   In the Tasks to Delegate dialog box, select the Create, Delete, and Manage User Accounts task. Complete the wizard.

LAB ANALYSIS TEST

1. What are the differences between a local user account and a domain user account?

    _____

    _____

2. What does an administrator need to create a domain user account?

    _____

    _____

3. List and explain the three scopes of influence contained with a Security and Distribution Group?

    _____

    _____

4. When moving an OU or container from one to the other, what happens to the original permissions?

    _____

    _____

5. Why would it be necessary to grant control of OUs or containers to other users?

    _____

    _____

KEY TERM QUIZ

Use the following vocabulary terms to complete the sentences below. Not all of the terms will be used. Definitions for these terms can be found in "Managing a Microsoft Windows 2000 Network Environment Study Guide."

> Active Directory (AD)
>
> Domain User Account
>
> Default User Profile
>
> Roaming User Profile
>
> Security Group
>
> Distribution Group
>
> Effective Permissions
>
> Delegation of Control Wizard
>
> Organizational unit
>
> Objects

1. A profile that is stored in a domain server is named a (an) _____.

2. An entity such as a file, folder, group, or user in Active Directory is considered a (an) _____.

3. _____ is a centralized system that automates network management.

4. A combination of all inherited rights a user can gain from group memberships is named _____.

5. A _____ allows a user to log on to a domain and gain access to resources.

LAB SOLUTIONS FOR CHAPTER 5

In this section, you'll find solutions to the lab exercises, Lab Analysis Test, and Key Term Quiz.

Lab Solution 5.01

Your task in this lab scenario is to create user accounts on new hires today, Friday, before they start work on Monday. This list of new hires was given to you by the personnel department:

Last Name	First Name	User Name	Password	Change Password
Reeves	Allen	Areeves	flowers	Must
Campbell	Harold	Hcampbell	(blank)	Must
DiMiele	Susan	Sdimiele	(blank)	Must
Sposo	Ellen	Esposo	Floppy	Must
Giubotto	William	Wgiubotto	Spring	Cannot

The purpose behind a user account is to provide that user access to the resources on that network. This includes not only access to information and resources on their local computer, but also access to shared information and resources on the network—files, databases, printers, applications, and web access.

In this lab, you created and configured accounts for domain users. By the end of this lab, you were able to

- Create a domain user account and configure its properties.
- Rename, disable, and delete an account.

The lab will be performed in three different stages. First, we'll create several domain user accounts. Second, we'll configure the associated account properties. Third, we'll disable and delete an account, and fourth, we'll create a roaming profile. To begin creating accounts, perform the following steps.

Step 1. Log on to your domain with your Administrator account. Access the Active Directory Users and Computers console. Click Start | Programs | Administrative Tools and select the Active Directory Users and Computers item from the list, as shown in Figure 5-1.

Step 2. In the left pane of the window, expand Active Directory Users and Computers and the domain name under it. This folder contains the default user accounts created during the Windows 2000 Server build. Right-click the Users folder and from the New menu choose User, as shown next. This will open the New Object - User dialog box.

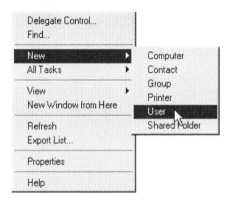

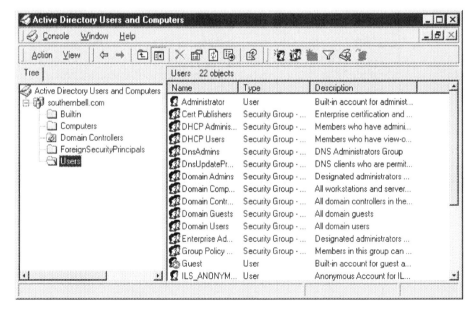

FIGURE 5-1

The right pane displays the user objects contained in the Users folder.

Step 3. When creating an Active Directory user account, you enter the user's first name, last name, and middle initial, as shown in Figure 5-2. The Full Name field is automatically filled in. Lastly, enter the user's login name. Enter Allen Reeves' information first. The domain name is auto-filled for you. The user login name in combination with the domain name is the user's full logon name. This will be the user's unique identifier throughout the directory. For Allen, it will be areeves@<domain name.com>.

lab
🛈int *User accounts can also be created using the New | User option in the Action menu.*

Step 4. Enter the information in the New Object - User Account Parameters window; this includes their password and password options. Type in Allen's password, and confirm it in the Confirm Password box, as shown next. If no password is being assigned, you leave the fields blank.

Password:	*******
Confirm password:	*******

☑ User must change password at next logon
☐ User cannot change password
☐ Password never expires
☐ Account is disabled

Step 5. We have four options for manipulating the password: the user will need to change it at first logon, the password is permanent, the user is not allowed to change the password, and the account is disabled. In Allen's case, we check off User Must Change Password at Next Logon.

Step 6. Repeat steps 3 and 4 for each of the remaining users.

Step 7. Come Monday, there is an e-mail from personnel regarding the new hires. There are some changes that need to be made to three of them. The first deals with Allen Reeves. His start date will be delayed two weeks, so you need to disable the account for the time being.

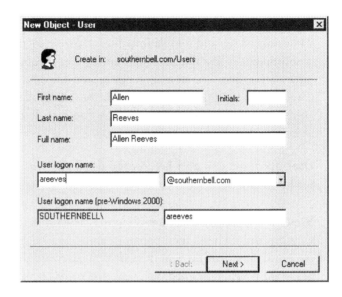

Step 8. Be sure that you are logged on with your Administrator account. Open the Active Directory Users and Computers console. Access the Active Directory Users and Computers console. Click Start | Programs | Administrative Tools and select the Active Directory Users and Computers item from the list. Expand the Active Directory Users and Computers tree, if necessary.

Step 9. Right-click the Allen Reeves user object and select Disable Account from the pop-up menu, as shown here. A message will notify you that the account has been disabled. Close out of the message box. Using the details pane of the console, how can you tell that the user account has been disabled? The object is marked with a red X.

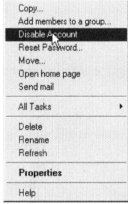

Step 10. Log off as Administrator and attempt to log on as Allen Reeves to confirm that the account is disabled.

Step 11. Ellen Sposo has gotten married since she applied for the temporary job. You need to change her now maiden name to her new married name, Esposato. Log in with your Administrator account.

Step 12. Right-click her domain user account object on the right pane of the Active Directory Users and Computers window. From the menu, select Rename. Enter the new logon name for Ellen, as shown in Figure 5-3. Click OK to finish.

Step 13. The last change is for Harold Campbell's user account. The e-mail states that he is not going to be working here after all. You need to delete the account.

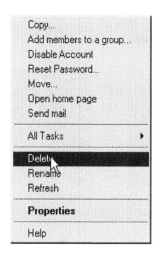

Step 14. Right-click his domain user account object on the right pane of the Active Directory Users and Computers window. From the menu, select Delete, as shown here, and confirm by clicking Yes. You are now done with all your changes. You may close or minimize the Active Directory Users and Computers console.

lab
Hint

If you've created a user account with special access parameters to fit a particular job function and you delete that account, you will have to re-create that account along with its attributes once a new worker is hired. An easier way of administering this scenario is to disable the account instead. It will keep the account and its attributes intact, and when the new person is hired, all you need to do is change the user's first name, last name, and logon name.

Lab Solution 5.02

Your organization is implementing new network standards. All Windows 2000 Professional users to have the same desktop settings, and an icon linked to an interest rate monitor program will be present on the desktop. Your job is to create a default template with those settings and test it out on a domain user account.

In this lab, you created a default user profile. The property values entered in the user template for that container are then copied into the new user object as it is created.

The template information is First Name - Profile, Last Name - Template, Logon Name - ptemplate, Password - (blank), Desktop Settings - Slate.

The test user will be First Name - William, Last Name - Giubotto, Logon Name - wgiubotto, Password - Spring, Password Change - Cannot.

FIGURE 5-3

A Rename User
dialog box
displays the
object's basic
information.

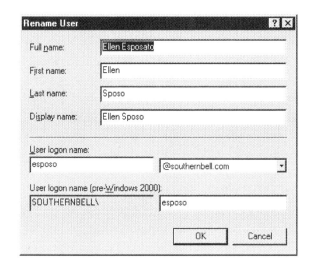

By the end of this lab, you were able to

■ Understand the difference between a local user profile, a roaming (default)
user profile, and a mandatory user profile.

■ Create a default user profile.

To create a default user profile, perform the following steps:

Step 1. Log on with the Administrator account. Access the Active Directory
Users and Computers console. Click Start | Programs | Administrative Tools and
select the Active Directory Users and Computers item from the list. Right-click the
Users folder and choose User from the New menu to create a new object named
Profile Template.

Step 2. Enter the templates first name (Profile), last name (Template), user logon
name (ptemplate), and an empty password field, as shown in Figure 5-4. The
password will not change or expire.

lab

①arning *You need to grant the template membership to the Domain Users group.
Right-click User Object, select Properties, select Member Of tab.*

FIGURE 5-4

Enter the template's information as you would a regular user.

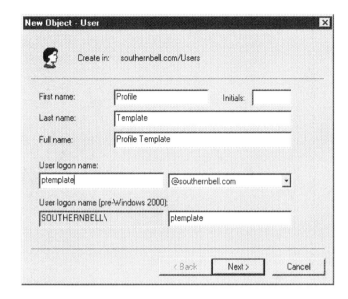

Step 3. Log off as Administrator. Log on as the template user. Change the Display Properties Appearance to Slate. Right-click anywhere on the desktop to open the context menu. Select Properties. This opens the Display Properties dialog box.

Step 4. Click the Appearance tab and select the Slate scheme from the Scheme list window, as shown in Figure 5-5.

Step 5. Add a shortcut to the desktop. Again, the purpose for this is to make a template by which all user object accounts associated will this template will receive their logon settings.

Step 6. Log off as the template account. Log on with the Administrator account. Click Start | Settings | Control Panel. Double-click the System icon.

Step 7. Select the Users Profiles tab, which lists profiles that stored on this computer. Click the Profile Template and click Copy To. A Copy To dialog box opens. Click Browse, then locate and click the William Giubotto user account object. Click OK in the Browse for Folder dialog box.

FIGURE 5-5

Change the
Display
Properties by
selecting a
different scheme
from the
pull-down menu.

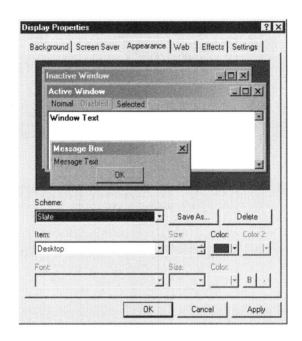

Step 8. It's also necessary to change the account permissions. In the Permitted to Use section of the dialog box, click Change. Select the William Giubotto user account object. Click OK in the Select User or Group dialog box. Complete the copy process by clicking OK. Click Yes to confirm the copy process. Close out of the System Properties window.

Lab Solution 5.03

You have an office that's running 11 Windows 2000 Professional computers and a Windows 2000 Server. You needed to provide a higher level of access to the three ophthalmologists and create a global group for the three ophthalmologists. How would you create and add the ophthalmologists listed in the following table to this group?

Last Name	First Name	User Name	Password	Change Password
Righter	Simon	Srighter	Iris	Must
Stigmah	Haye	Hstigmah	Cornea	Must
Dialatter	Herbert	Hdialatter	Eyedrop	Must

In this lab, you created a group object and populated it with members. By the end of this lab, you were able to

■   Create a Global Group and add members to the Global Group.

lab
Hint   *Before beginning the Global Group process, we need to create the users listed in the lab scenario. By this point, you can perform the steps without any assistance.*

To create a Global Group and add users to the group, perform the following steps:

Step 1.   Log on with the Administrator account. Access the Active Directory Users and Computers console. Click Start | Programs | Administrative Tools and select the Active Directory Users and Computers item from the list. Expand your domain to view the list of current objects.

Step 2.   Create a new group named *Administration*. Right-click the Users folder and choose Group from the New menu to create a New Object named Profile Template, as shown here. This will open the New Object - Group dialog box.

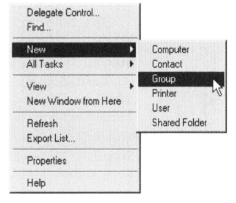

Step 3.   In the Group Name box, type **Administration**. Select Global in the Global Scope box, and select Security in the Global Type box, as shown in Figure 5-6. These settings will give the members a broader access scope than domain local groups. This group has possible access to resources in other domains.

Step 4.   Click OK to apply your Global Group. The Global Group icon will appear in the right pane of the window.

Step 5.   Now you need to add the members listed in the previous table. Be sure that your domain tree is expanded to view the list of current objects. In the right pane of the window, double-click the Administration group object you just created. This will display the Properties window.

FIGURE 5-6

Enter the group's name and select its group settings.

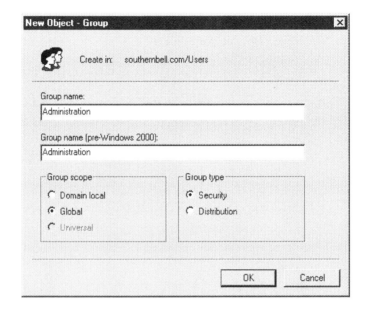

Step 6. There are several tabs in this window—we will be selecting the Members tab. You'll notice that there are no members at this time. Click Add to open the Select Users, Contacts, or Computers dialog box. Select the users you created as a prerequisite for this lab, as shown in Figure 5-7.

Step 7. Once the users have been added, click OK to permanently add them to the group, as shown in Figure 5-8. Click OK to close the Administration Properties window.

Lab Solution 5.04

In part two of the previous lab scenario, we needed to take the two nurse professionals listed in the following table and place them in their own organizational unit (container) named Nurse Managers, and then place them in the (container name) container.

Last Name	First Name	User Name	Password	Change Password
Nearse	Ivy	Inearse	Stick	Must
Fleat	AnnaMay	Afleat	flush	Must

FIGURE 5-7

Select the users you wish to be members of the group.

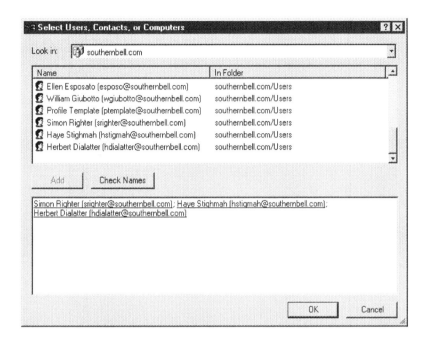

FIGURE 5-8

Once the users have been added, they will be listed in the Members window.

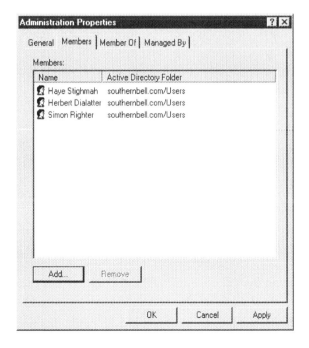

In controlling access to Active Directory objects, there are two things to consider: the permissions that you are allowed to attach to the object, and the ways in which you can attach these permissions in order to delegate administrative responsibility for Active Directory objects.

In this lab, you created a container object, added two users, and moved the object within a domain. By the end of this lab, you were able to

- Know the difference between standard permissions and special permissions.

- Understand permission inheritance.

- Create an organizational unit (OU) with two user accounts.

- Move an object within a domain.

First, we created an OU and added two users. Then, we looked at the default security settings, and moved the object (the OU) within a domain. To make this happen, perform the following steps:

Step 1. Log on with the Administrator account. Access the Active Directory Users and Computers console. Click Start | Programs | Administrative Tools and select the Active Directory Users and Computers item from the list. Expand your domain to view the list of current objects.

Step 2. Right-click the domain object | New | Organizational Unit, as shown here.

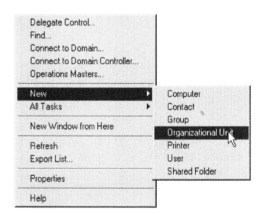

In the Name text box, type **Nurse Managers** and click OK. In the Managers OU, create the user objects listed above with the first name, last name, password, and logon name in the New Object - User dialog box. Click Next to continue.

Step 3. Part two of the New Object - User dialog box asks you to enter and confirm a password in the appropriate fields. Click User Must Change Password at Next Logon option.

Step 4.   Grant both users membership in the Administration group with the logon rights to the domain controller. View the default permissions for the newly created OU—Administration.

lab
ⓗint   *To grant users member to a group, right-click the user object, select Properties, and select the Member Of tab.*

Step 5.   Click View and choose Advance Features from the menu. This allows you to review and configure Active Directory permissions. Now, right-click the Managers object in the console tree.

Step 6.   Select Properties from the Managers object pop-up menu. Click the Security tab. Select the Domain Admins group and list the assigned permissions for the OU, as shown in Figure 5-9.

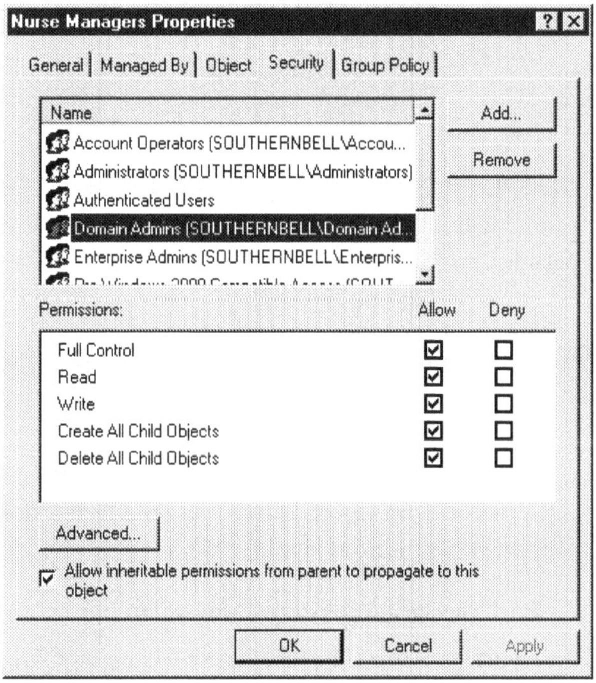

FIGURE 5-9

This window displays the security permissions of the highlighted object.

Nurse Managers Properties

General | Managed By | Object | Security | Group Policy

Name	
Account Operators (SOUTHERNBELL\Accou...	Add...
Administrators (SOUTHERNBELL\Administrators)	Remove
Authenticated Users	
Domain Admins (SOUTHERNBELL\Domain Ad...	
Enterprise Admins (SOUTHERNBELL\Enterpris...	
Pre-Windows 2000 Compatible Access (SOUT...	

Permissions:	Allow	Deny
Full Control	☑	☐
Read	☑	☐
Write	☑	☐
Create All Child Objects	☑	☐
Delete All Child Objects	☑	☐

Advanced...

☑ Allow inheritable permissions from parent to propagate to this object

OK | Cancel | Apply

Step 7. Next, we need to move the object within the domain. We want to reduce overhead by placing objects with similar security needs into their own OU or container. The occupants inherit the permissions assigned to the OU or container.

Step 8. In the console tree, right-click the OU we need to move. From the pop-up menu, select Move to open the Move dialog box, and select the OU or container to which you wish to move the object, as shown here:

Step 9. When the move is complete, as shown in Figure 5-10, the OU that was moved will inherit the permissions of its new location. The OU relinquishes its old permissions; they're no longer in force. Click OK to complete the move process.

Lab Solution 5.05

In this final part of the scenario, we need to assign Hebert Dialatter, ophthalmologist, as a container administrator. He will have administrative control over the users within that container.

In this lab, you learned how to use the Delegation of Control Wizard. By the end of this lab, you were able to

■ Delegate administrative control of objects and OUs.

To delegate control of the Nurse Managers OU, perform the following steps:

FIGURE 5-10

The Nurse Managers container is now within the Domain Controllers container.

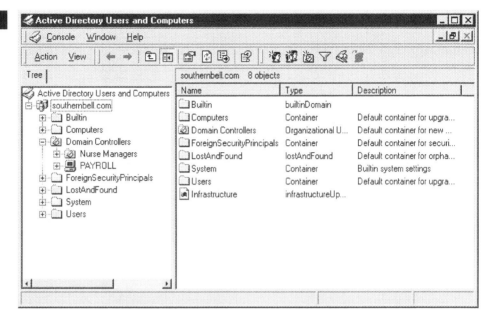

Step 1. Log on with the Administrator account. Access the Active Directory Users and Computers console. Click Start | Programs | Administrative Tools and select the Active Directory Users and Computers item from the list. Expand your domain to view the list of current objects.

Step 2. Right-click the Nurse Managers OU. From the pop-menu, activate the Delegation of Control Wizard. Click past the Welcome page. This opens the Users Or Groups window. The window is empty of users or groups at this time.

Step 3. Click Add within the Select Users, Computers, or Groups window. Select hdialatter and click Add to give him control of the Nurse Managers OU, as shown in Figure 5-11. Click OK.

Step 4. Click Next. This opens the Tasks to Delegate dialog box. Here you choose the common tasks you wish to assign to the container administrator. Select the Create, Delete, and Manage User Accounts task.

Step 5. Also click the Delegate the Following Common Tasks radio button, as shown in Figure 5-12. Click Next to display the Completing the Delegation

FIGURE 5-11

The user has been added as container administrator.

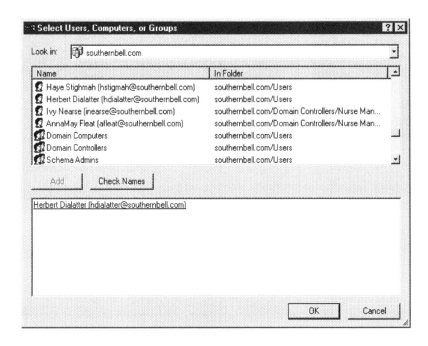

Control Wizard page. Review the Summary page and click Finish. The delegation process is complete.

FIGURE 5-12

Select the common tasks that are available to the container administrator.

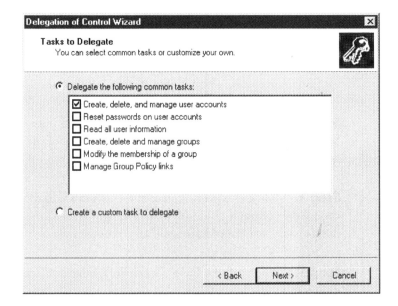

ANSWERS TO LAB ANALYSIS

1. Local user accounts let a user log on and have access to resources only on the computer that he or she sits at. Domain user accounts let a user log on to a domain using any computer attached to that network, gaining access to resources based on his or her permissions.

2. All that's required is a first or last name, and a logon name. The Full Name field is auto-filled.

3. The three types of scopes are as follows: The Domain Local Group is used to grant permission to users within a domain. A Global Group is used to grant permission anywhere within the forest. Finally, the Universal Group is used to provide access in a multidomain network; users can be added into this group from any domain or forest.

4. The object inherits permissions from the new OU or container. Permissions inherited from its original OU or container are no longer in effect.

5. It is more efficient to make a user a manager of objects contained in an OU or container, giving the user responsibility to maintain, add, or remove those objects.

ANSWERS TO KEY TERM QUIZ

1. Roaming User Profile
2. Objects
3. Active Directory (AD)
4. Effective Permissions
5. Domain User Account

6

Implementing
Security Policies

LAB EXERCISES

6.01   Using Group Policies to Apply
        Security Settings

6.02   Using Group Policy to Configure
        an Audit Policy

6.03   Delegating Group Policy Authority

6.04   Troubleshooting Group Policy

▓   Lab Analysis Test

▓   Key Term Quiz

▓   Lab Solutions

W indows 2000 provides a centralized method of defining security with a Microsoft Management Console (MMC) tool, a Security Settings snap-in. Functioning as a single point of entry, it provides a full range of system security which can be viewed, adjusted, and applied to a local computer or imported to a Group policy object. This snap-in console does not introduce any new security parameters; rather, it takes the existing security attributes and organizes them all in one place for easy security administration. Security settings appear under the Computer Configuration and User Configuration folders. User configuration settings are applied to users regardless of which computer they log on from. Computer configuration settings are applied to computers regardless of who logs on to that computer. Most networks will implement security policies under Computer Configuration. The following is a list of the nine different areas of security settings that can be applied to computers:

- **Account policies**   Provides security for passwords and logon procedures.
- **Local policies**   Provides security for auditing security events and user rights, and for security options.
- **Event log**   Defines attributes related to application, security, and system events.
- **Restricted groups**   Provides security for default Windows 2000 groups.
- **Registry**   Provides security for local registry keys.
- **File system**   Provides security for the local file system.
- **Public key**   Provides security for certificate settings.
- **System services**   Provides security for permissions and startup settings.
- **IP security**   Provides security by way of encryption.

You can import security settings to a group policy object. Any computer or user accounts in the site, domain, or organizational unit to which the group policy object is applied will receive the security settings.

Because a group policy object defines access, configuration, and usage settings for accounts and resources, importing security settings to a group policy object eases domain administration by configuring security for multiple computers at once. These settings are contained in a security template saved as a text-based .inf file, which enables the administrator to copy, paste, import, or export some or all of the template attributes. With the exceptions of IP security and public key policies, all security attributes can be contained in a security template.

When there are conflicts, security settings defined globally via Active Directory always override security settings defined on the local machine. Security settings for an organizational unit (OU) always override security settings defined in any parent OUs or on the domain itself.

Somewhere along the way, configuration settings within a group policy appear to not have taken effect. It will become necessary to determine exactly what the cause may be. Through the use of the group policy auditing process, an audit review will help you solve the issue—or, at the very least, point you in the right direction.

In this chapter, we'll look at how to apply security settings to a domain or OU through the use of group policy; how to implement an audit policy using group policy; and how to implement auditing on group policy for more extensive checking of how group policy objects (GPOs) are processed.

cross
Reference

For information about the Group Policies, refer to Chapter 2 of "Managing a Microsoft Windows 2000 Network Environment Study Guide."

CERTIFICATION OBJECTIVE 6.01

Using Group Policies to Apply Security Settings

20 Minutes

You have been asked by your CIO to configure DC security settings that will be applied to the domain controller within the Montreal site of the major car manufacturer that you work for as a network administrator. You need to import an already created template and apply it to the domain controller. How would you go about accomplishing this goal?

Learning Objectives

Security policy is to computers what security groups are to users. Just as security groups let you grant a standardized set of rights to a group of users, security policy lets you apply a single security profile to multiple computers. It enforces consistency and provides easy administration. Security policy objects contain permissions and parameters that implement multiple types of security strategies. By default, security policy is installed on local computers. However, Active Directory must be installed on a server before you can edit and apply domain-wide security policy objects.

There are some considerations when applying security policies using group policy. It is wise to keep the number of group policy objects to a minimum, including security policy objects. This applies to users and computers alike. You do this first, because each computer and user group policy object must be loaded to a computer during startup and to user profiles at logon. Having many group policy objects will increase the time it takes for computer startup and the time it takes for the user to log on. Secondly, it becomes difficult to troubleshoot policy conflicts where there are multiple group policy objects.

Generally, group policy can be passed down from parent to child sites, domains, and organizational units. When assigning a specific group policy to an upper-level parent, determining which group policy will apply to all organizational units beneath that parent, including the user and computer objects in each container, will become increasingly more difficult to troubleshoot.

Security templates may be applied to local computer policy, imported to a group policy object, and used for system security analysis. These templates represent a security configuration—a single file containing a group of security settings. Importing a security template to a group policy object ensures that any accounts to which the group policy object is applied will automatically receive the template's security settings when the group policy settings are refreshed. You can directly apply a security template to a local computer policy even when a computer is not part of a domain. The system is immediately configured with the new template settings.

In this lab, you'll apply security settings using group policy. By the end of this lab, you'll be able to

- Recognize security settings in a group policy object.
- Recognize the type of policies in the Security Settings snap-in.
- Apply security settings using group policy.
- Import a security template into a group policy object.

Lab Materials and Setup

For this lab exercise, you'll need

- A working computer
- Installed network card (NIC)

- Windows 2000 Server software (installed)
- TCP/IP installed
- Active Directory (AD) installed

Getting Down to Business

To import and apply a security template, perform the following steps:

Step 1. Access the Active Directory Users and Computers console. Open the Properties window of the GPO domain. View the Group Policy tab window and select the Default Domain Policy object. Access the Edit window.

Step 2. Expand the Group Policy tree down to the Security Settings for Computer Configurations. Notice the nine different security areas that can be applied to a computer. Items within each category can be manually modified. They will not be saved, however, as a security template. Existing templates can be imported and have their settings applied within the GPO.

Step 3. Import a security template, DC Security, using the Import Policy option. This will open the Import Policy dialog window. From the listing, locate the path and filename of the DC security template you wish to import and apply.

Step 4. Once selected, complete the import process and exit out of the Editor window. Do not close the Active Directory Users and Computers window.

CERTIFICATION OBJECTIVE 6.02

Using Group Policy to Configure an Audit Policy

15 Minutes

You are the network administrator for the HRware software company. Your company produces software solutions for human resource and payroll departments to process and track employee information, benefits, and payroll processing. As part of your security scheme, you wish to track access to Directory Services objects by all users in the domain. You know that the best way to accomplish this is to create an audit policy for the Domain Users object. Additionally, there have been occurrences of users not logging off when they leave work, thereby leaving the logon account open. You wish to have their connection terminated when their logon time expires. What steps do you need to perform to achieve these goals?

Learning Objectives

An important facet of security is to establish some form of an audit trail. By monitoring the creation or modification of objects, you can track potential security problems and assure user accountability, and it can provide evidence in case of a security breach.

To implement security-related auditing for a system, there are three main steps. You must first turn on the categories of events you wish to audit (for example, user logon and logoff). The categories of events you select make up your audit policy. Audit Policy is a component of security policy, which enables the administrator to monitor security-related events. When you build a Windows 2000 server, no categories are selected. You can see a list of event categories for auditing in Computer Management. Your second step would be to configure the security log settings. And finally, selecting either the Audit directory service access category or the Audit object access category requires that you determine the objects to which you want to monitor access and modify their security descriptors. An example would be to audit an account logon attempt—you can track either a successful logon attempt or a failed logon attempt.

The event categories that you can select are Audit Account Logon Events, Audit Account Management, Audit Directory Service Access, Audit Logon Events, Audit Object Access, Audit Policy Change, Audit Privilege Use, Audit Process Tracking, and Audit System Events.

Each object has security information, or a security descriptor, attached to it. Part of the security descriptor specifies the groups or users that can access an object and the types of permissions granted to those groups or users, known as a discretionary access control list (DACL). It also contains an auditing information descriptor that specifies the group or user accounts to audit when accessing an object, and which events to audit—the success or failure of the action. This auditing information is known as a system access control list (SACL). This success or failure of the action is based on the permissions granted to each group and user in the object's DACL.

In this lab, you'll configure an audit policy for more than one computer by using group policy. By the end of this lab, you'll be able to

- Set an audit policy.
- Make use of group policy.
- Configure an audit policy using group policy.

Lab Materials and Setup

For this lab exercise, you will need

- A working computer
- Installed network card (NIC)
- Windows 2000 Server software (installed)
- TCP/IP installed
- Active Directory (AD) installed

Getting Down to Business

To configure an audit policy using group policy, perform the following steps:

Step 1.   Access the Active Directory Users and Computers console. Open the Properties window of the GPO domain. View the Group Policy tab window and select the Default Domain Policy object. Access the Edit window.

Step 2.   Expand the Group Policy tree down to the Security Settings for Computer Configurations. Now select the Local Policies folder. This shows the audit policies and to which areas of the system they are applied.

Step 3.   Double-click the audit event we wish to track—Directory Services. This opens the Setting Definition dialog window. Define the policy settings to track the success and failure of the attempts. Save the changes.

Step 4.   Within the Security options in the Local Policies, change the audit policy for the Automatic Log Off of Users When Logon Time Expires to Enabled. Save the change and complete the process.

Delegating Group Policy Authority

15 Minutes

Your company, BellaScooters Intl., has expanded in the New England area of the United States. It has a sales marketing center of six people. They will be directly associated with the United States headquarters in New Jersey. The company wants you to delegate group policy authority for the center by creating an OU for the BellaScooterNE and assigning an administrator, Gino Sottovoce (his password will be motoscooter), the ability to manage the sales staff on the network. You also create the first sales associate, Gina A. Barbutta (her password will be passaretto). What steps must you take to create the OU and assign authority to the newly appointed administrator?

Learning Objectives

By creating organizational units within a domain and delegating administrative control for specific organizational units to a particular user or group, you can assign administrative control to any level of a domain tree. For example, you may want to grant administrative control to a group of users and computers within an organizational unit in all locations for a particular department, such as a sales or marketing group.

Delegating administrative responsibilities can help eliminate the need for multiple administrative accounts with broad authority, such as an entire domain. Although you likely will still use the predefined Domain Admins group for administration of the entire domain, you can limit the accounts that are members of the Domain Admins group to highly trusted administrative users.

In this lab, you'll delegate authority to an organizational unit administrator with the ability to manage users in a particular department. By the end of this lab, you'll be able to

- Create an OU for a department and add a user account for the administrator.

- Assign control of the OU to an administrative role.

Lab Materials and Setup

For this lab exercise, you will need

- A working computer
- Installed network card (NIC)
- Windows 2000 Server software (installed)
- TCP/IP installed
- Active Directory (AD) installed

Getting Down to Business

To delegate authority of the OU to an administrator, perform the following steps:

Step 1.   First, we need to create the organizational unit and create the user account within the OU. Access the Active Directory Users and Computers console. Create a new OU in the domain. To delegate control for the new OU, create the new user listed in the scenario who will be the OU's administrator. Enter the user's full name, logon name, and password.

Step 2.   Next, you need to delegate control of the new OU to the new administrator. Access the Delegate Control utility on the OU and add the new user as manager in the Users and Groups window. Be sure the new administrator can create, delete, and manage user accounts in the OU. Click Next and complete the process. Close all windows and log off.

Step 3.   Last, we need to test the new administrator's ability to create a new user account, so log in as new administrator. Access the Active Directory Users and Computers console.

Step 4.   Click the new OU and create a new user. Enter the user's full name, logon name. Enter the user's password in the next window. Click Next and complete the process. Close all windows and log off.

CERTIFICATION OBJECTIVE 6.04

Troubleshooting Group Policy

15 Minutes

As a seasoned network administrator, you've learned to stay ahead of potential problems when it comes to managing users through the use of group policy. You pass on this knowledge to a newly promoted network administrator at the Verona, Italy office of the fashion import enterprise you work for. Despite the best planning, common group policy problems may "rear their ugly heads." To avoid this, you suggest that she audit the following access entries on the Domain Users object and their successful or failed attempts at performing a particular task: the failed attempt at Delete, Delete Subtree, and Modify Permissions; and the successful attempt at Read Permissions.

Learning Objectives

As an administrator, you may see several common scenarios when troubleshooting group policy. For example, you may see that policy settings aren't being applied, that policy settings are applied inconsistently, or that you are simply unable to manage group policy due to delegation or permission issues. Four strategies can help minimize problems:

- Keep objects to a minimum. One domain-level GPO can satisfy most business requirements.

- Keep good documentation by mapping your Group Policies in a diagram in the same way you would map network configurations. Be sure to test new policies and ensure that they are working properly before you deploy them.

- Some other guidelines include the need to plan your group policy implementation, asking yourself what it is you are trying to accomplish. Configure GPO settings for users rather than computers. Settings applied to users travel with the users no matter where they log on from.

- Be prudent when delegating administrative control over a GPO to someone else. The adage of "too many cooks spoil the broth" applies here.

In this lab, you'll apply preventive measures in the form of auditing group policy. It's a way of being proactive rather than reactive. (This is very different from the previous lab scenario where we used a GPO to apply auditing on computers.) By the end of this lab, you'll be able to

■ Configure auditing for a group policy object.

Lab Materials and Setup

For this lab exercise, you will need

■ A working computer
■ Installed network card (NIC)
■ Windows 2000 Server software (installed)
■ TCP/IP installed
■ Active Directory (AD) installed

Getting Down to Business

To configure auditing for a GPO, perform the following steps:

Step 1.   Access the Active Directory Users and Computers console. Open the Properties window of the GPO domain. View the Group Policy tab window and select the Default Domain Policy object. Open the Properties window for this object.

Step 2.   Open the Auditing window of the object through the Security and Advanced tabs. The window displays the auditing configuration that is presently set. This window also contains a message section below the buttons. If there is a message stating that the auditing configuration is inherited from a parent container, you'll need to move one level up the tree to make the change. Since we are working the domain level, there should not be a message.

Step 3.   Add the audit settings for the Domain Users object. When presented with the Audit Entry dialog window, select the following permissions and whether to track their success or failure: Delete, Failure; Delete Subtree, Failure; Modify Permissions, Failure; Read Permissions, Success.

Step 4.   Once the selections have been made, Click OK to save the settings and complete the process. Exit out of all windows, including the Active Directory Users and Computers console.

LAB ANALYSIS TEST

1. What function does a Security Settings snap-in provide for a network administrator?

   _____

   _____

2. What are the two types of group policy settings and how are they used?

   _____

   _____

3. To help minimize problems that are associated with group policy, consider three strategies. Explain these three strategies.

   _____

   _____

4. What does the term No Override / Force group policy mean?

   _____

   _____

5. Security templates may be applied to a local computer policy or imported to a group policy object. Explain the function and purpose of a security template.

   _____

   _____

KEY TERM QUIZ

Use the following vocabulary terms to complete the sentences below. Not all of the terms will be used. Definitions for these terms can be found in "Managing a Microsoft Windows 2000 Network Environment Study Guide."

Security template

Account polices

Local policies

Audit policy

Discretionary access control list (DACL)

System access control list (SACL)

Block inheritance

No override

Group policy object

Security policy

1. A _____ is a text file that contains settings that enable the administrator to copy, paste, import, or export some or all of the template attributes to enforce security on users and computers.

2. A(n) _____ provides security for passwords and logon procedures.

3. Categories of security-related events make up your _____. This policy is a component of security policy, which enables the administrator to monitor security-related events.

4. Part of the security descriptor that specifies the groups or users that can access an object, and the types of permissions granted to those groups or users, is known as a _____.

5. _____ prevents policies applied above a container or OU from filtering down into the container or OU where the GPO is being configured.

LAB SOLUTIONS FOR CHAPTER 6

In this section, you'll find solutions to the lab exercises, Lab Analysis Test, and Key Term Quiz.

Lab Solution 6.01

You have been asked by your CIO to configure DC security settings that will be applied to the domain controller within the Montreal site of the major car manufacturer that you work for as a network administrator. In this situation, you need to use a security template, namely the DC template, to configure the security settings. You would use the Active Directory Users and Computer console to access the Group Policy Editor to accomplish this task.

Security templates may be applied to a local computer policy, imported to a group policy object, or used for system security analysis. These templates represent a security configuration—a single file containing a group of security settings. Importing a security template to a group policy object ensures that any accounts to which the group policy object is applied will automatically receive the template's security settings when the group policy settings are refreshed. You can directly apply a security template to local computer policy when a computer is not part of a domain. The system is immediately configured with the new template settings.

In this lab, you applied security settings using group policy. By the end of this lab, you were able to

■ Recognize security settings in a group policy object.

■ Recognize the type of policies in the Security Settings snap-in.

■ Apply security settings using group policy.

■ Import a security template into a group policy object.

To import and apply a security template, perform the following steps:

Step 1.   Access the Active Directory Users and Computers console. Click Start | Programs | Administrative Tools and select the Active Directory Users and Computers item from the list. Right-click the GPO domain and select Properties, as shown here.

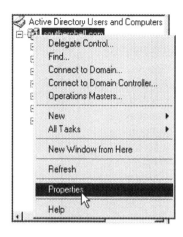

Click the Group Policy tab window and select the Default Domain Policy object, as shown next. This GPO contains the security settings propagated to objects within its scope. Click Edit to access the Group Policy Editor.

Step 2.   Expand the Group Policy tree down to the Security Settings for Computer Configurations, as shown in Figure 6-1. Items within each category can be manually modified. They will not be saved, however, as a security template. Existing templates can be imported and have their settings applied within the GPO.

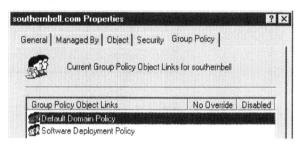

Step 3.   To import the security template, DC Security, right-click Security Settings and choose Import Policy, as shown here.

This will open the Import Policy dialog window. From the listing, locate the path and filename of the DC security template that we wish to import and apply, as shown in Figure 6-2.

Step 4.   Select DC Security and click Open. The template will be imported when the Browse window closes. You are now back at the Group Policy Editor. Complete the import process by closing the Group Policy Editor window. Exit out of the Active Directory Users and Computers window when finished.

FIGURE 6-1

Notice the nine
different security
areas that can
be applied to
a computer
listed under
the Security
Settings folder.

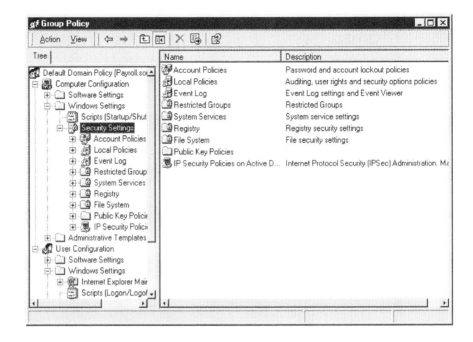

Lab Solution 6.02

You have two goals here. You wish to track access to Directory Services objects by all users in the domain, and you wish to automatically terminate open connections when a user's logon time expires. You need to apply security polices domain-wide using group policy. The group policy object is Domain Users.

FIGURE 6-2

The Browse
window lets you
locate a security
template that you
wish to import
and apply.

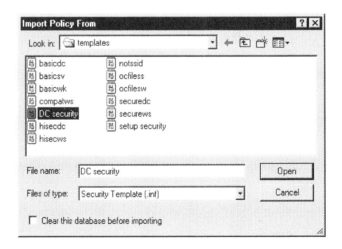

Security policy is to computers what security groups are to users. Just as security groups let you grant a standardized set of rights to a group of users, security policy lets you apply a single security profile to multiple computers. It enforces consistency and provides easy administration.

In this lab, you applied security settings using group policy. By the end of this lab, you were able to

■ Recognize security settings in a group policy object.

■ Recognize the type of policies in the Security Settings snap-in.

■ Apply security settings using group policy.

■ Import a security template into a group policy object.

Step 1.   Access the Active Directory Users and Computers console. Click Start | Programs | Administrative Tools and select the Active Directory Users and Computers item from the list. Right-click the GPO domain and select Properties. Click the Group Policy tab window and select the Default Domain Policy object. This GPO contains the security settings propagated to objects within its scope. Click Edit to access the Group Policy Editor.

Step 2.   Expand the Group Policy tree | Computer Configuration | Windows Settings, down to the Security Settings for Computer Configurations. Now select the Audit Policies folder, as shown in Figure 6-3.

Step 3.   Double-click the audit event we wish to track—Directory Services. This opens the Setting Definition dialog window. Click the Define These Policy Settings check box along with the Success and Failure check boxes, as shown next. Click OK to save the changes.

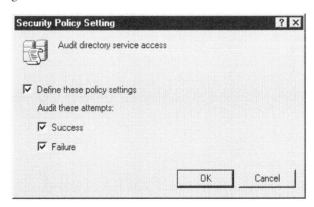

FIGURE 6-3

This shows the audit policies and the areas of the system in which they are applied.

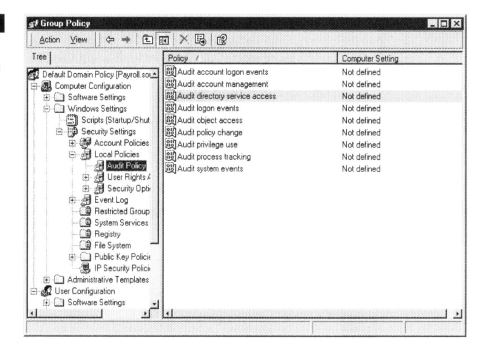

Step 4. Within the Security options in the Local Policies, change the audit policy for Automatically Log Off Users when Logon Time Expires to Enabled, as shown next. Click OK to save the change. Complete the audit function by closing the Group Policy Editor window. Exit out of the Active Directory Users and Computers window when finished.

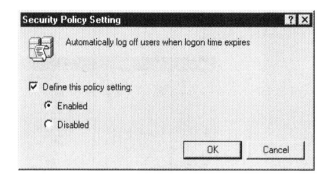

Lab Solution 6.03

Your company, BellaScooters Intl., has expanded in the New England area of the United States. It has a sales marketing center of six people. You need to delegate group policy authority for the center by creating an OU for the BellaScooterNE and assigning an administrator the ability to manage the sales staff on the network.

Delegating administrative responsibilities can help eliminate the need for multiple administrative accounts with broad authority, such as an entire domain. Although you likely will still use the predefined Domain Admins group for administration of the entire domain, you can limit the accounts that are members of the Domain Admins group to highly trusted administrative users.

In this lab, you'll delegate authority to an organizational unit administrator with the ability to manage users in a particular department. By the end of this lab, you'll be able to

■ Create an OU for a department and add a user account for the administrator.

■ Assign control of the OU to an administrative role.

To delegate authority of the OU to an administrator, perform the following steps:

Step 1.   First, we need to create the organizational unit and create the user account within the OU. Click Start | Programs | Administrative Tools, then select Active Directory Users and Computers. In the left pane of the console, right-click the domain, select New and then Organizational Unit from the context menu, as shown here:

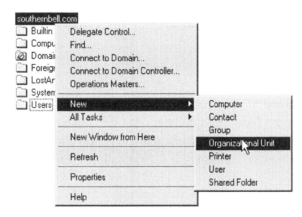

Enter **BellaScooterNE** as the name of the OU, as shown next. Click OK.

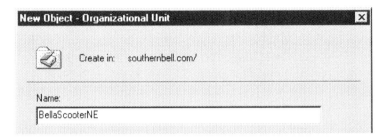

Step 2.   Next, we need to create the new administrator for the BellaScooterNE OU. Right-click the OU, select New and then User from the context menu. Type the name of the new administrator, **Nino Sottovoce**, and then his login name, **nsottovoce**. Click Next and enter his password, **motoscotter**. Click Next and then Finish.

Step 3.   Next, we need to delegate control of the new OU to the new administrator. Right-click the BellaScooterNE OU and select Delegate Control. Click Next at the Welcome screen. In the Users and Groups window, click Add. Double-click our new administrator, Nino Sottovoce, and click OK, as shown in Figure 6-4. Click Next. Be sure the new administrator can create, delete, and manage user accounts in the OU by checking the appropriate boxes, as shown in Figure 6-5. Click Next and then Finish. Close all windows and log off.

Step 4.   Last, we need to test the new administrator's ability to create a new user account. Log in as Nino Sottovoce, the new administrator. His password is motoscooter. Click Start | Programs | Administrative Tools and select Access the Active Directory Users and Computers.

Step 5.   To create a new sales associate, Gina A. Barbutta, right-click BellaScooterNE, select New and then User from the context menu. Enter Gina's full name and then her logon name, **gbarbutta**. Click Next and enter her password, **passaretto**, in the password window. Click Next and then Finish. Close all windows and log off.

FIGURE 6-4

Select and add the user, Nino Sottovoce, that will administer the OU.

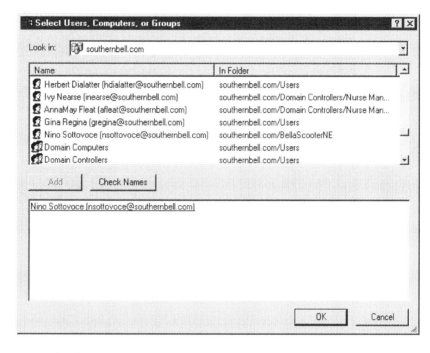

FIGURE 6-5

Select the common tasks— Create, Delete, and Manage User Accounts—that the administrator can perform.

Lab Solution 6.04

As an administrator, you may see several common scenarios when troubleshooting group policy. Three strategies that can help minimize problems are keeping objects to a minimum, keeping good documentation by mapping your Group Policies in a diagram in the same way you would map network configurations, and, lastly, being sure to test new policies and ensuring that they are working properly before you deploy them.

In this lab, you applied preventive measures in the form of auditing group policy. It's a way of being proactive rather than reactive. (This is very different from the previous lab scenario where we used a GPO to apply auditing on computers.) By the end of this lab, you were able to

■ Configure auditing for a group policy object.

To configure auditing for a GPO, perform the following steps:

Step 1. Access the Active Directory Users and Computers console. Click Start | Programs | Administrative Tools and select the Active Directory Users and Computers item from the list. Right-click the GPO domain and select Properties. Click the Group Policy tab window and select the Default Domain Policy object. This GPO contains the security settings propagated to objects within its scope. Click Edit to access the Group Policy Editor.

Step 2. Select the Security tab in the Group Policy Properties dialog window. Now, click Advance to open the Advanced Security settings dialog window, as shown in Figure 6-6. This window also contains a message section below the buttons. If there is a message stating that the auditing configuration is inherited from a parent container, you'll need to move one level up the tree to make the change. Since we are working at the domain level, there should not be a message.

Step 3. Add the audit settings for the domain users by clicking the Add button and selecting the Domain Users object, as shown here:

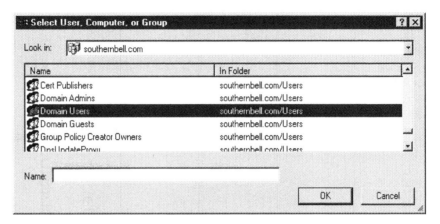

You will now be presented with the Audit Entry dialog window, as shown in Figure 6-7. Select the following access permissions: Delete, Failed; Delete Subtree, Failed; Modify Permissions, Failed; Read Permissions, Success.

FIGURE 6-6

The window displays the auditing configuration that is presently set, and a message stating that the audit entry is defined directly on the object.

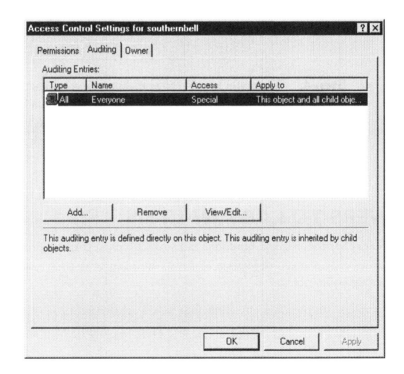

FIGURE 6-7

Select the access
permissions and
whether to track
their success
or failure.

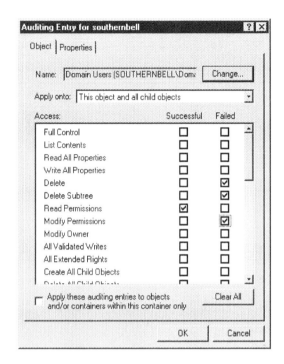

Step 4. When you have finished making the selections, click OK to save the settings. Notice that the Domain Users object has been added to the Audit dialog box of the Access Control Settings window, as shown in Figure 6-8. Click OK to apply and exit out of the Access Control Settings window. Click OK to close the GPO Properties window and to save your settings. Click OK to close the Active Directory Users and Computers console.

ANSWERS TO LAB ANALYSIS

1. A Security Settings snap-in functions as a single point of entry; it provides a full range of system security that can be viewed, adjusted, and applied to a local computer or imported to a group policy object.

2. User configuration settings are applied to users regardless of which computer they log on from. Computer configuration settings are applied to computers regardless of who logs on to that computer.

3. One, keep objects to a minimum by placing users and computers in the same container or OU, and by limiting the use of Block Policy Inheritance and No Override. Less is more. Two, one domain-level GPO can satisfy most business requirements. Fewer GPOs decrease your chances of potential problems. Three, keep good documentation by mapping your group policies

FIGURE 6-8

A final look at the objects on which audit settings have been applied.

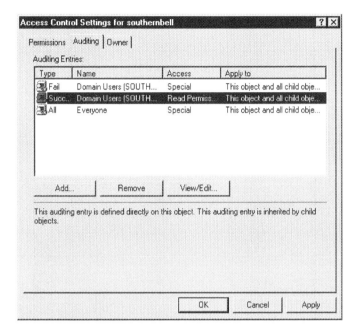

in a diagram. A visual schematic can help pinpoint where policies may be failing. And four, be sure to test new policies and ensure that they are working properly before you deploy them.

4. The Override/Forcing group policy does not allow a container's or OU's GPO to override a domain-wide policy from above, and thereby avoids having to create multiple GPOs with potential conflicting policies that apply to the same users or computers.

5. Security templates are used to enforce security settings for users and computers, and for system security analysis. These templates represent a security configuration—a single file containing a group of security settings. Importing a security template to a group policy object ensures that any accounts to which the group policy object is applied will automatically receive the template's security settings when the group policy settings are refreshed. You can directly apply a security template to local computer policy when a computer is not part of a domain.

ANSWERS TO KEY TERM QUIZ

1. Security template
2. Account policy
3. Audit policy
4. Discretionary access control list (DACL)
5. Block Policy Inheritance

7

Publishing Resources in Active Directory

LAB EXERCISES

7.01   Publishing Shared Folders

7.02   Publishing Shared Printers

7.03   Publishing Network Services

■   Lab Analysis Test

■   Key Term Quiz

■   Lab Solutions

N etwork administration is not without its moments of challenges, especially in a large network. One challenge (and reason for creating networked computers) is to provide information about network resources to authorized users on a network, while at the same time keeping this information secured from unauthorized access. At the same time, an administrator needs to make the information easy to find on the network.

By storing information about all network objects, the Active Directory database services was meant to meet these challenges by offering rapid information retrieval and providing security mechanisms that control access. Resources that you can make available (publish) in Active Directory database services include objects, such as users, computers, printers, files, folders, and network services. Publishing information about shared resources, such as folders, files, and printers, makes it easy for users to find these resources on the network.

In this chapter, we will look at how we publish these resources, especially the more commonly needed objects, folders, printers, and particular network-enabled services.

CERTIFICATION OBJECTIVE 7.01

Publishing Shared Folders

15 Minutes

Your sales department manager wants to provide her staff with a shared folder that will contain updated sales figures. She also wants to make sure that they are easy to access and locate. What steps do you need to take in creating, sharing, and publishing this folder?

Learning Objectives

Any shared network folder, including a Distributed File System (DFS) folder, can be published in the directory. A DFS provides drive maps to, and a uniform naming convention for, an array of servers, shares, and files. It also adds the capability of organizing file servers and their shares into a logical hierarchy, making it considerably easier to manage and use information resources. Creating a Shared Folder object in the directory does not automatically publish the folder. This is a two-step process: you must first share the folder, and then publish it in the directory.

In this lab, you'll give access to documents, spreadsheets, or presentations. By the end of this lab, you'll be able to

■ Share and publish a folder.

Lab Materials and Setup

For this lab exercise, you'll need

■ A working computer
■ Installed network card (NIC)
■ Windows 2000 Server software (installed)
■ TCP/IP installed
■ Domain Name System (DNS) installed
■ Active Directory (AD) installed

Getting Down to Business

To create, share, and publish a shared folder, perform the following steps:

Step 1. As mentioned, we first need to create a folder and share it out. Log on to your domain with your Administrator account. Create a folder named Marketing Documents on a drive.

Step 2. Right-click the folder and select the Sharing option. Share out the folder with the Marketing Documents title. Click OK to create the share.

Step 3. Now we need to publish the folder. Access the Active Directory Users and Computers console. Expand your domain to view the list of current objects. Select the Users container, in which we will create the Shared Folder object.

Step 4. From the New menu, choose Shared Folder and name it Marketing Documents. In the Network Path text box, use the Universal Naming Convention (UNC) notation pointing to the drive where the folder was created. UNC is the full Windows 2000 name of a resource on a network. Click OK to complete.

Step 5. The Users folder will now contain the Marketing Documents folder.

CERTIFICATION OBJECTIVE 7.02

Publishing Shared Printers

15 Minutes

Steve, the network administrator for Hands-for-Hire Employment Agency, has just acquired a second printer for the office. The printer will be managed by a Windows 2000 server. What steps does Steve need to take to make this available to the office staff?

Learning Objectives

Ease of access and use is a main concern of the network administrator. Publishing information about these shared resources makes it easy for users to locate them on the network. When installing a printer on a Windows 2000 server, the operating system automatically creates an object for the printer in the Active Directory database service.

In this lab, you'll share a printer on the network. By the end of this lab, you'll be able to

- Share and publish a printer.
- Search for a printer in Active Directory.

Lab Materials and Setup

For this lab exercise, you'll need

- A working computer
- Installed network card (NIC)
- Windows 2000 Server software (installed)
- TCP/IP installed
- Domain Name System (DNS) installed
- Active Directory (AD) installed

Getting Down to Business

To create, share, and publish a shared printer, perform the following steps:

Step 1. In Windows 2000, follow the steps to add a printer. Follow the instructions to create the printer.

Step 2. After you have created and shared the printer, the Listed in the Directory check box should be selected. The Printer object is published under the Computer object to which it is attached.

lab

(h)int

In Windows 2000 Server, the Add Printer Wizard shares the printer and publishes it in Active Directory by default, unless you click Do Not Share this Printer in the wizard's Printer Sharing dialog box.

Step 3. Active Directory client users can browse for, submit jobs to, and even install printer drivers directly from the server to printers published in Active Directory. From the Start button, search for printers in Windows 2000.

Step 4. Using the Locate Your Printer box, search for your installed printer. Once the printer is found, view the current printer queue.

CERTIFICATION OBJECTIVE 7.03

Publishing Network Services

15 Minutes

Gina, a network administrator, works for you at the world headquarters of a large financial firm. Your Windows 2000 network consists of one hundred and seventy-five client computers, six domain controllers, and two application servers. You wish to assign her the task of centrally managing the Certificate Authority service using the Active Directory Sites and Services utility. What steps do you need to take to make this available to Gina?

Learning Objectives

Network-enabled services, such as Certificate Services, can be published in the directory so administrators can locate and administer them using the Active Directory Sites and Services utility. Certificates provide for authentication and secure exchange of information on an unsecured network. By publishing a service, rather than computers or servers, administrators can focus on managing the service regardless of where the computer is located.

There are two common types of information published using the Active Directory services: binding information, which enables clients to connect to not so well-known bindings that do not conform to service-based systems (usually legacy flat-file type of operating systems); and configuration information, which allows an administrator to distribute the information for the applications to client computers.

In this lab, you'll learn how to publish a network service. By the end of this lab, you'll be able to

- Use Active Directory Sites and Services.
- Publish a network service.

Lab Materials and Setup

For this lab exercise, you'll need

- A working computer
- Installed network card (NIC)
- Windows 2000 Server software (installed)
- TCP/IP installed
- Domain Name System (DNS) installed
- Active Directory (AD) installed
- A user account for Gina

Getting Down to Business

To set security permissions and delegate control of certificate templates, perform the following steps:

Step 1. Access Active Directory Sites and Services. From the View menu, select Show Services Node.

Step 2. Expand the Active Directory Sites and Services until you reach the Certificate Templates icon. Select the Certificate Authority template and open the Properties dialog window.

Step 3. Set appropriate security permissions through the Security tab for Gina. Click OK and complete the process. This will set the security permission and delegate control of the certificate template in the OU.

LAB ANALYSIS TEST

1. What is the purpose of publishing shared resources in AD services?

   _____

   _____

2. What are some of the challenges that a network administrator faces?

   _____

   _____

3. What benefit is there to publishing a service rather than a computer or server?

   _____

   _____

4. What can Active Directory clients perform with published printers in the Active Directory database?

   _____

   _____

5. List and describe the two types of information categories that are frequently published using Active Directory services.

   _____

   _____

KEY TERM QUIZ

Use the following vocabulary terms to complete the sentences below. Not all of the terms will be used. Definitions for these terms can be found in "Managing a Microsoft Windows 2000 Network Environment Study Guide."

Universal Naming Convention (UNC)

Binding information

Configuration information

Distributed File System (DFS)

Group Policies

Scope

Publish

Replication policy

Security permissions

Certificate

1. A type of information that lets clients connect to services that do not conform to a service-centric network model is named _____.

2. _____ is the full Windows 2000 name of a resource on a network.

3. A _____ is a collection of data used for authenticating and securing information on an unsecured network.

4. To make data available for replication, you _____ it on the network.

5. _____ lets you distribute current configuration information for an application to all clients in the domain.

LAB SOLUTIONS FOR CHAPTER 7

In this section, you'll find solutions to the lab exercises, Lab Analysis Test, and Key Term Quiz.

Lab Solution 7.01

Any shared network folder, including a Distributed File System (DFS) folder, can be published in the directory. Creating a Shared Folder object in the directory does not automatically publish the folder. This is a two-step process: you must first share the folder, and then publish it in the directory.

In this lab, you gave access to documents, spreadsheets, or presentations. By the end of this lab, you were able to

■ Share and publish a folder.

To create, share, and publish a shared folder, perform the following steps:

Step 1.   As mentioned, we first need to create a folder and share it out. Log on to your domain with your Administrator account. Open Windows Explorer, or access your hard drive through My Computer, and create a folder named Marketing Documents on that drive, as shown in Figure 7-1. The new folder is displayed in the hard drive contents window.

Step 2.   Right-click the newly created folder and from the pop-up menu select Sharing. Select Share this Folder, and in the Share Name box enter **Marketing Documents**, as shown next. Click OK to create the share.

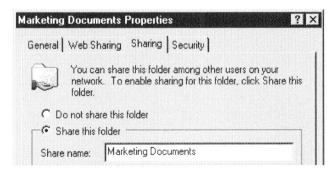

FIGURE 7-1   Create a new Marketing Documents folder for sharing purposes.

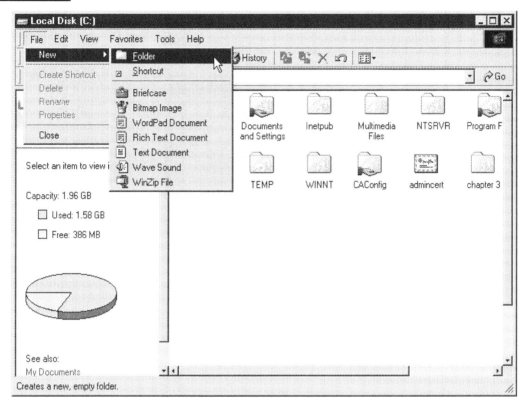

Step 3.   Now we need to publish the folder. Access the Active Directory Users and Computers console. Click Start | Programs | Administrative Tools and select the Active Directory Users and Computers item from the list. Expand your domain to view the list of current objects. Right-click the Users folder, in which we will create the Shared Folder object.

Step 4. From the New menu, choose Shared Folder, as shown next. This opens the New Object - Shared Folder dialog window.

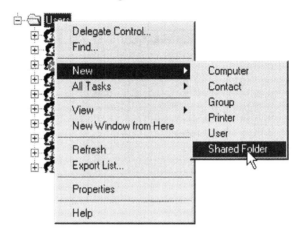

Step 5. In the Name text box, enter **Marketing Documents**. In the Network Path text box, using the Universal Naming Convention (UNC) notation, point to the drive where the folder was created. Both of these entries are shown next. Click OK to complete.

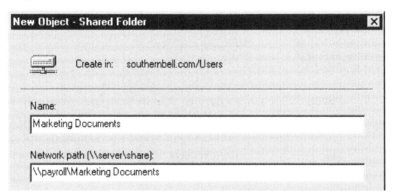

Step 6. The Users folder will now contain the Marketing Documents folder, as shown in Figure 7-2.

FIGURE 7-2   The new share shows in the right pane of the window with a Shared Drive icon.

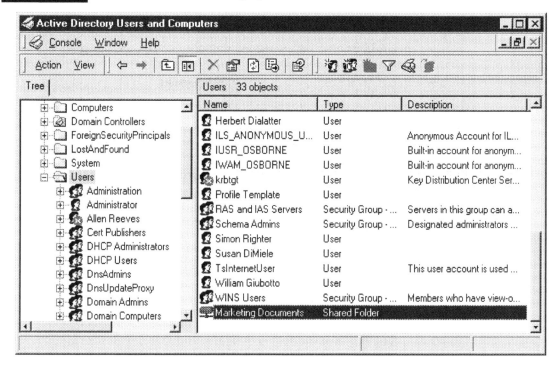

Lab Solution 7.02

Ease of access and use is a main concern of the network administrator. Publishing information about these shared resources makes it easy for users to locate them on the network.

In this lab, you shared a printer on the network. By the end of this lab, you were able to

- Share and publish a printer.
- Search for a printer in Active Directory.

To create, share, and publish a shared printer, perform the following steps:

Step 1. In Windows 2000, follow the steps to add a printer. Click Start | Settings | and then click Add Printer. Follow the instructions to create the printer.

Step 2. After you have created and shared the printer, the Listed in the Directory check box should be selected. Right-click the printer and select Properties to view this setting. The Printer object is published under the Computer object in the Active Directory Users and Computers console.

lab
ⓗint
In Windows 2000 Server, the Add Printer Wizard shares the printer and publishes it in Active Directory by default, unless you click Do Not Share this Printer in the wizard's Printer Sharing dialog box.

Step 3. Active Directory client users can browse for, submit jobs to, and even install printer drivers directly from the server to printers published in Active Directory. From the Start button, search for printers in Windows 2000.

Step 4. Click Start | Search and then click For Printers. In the Locate Your Printer box, click the Type the Printer Name, or click Next to Browse for a Printer radio button, as shown in Figure 7-3. Click Find Now. Once the printer is found and added, right-click the Printer icon to view the current printer queue.

Lab Solution 7.03

Network-enabled services, such as Certificate Services, can be published in the directory so administrators can locate and administer them using the Active Directory Sites and Services utility. By publishing a service, rather than computers or servers, administrators can focus on managing the service regardless of where the computer is located.

There are two common types of information published using the Active Directory services: binding information and configuration information.

In this lab, you learned how to publish a network service. By the end of this lab, you were able to

- Use Active Directory Sites and Services.
- Publish a network service.

FIGURE 7-3

Browse for the
printer that is
advertising itself
on the network.

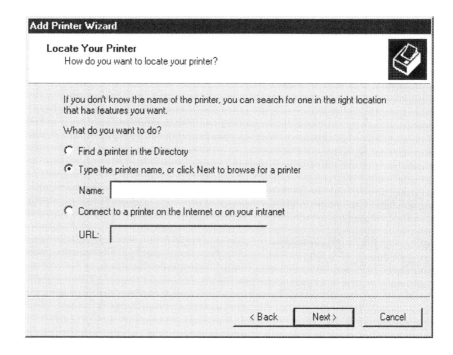

To set security permissions and delegate control of certificate templates, perform
the following steps:

Step 1. Click Start | Programs | Administrative Tools, to access Active Directory
Sites and Services. From the View menu, select Show Services Node, as shown here:

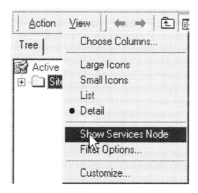

Step 2. Expand the Active Directory Sites and Services until you reach the Certificate Templates icon. Select the Certificate Authority template and open the Properties dialog window, as shown in Figure 7-4.

Step 3. Set appropriate security permissions through the Security tab for Gina, as shown in Figure 7-5. Click OK and complete the process. This will set the security permission and delegate control of the certificate template in the OU.

FIGURE 7-4 The right pane displays all available certificate templates. Choose the CA (Certificate Authority) template.

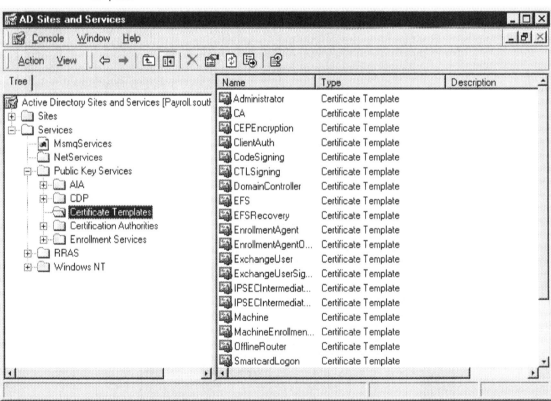

Add the user
to the access
control list in the
Security dialog
window. Allow
her full control
of the service.

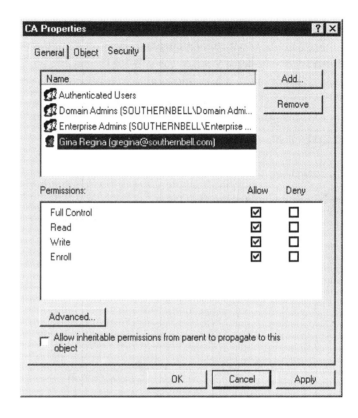

ANSWERS TO LAB ANALYSIS

1. Publishing information about shared resources makes it easy for users to locate them on the network.

2. One challenge is to provide information about network resources to authorized users on a network, while at the same time keeping this information secured from unauthorized access. At the same time, an administrator needs to make the information easy to find on the network.

3. By publishing a service, rather than computers or servers, administrators can focus on managing the service regardless of where the computer is located.

4. Active Directory client users can browse for, submit jobs to, and even install printer drivers directly from the server to printers published in Active Directory.

5. The two common types of information published using the Active Directory services are binding information, which enables clients to connect to not so well-known bindings that do not conform to service-based systems (usually legacy flat-file type of operating systems); and configuration information, which allows an administrator to distribute the information for the application to client computers.

ANSWERS TO KEY TERM QUIZ

1. Binding information

2. Universal Naming Convention (UNC)

3. Certificate

4. Publish

5. Configuration information

MICROSOFT CERTIFIED SYSTEMS ASSOCIATE

8

Deploying Software with Group Policies

LAB EXERCISES

8.01 Using Group Policies to Deploy
      Software

8.02 Using Group Policies to Set Up
      Application Categories

8.03 Using Group Policies to Remove
      Software

■ Lab Analysis Test

■ Key Term Quiz

■ Lab Solutions

I n an Active Directory environment, group policies allow us to distribute software to users and computers. When software is deployed (made available for activation) using a group policy, the user needs no special privileges since the software is installed using the elevated privileges of policy. If a vendor does not provide an .msi file for their software (this is a file that contains instructions about the installation and removal of specific applications— Microsoft software installer), you can use a repackaging program, such as WinInstall LE (found on the Windows 2000 CD) to create one.

When deploying software via group policy, the two options available are to either assign it or publish it. When you assign it to a group, the software will be available to users (roams with the users), regardless of which computer they log on from. The application appears on the Start menu as a shortcut. The software is installed when the user clicks on that shortcut. When assigned to a computer, the software is installed automatically on that computer the next time it reboots. It then becomes available to all users on that computer. When you publish it (which can only be done to users, not computers), the software is available to install from Add/Remove programs, or by document invocation (when a user clicks on a file type associated with that application).

Publishing software makes it available to users, giving the option to install the application to the user. The user chooses if and when to install it. An application can also be published using a .zap file (an existing setup program that installs an application by using its original Setup.exe program) if an .msi does not exist or if one cannot be created. A .zap file is an ASCII text file that has information relative to the installation of the application, similar to a batch file. Keep in mind that if a .zap file is used, the user will need the appropriate administrative rights to install the application. And, software deployment options only apply to Windows 2000–based systems and not other 9x systems.

Working together with Group Policy and Active Directory services, the Software Installation extension snap-in sets a group-policy-based software management system that lets you centrally manage the four stages of the distribution life cycle:

- **Preparation**   The prep work necessary prior to the actual release of the software. This may include the process of packaging software that is not in an .msi or .zap format.

■ **Deployment** When you actually get the software out to the users and/or computers. This is where you also decide to either assign or publish the software.

■ **Upgrades** Over time, new updates, patches, fixes, or revisions will be posted on a software company's web site or sent to you on a CD. So you need to ensure currency of, or proper repair of, the software.

■ **Removal** Once all users have installed or updated the software, it is no longer necessary for it to take up hard drive space or clutter up the Start menu.

What makes the deployment of applications to users through the use of Group Policies is the technology of Windows Installer. This technology consists of two components: Windows Installer Service and Windows Installer Package. It was developed to improve the installation and deinstallation of programs, to make software deployment on networks easier, and to solve common problems such as shared .dll conflicts. The Windows Installer Service is a default service on all Windows 2000 computers. It facilitates the automated function of deploying software. The Windows Installer package is the application product that contains all the necessary files and information to install or remove the application. The packaged product has the .msi extension. Think of it as Microsoft's version of PKZIP, or a self-extracting .exe program.

In this lab chapter, we'll first work through the steps to deploy a software application to all users. We'll then look at how to distribute software upgrades. Finally, we'll remove software applications using group policies.

CERTIFICATION OBJECTIVE 8.01

Using Group Policies to Deploy Software

15 Minutes

You are the senior network administrator for a large global corporation with offices in all the major countries of the world. Your headquarters are in Boston, MA. Your senior network engineer, the person you report to, wants you to distribute the new Windows 2000 Resource Kit as a software option for all users throughout the organization. He needs to make sure that the software application gets deployed.

Learning Objectives

You can use group policies to assign or publish software for users computers in a domain rather than creating a Group Policy object (GPO) (which is an object within Active Directory (AD) enabling an administrator to configure deployment settings, security, and templates—it helps enforce company rules for users and computers) for each organizational unit (OU). An organizational unit is a subsection of a domain, a container of users categorized either by geographical location and/or by department grouping. Group Policy objects (GPOs) are normally applied only to members of organizational units (OUs) linked to the GPO. Assigning the software to the user, as will be our case, means that the icon will be available for installation by the user, and it will be up to the user whether to install it or not. Selecting the application's icon will cause the installation to take place. The option is up to the user.

If we were to assign the software to computers instead, when the computer processes its Group Policy settings it will notice the assigned software and automatically install it on the computer to make it available to all users on that computer.

In this lab, you'll assign software through the use of Group Policy. By the end of this lab, you'll be able to

■ Deploy software using Group Policy.

■ Configure software distribution for a user or group.

Lab Materials and Setup

For this lab exercise, you'll need

■ A working computer

■ Installed network card (NIC)

■ Windows 2000 Server software (installed)

■ TCP/IP installed

■ Active Directory (AD) installed

■ Windows 2000 Server CD

lab Hint *A ready-made MSI file is available for use, in this lab scenario, in the Windows 2000 Server CD in the support\tools folder.*

Getting Down to Business

To deploy a software application using Group Policy, perform the following steps:

Step 1.   First, we need to set up a software distribution point by sharing the folder where the software is located. The share name will be Share Folder. Remove the Full Control and Change Permissions options from the Everyone group. The purpose of this is to prevent accidental modification or deletion of the file.

Step 2.   Next, we need to assign the application to users. Access the Active Directory Users and Computer console. Access the domain in which you want to configure a Group Policy object (GPO). Create a new GPO, which you will use to deploy the software application.

Step 3.   Open the Group Policy Editor to configure software deployment. Click the Group Policy tab and click New to create a new GPO, which we will use to deploy software. Enter the new GPO name—**Software Deployment Policy**. Click OK to accept.

Step 4.   Next, we need to add a new software installation package. Open the Properties window of the Software Deployment Policy object. Select Software Installation under the User Configuration object and create a new package. Browse the network to the 2000RKST application that we are going to assign. Select Assigned in the Deploy Software dialog window. Click OK to create the software package.

lab Warning *Do not browse your local drive to assign the application. You need to browse by way of My Network Places. This will ensure that the path is that of a network share.*

Step 5.   Open the Properties window of the newly created package. Check the default settings for the deployment options. Notice that the Auto-install by file extension activation radio button is selected and grayed out. This will ensure that the application will install even if activated through file extension. Click OK and complete the process. The package is now available for user deployment.

CERTIFICATION OBJECTIVE 8.02

Using Group Policies to Set Up Application Categories

20 Minutes

There is a second requirement to this software deployment process. Remember, you are the senior network administrator for a large global corporation with offices in all the major countries of the world. Your headquarters are in Boston, MA. Your senior network engineer, the person you report to, wants you to distribute the new Windows 2000 Resource Kit, 2000 RKST, as a software option for all users throughout the organization. He also wants it to be available in an application category within the user's Start menu. What do you need to configure to meet this requirement?

Learning Objectives

As we know, easy access to software applications and utilities is one of the goals of network administration. It may be beneficial to create software categories for particular applications that are to be deployed, especially on a voluntary basis. Creating software categories also changes the Add/Remove Programs window by including the Add Programs from your network option.

Without the Categories option, if there are many applications available for installation, there would be one single list of these applications. The user would have to scroll the list to find the needed application. Using software categories, the list is shorter by showing the categories first. Then, once the user finds the category, the grouped applications are listed in a drop-down menu box for the user to select. The list is limited to only the software that was placed in that category.

In this lab, you'll organize a software package by placing it in a category to make it easier for a user to locate. By the end of this lab, you'll be able to

- Create a software category.
- Assign a software package to a category.

Lab Materials and Setup

For this lab exercise, you will need

- A working computer
- Installed network card (NIC)
- Windows 2000 Server software (installed)
- TCP/IP installed
- Active Directory (AD) installed

Getting Down to Business

To create a software category and assign a software package, perform the following steps:

Step 1.   Access the Group Policy Editor. Expand the User Configuration folder and open the Software Installation Properties window. Switch to the Categories tab to display the Categories dialog window.

Step 2.   Add the category that will contain the .msi file from the previous lab. It will be named Utilities. Close the Editor to apply your changes. Do not close out of the Group Policy window.

lab
Hint   *It's important to note that when categories are configured in a GPO on a domain, it will be available throughout that domain. Any OU in that domain will have access to that category.*

Step 3.   Select the software package that you will assign to a category. Open the Properties window of the package. Switch to the Categories tab. Select and assign the package to our Utilities category.

Step 4.   If you ever need to remove the application from the category, you would highlight the application under the Selected categories and click Remove. Close the Editor to apply your changes. Exit out of all open windows and consoles.

Using Group Policies to Remove Software

10 Minutes

Sixty days have passed since your senior network engineer wanted you to distribute the new Windows 2000 Resource Kit, 2000 RKST, as a software option for all users throughout the organization. Now you need to remove the software package. What needs to be done to make this happen?

Learning Objectives

There will come a time, once all users have installed the software, that a software package will no longer be needed. You need to remove the software application. There are two choices that affect the removal process decision within the Software Installation snap-in. The first is an optional, or conditional, removal specified by selecting the Immediately Uninstall Software from Users and Computers option when configuring the removal of the software package. You remove the software from management without forcing the (physical) removal of the software from the computers of users who are still using the software. Users can continue to use the software until they remove it themselves. In this scenario, no one is able to install the older version of the software from the Start menu by using Add/Remove Programs or by document invocation.

The second is a forced, or mandatory, removal specified by selecting the Allow Users to Continue to Use the Software But Prevent New Installations option. The decision is made that it is best that the software no longer be used. With forced removal, the software is automatically removed from a computer, either the next time the computer is turned on (when the software is assigned to the computer) or the next time the user logs on (when the software is assigned to the user).

In this lab, you'll remove a software package by using the Optional Removal option. By the end of this lab, you'll be able to

■   Remove a package using Group Policy.

Lab Materials and Setup

For this lab exercise, you will need

- A working computer
- Installed network card (NIC)
- Windows 2000 Server software (installed)
- TCP/IP installed
- Active Directory (AD) installed

Getting Down to Business

To remove a software package using a Group Policy, perform the following steps:

Step 1. Access the Active Directory Users and Computers console. Access the Properties windows of the GPO domain. Open the Group Policy Editor of the GPO.

Step 2. Locate the software package folder, right-click the icon, and select Remove. Complete the removal process and close out of the editor to apply the changes.

LAB ANALYSIS TEST

1. One of your interns, Phil, is watching you deploying software via a group policy. He has read about this in his MCSA study guide, but forgot the two available options. Refresh Phil's memory and explain the two options that are available.

   _____

   _____

2. You give Marcy, a junior network administrator, the task of removing the availability of a packaged software application from the users. You tell her that you don't want the software to be available to the users any longer. You're asked to explain the two choices available within the Software Installation snap-in, and which one to use.

   _____

   _____

3. If your company has many software application packages available for deployment, how can it be made easier for users to find the application they want?

   _____

   _____

4. Why would a software package remove files when being deployed?

   _____

   _____

5. Why would you assign an application to a computer rather than a user?

   _____

   _____

KEY TERM QUIZ

Use the following vocabulary terms to complete the sentences below. Not all of the terms will be used. Definitions for these terms can be found in "Managing a Microsoft Windows 2000 Network Environment Study Guide."

.msi file

.zap file

Group Policy object (GPO)

Optional removal

Forced removal

Organizational unit (OU)

Group Policy

Deployment

Windows Installer service

Repackage

1. When you remove software from management without forcing the (physical) removal of the software from the computers of users who are still using the software, this is called
   _____.

2. The _____ is a default service on all Windows 2000 computers. It facilitates the automated function of deploying software.

3. _____ is when you actually get the software out to the users and/or computers.

4. An object within Active Directory (AD) that enables an administrator to configure deployment settings, security, and templates, and helps to enforce company rules for users and computers, is known as _____.

5. A _____ is a file that contains instructions about the installation and removal of specific applications.

LAB SOLUTIONS FOR CHAPTER 8

In this section, you'll find solutions to the lab exercises, Lab Analysis Test, and Key Term Quiz.

Lab Solution 8.01

You can use group policies to assign or publish software for users or computers in a domain. Assigning the software to the user, as will be our case, means that the icon will be available for installation by the user, and it will be up to the user whether to install it or not.

In this lab, you assigned software through the use of Group Policy. By the end of this lab, you were able to

- Deploy software using Group Policy.
- Configure software distribution for a user or group.

lab

Hint *A ready-made MSI file is available for use, in this lab scenario, in the Windows 2000 Server CD in the support\tools folder.*

To deploy a software application using Group Policy, perform the following steps:

Step 1. First, we need to set up a software distribution point by sharing the folder where the software is located. The share name will be Share Folder. Remove the Full Control and Change Permissions options from the Everyone group. The purpose of this is to prevent accidental modification or deletion of the file.

Step 2. Next, we need to assign the application to users. Access the Active Directory Users and Computer console. Click Start | Programs | Administrative Tools and select the Active Directory Users and Computers item from the list.

Right-click the domain where we will configure the GPO and select Properties, as shown here:

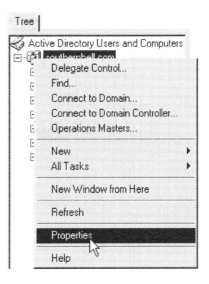

Step 3.   Click the Group Policy tab and click New to create a new GPO, which we will use to deploy software, as shown here:

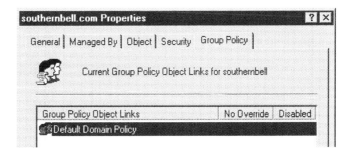

Enter the new GPO name, **Software Deployment Policy**. Click OK to accept. The new GPO is added to the list, as shown here:

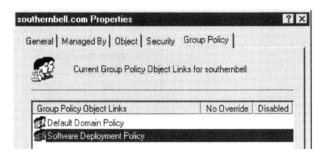

Step 4. Open the Group Policy Editor to configure software deployment by selecting Software Deployment Policy and clicking Edit. Expand the Software Settings folder for users. Right-click the Software Installation icon to create a new package. Select New, then Package from the context menu, as shown here.

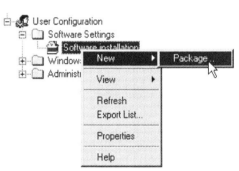

Step 5. Browse the network to the 2000RKST application that we are going to assign, as shown here:

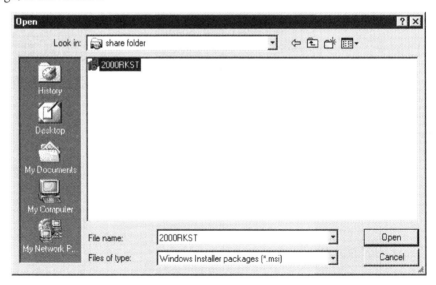

Click Open. Select Assigned in the Deploy Software dialog window that appears. This dialog window appears because we have decided to assign the software application package to the users of Group Policy, as shown next. Click OK to create the software package.

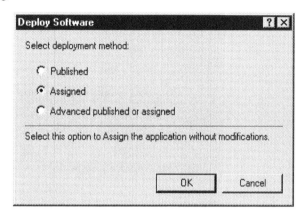

lab
Warning   *Do not browse your local drive to assign the application. You need to browse by way of My Network Places. This will ensure that the path is that of a network share.*

Step 6.   Right-click the new package and select Properties. Check the default settings for the deployment options and notice that the Auto-install by File Extension Activation radio button is selected, as shown in Figure 8-1. This will ensure that the application will be installed even if activated through file extension.

Step 7.   Click OK to close the dialog window. Close the Group Policy Editor and click OK to close the Group Policy Container Properties dialog window. The package is now available for user deployment.

Lab Solution 8.02

The second requirement is to distribute the new Windows 2000 Resource Kit, 2000 RKST, as a software option for all users throughout the organization within the user's Start menu. Easy access to software applications and utilities is our goal here. Creating software categories provides a benefit when choosing a particular application from a list. When using software categories, the list is shorter by showing the categories first. Then, once the user finds the category, the grouped applications are listed in a drop-down menu box for the user to select. The list is limited to only

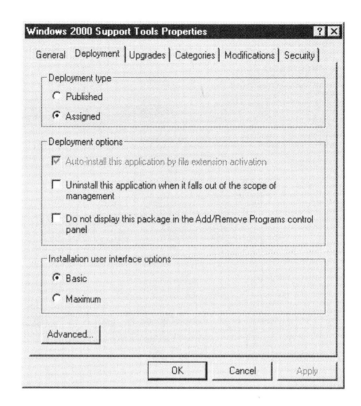

FIGURE 8-1

The package's Deployment tab window displays the Auto-install option selected.

the software that was placed in that category. To create a software category and assign a software package, perform the following steps:

Step 1. Access the Active Directory Users and Computer console. Click Start | Programs | Administrative Tools and select the Active Directory Users and Computers item from the list. Right-click the domain and select Properties. Select the GPO we created (Software Deployment Policy) and click Edit. This will open the Group Policy Editor. Expand the User Configuration folder and the Software Settings folder.

Step 2. Right-click Software Installation to open the Properties window. Click the Categories tab to display the Categories dialog window and a list of any currently configured categories, as shown in Figure 8-2.

FIGURE 8-2

The Categories
tab lists any
currently
configured
categories.

Software installation Properties

General | File Extensions | Categories |

Categories for southernbell.com

Step 3. To add a category that will contain the .msi file from the previous lab, click Add. A New Category dialog box will appear. Enter the new category name as **Utilities**, as shown here.

Click OK. The new category
now appears in the Software
Installation Properties window, as
shown next. Click OK to accept
the new category. Close the
Software Installation Properties
window. Do not close out of the
Group Policy window.

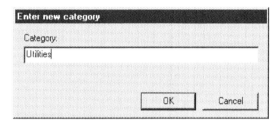

Enter new category

Category:

Utilities

OK   Cancel

Software installation Properties

General | File Extensions | Categories |

Categories for southernbell.com

Utilities

lab
Hint *It's important to note that when categories are configured in a GPO on a domain, it will be available throughout that domain. Any OU in that domain will have access to that category.*

Step 4. Now we need to assign the software application to the category. Highlight the software package on the right pane of the window. Right-click the package and select Properties.

Step 5. To see the list of available categories, click the Categories tab. Select and assign the package to our Utilities category, and click Add. It now appears under Selected Categories, as shown in Figure 8-3. If you ever need to remove the

FIGURE 8-3

The new category, Utilities, has been added to the Selected Categories list.

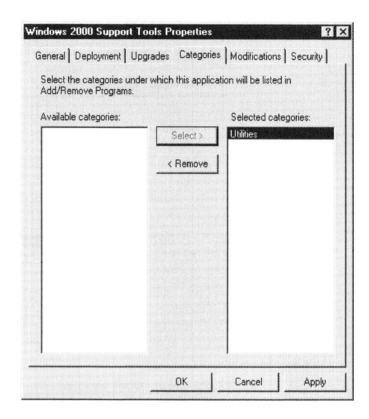

application from the category, you would highlight the application under Selected Categories and click Remove.

Step 6. Click OK to accept the category. Exit out of all Properties windows, the Group Policy window, and the Active Directory Users and Computers console.

Lab Solution 8.03

Sixty days have passed since your senior network engineer wanted you to distribute the new Windows 2000 Resource Kit. Now you need to remove the software package. To remove a software package using a Group Policy, perform the following steps:

Step 1. Access the Active Directory Users and Computers console. Click Start | Programs | Administrative Tools and select the Active Directory Users and

Computers item from the list. Right-click the container where the GPO is located. Select Properties.

Step 2. Select the Group Policy tab. Select the GPO, Software Deployment Policy, containing information on the software package we need to remove, then click Edit. This opens the Group Policy Editor of the GPO.

Step 3. Expand the container within the Software Installation folder and select the software package we need to remove that is on the right pane of the window. To remove the package, right-click the 2000RKST icon and choose All Tasks from the context menu; then click Remove, as shown here:

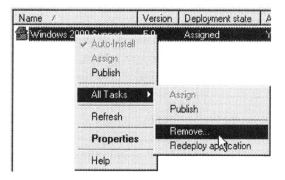

There are two methods to remove the software, and we will choose the first—Immediately Uninstall the Software from Users and Computers, as shown next. Click OK to apply our choice.

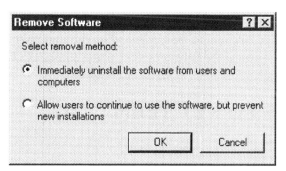

Step 4. The window closes and it returns you to the Group Policy Editor. Notice that the software package is no longer listed. Click OK to close out of the container Properties dialog window. Exit out of the Active Directory Users and Computers.

ANSWERS TO LAB ANALYSIS

1. When deploying software via group policy, the two options available are to assign it or to publish it. When you assign it to a group, the software will be available to users (roams with the users), regardless of which computer they log on from. The application will appear on the Start menu as a shortcut. The software is installed when the user clicks on that shortcut. When assigned to a computer, the software is installed automatically on that computer the next time it reboots. It then becomes available to all users on that computer. When you publish it (which can only be done to users, not computers), the software is available to install from Add/Remove programs, and can also be installed by document invocation.

2. The first is an optional removal, specified by selecting the Immediately Uninstall Software from Users and Computers option when configuring the removal of the software package. You remove the software only from management. Users have to remove the software themselves. The second is a forced removal, specified by selecting the Allow Users to Continue to Use the Software But Prevent New Installations option. The software is automatically removed from a computer the next time the computer is turned on or the next time the user logs on. This second option is the option of choice.

3. Using software categories, the application list displays the available categories first. Then, once the user finds the category, the grouped applications are listed in a drop-down menu box for the user to select. The list is limited to only the software that was placed in that category. Without the categories option, if there are many applications available for installation, there would be one single list of these applications. The user would have to scroll the list until finding the needed application.

4. There will come a time, once all users have installed the software, that the software package will no longer be needed.

5. After you assign software to computers, when the computer processes the Group Policy settings, it will notice the assigned software and automatically install it on the computers to make it available to all users on those computers.

ANSWERS TO KEY TERM QUIZ

1. Optional removal

2. Windows Installer service

3. Deployment

4. Group Policy object

5. .msi file

9

Managing and Troubleshooting Active Directory

LAB EXERCISES

9.01   Managing Active Directory Objects

9.02   Configuring a Global Catalog Server

9.03   Troubleshooting Active Directory Replication

▨   Lab Analysis Test

▧   Key Term Quiz

▧   Lab Solutions

A ctive Directory is Microsoft's answer to Novell's Directory Services. It supports a single unified view of all objects on a network (no matter what size) with the ability to locate and manage resources faster and easier. This directory service uses a structured data store as the basis for a logical, hierarchical organization of directory information. Active Directory allows organizations to centrally manage and share information relative to network resources and users while acting as the central authority for network security. In addition, Active Directory is designed to be a consolidation point for isolating, migrating, centrally managing, and reducing the number of directories that companies require.

An underlying integrated component of Active Directory is security. It is integrated with Active Directory through logon authentication and access control to objects in the directory. With a single network logon, an administrator can manage directory data throughout his or her network. Authorized network users can access resources anywhere on the network. Because administration is policy-based, it can ease the management of even the most complex network.

In this chapter, we will first look at how to manage Active Directory objects—specifically, the ability to delegate administrative control to portions of Active Directory to other users, by combining the use of organizational units and permissions. This is accomplished using the Delegation of Control Wizard. Next, we will look at the role of the global catalog server. The purpose of a catalog service is to compile information about each separate partition into one central data location. Lastly, we will look at how to troubleshoot replication. Nonproductive replication results in deteriorating Active Directory performance. This can result in new users not being recognized, out-of-date directory information, or unavailable domain controllers.

CERTIFICATION OBJECTIVE 9.01

Managing Active Directory Objects

20 Minutes

Cynthia works for Tread Lightly Tire Company. She is in charge of a network that has one Windows 2000 domain. The network has 700 users and services the entire company. For the past few weeks, Cynthia has been reevaluating the different departments on the network and looking to see which departments should control their own user accounts. After several discussions with the Human Resources department, an agreement has been reached where they will be responsible for the user accounts in that department.

The user information for the three test users in the Human Resources container is as follows:

Last Name	First Name	User Name	Password	Change Password
Packet	Helen	Hpacket	Employer	Must
Battey	Adele	Abattey	(blank)	Must
Cipollini	Paula	Pcipollini	(blank)	Must

What are the necessary steps she needs to perform?

Learning Objectives

Combining the use of organizational units (OUs) and permissions provides an administrator with the ability to delegate the management of portions of Active Directory to other trusted users. By giving a user or group permissions needed to manage an OU, you're effectively creating a local administrator or workgroup within a domain. Although you can use the Full Control permission to delegate control, the use of the Delegation of Control Wizard is best. This wizard lets you delegate complete or partial control of an OU.

In this lab, you'll create an OU that contains three user accounts (to test out the configuration before adding the 12 remaining users), and use the Delegation of Control Wizard to delegate control over objects in the OU to a user. By the end of this lab, you'll be able to

- Create an organizational unit (OU).
- Delegate control of an OU to a user.

Lab Materials and Setup

For this lab exercise, you'll need

- A working computer
- Installed network card (NIC)

- Windows 2000 Server software (installed)
- TCP/IP installed
- Active Directory (AD) installed

Getting Down to Business

To create an OU and delegate control of the OU and the objects contained within, perform the following steps:

Step 1. As administrator, log on to your domain. Access the Active Directory Users and Computers console. In the console tree, right-click your domain and open its context menu. Create the Human Resources OU.

Step 2. In the OU, create the three user objects using the information provided in the scenario. Accept the defaults for all other settings. Next, we'll view the default permissions of the users within the OU.

Step 3. Select the Advanced Features from the View menu. Access the Properties window of the OU object and select the Security tab. Add the newly created users to the list. Make note of the user accounts and their assigned permissions.

Step 4. Lastly, we need to delegate control of the OU. Access the context menu of the OU and select Delegate Control. This will activate the wizard. Add the user account, which will be responsible for administering the OU. The user selected is the director of the department, Helen Packet.

Step 5. Complete the delegation process by assigning the user the Create, delete, and manage user accounts permissions; the Reset passwords on user accounts permissions; and the Create, delete, and manage groups permissions. Exit the Active Directory Users and Computers console.

CERTIFICATION OBJECTIVE 9.02

Configuring a Global Catalog Server

10 Minutes

Steve is the administrator for a network that is part of an Active Directory tree. His network is divided into four different sites spread across two floors in a downtown historic building. He needs to assign one of the domain controllers as a global catalog server to provide schema and configuration information between the four sites, and also to make it easy to locate objects in the Active Directory tree. How would he configure the domain controller as a global catalog server?

Learning Objectives

A *global catalog server* is a domain controller that stores extra information. This information is used to glue together all the parts of the Active Directory. It ensures that the schema and configuration information is available to all the domains. It also provides a method of locating objects in Active Directory. The knowledge consistency checker (KCC) process creates a replication topology that ensures delivery of the contents of every directory partition to every global catalog server in the forest.

By default, the server on which you install Active Directory to create the first domain in a new forest is a global catalog server. The global catalog is designed to respond to user and program queries about objects anywhere in the forest with the most speed and least amount of network traffic. A request about an object can be resolved by a global catalog in the domain in which the query is initiated because it contains information about objects in all domains in the forest. Therefore, finding information in the directory does not produce unnecessary traffic across domain boundaries.

You can optionally configure any domain controller to host a global catalog, based on a company's requirements for servicing logon requests and search queries.

In this lab, you'll configure a server to be a global catalog server. By the end of this lab, you'll be able to

▧ Create a global catalog server.

Lab Materials and Setup

For this lab exercise, you'll need

- A working computer
- Installed network card (NIC)
- Windows 2000 Server software (installed)
- TCP/IP installed
- Active Directory (AD) installed

Getting Down to Business

To create a global catalog server, perform the following steps:

Step 1.   As administrator, log on to your domain. Access the Active Directory Sites and Services console. Expand the Sites folder until the server is visible.

Step 2.   Access the Properties window of the NTDS Settings object. Designate this server to be a global catalog server. Accept the settings and exit the Active Directory Sites and Services console.

CERTIFICATION OBJECTIVE 9.03

Troubleshooting Active Directory Replication

10 Minutes

You have two sites that are linked using a fractional T1 connection. You are working to optimize the replication traffic between the sites. A high-end domain controller is at each site, already functioning as a global catalog server. Connection objects have been created that link the two servers. What additional configuration must you perform to make these the main servers for all site links using the TCP/IP protocol?

Learning Objectives

Windows 2000 uses multimaster replication for the Active Directory. In multimaster environments, all domain controllers function as peers and all replicate Active Directory database changes to each other. There is no single master replicator, but all domain controllers are responsible for the replication tasks. Multimaster replication is effective because changes to the Active Directory can be made at any domain controller. The purpose of replication is to ensure that all domain controllers have accurate Active Directory data. For example, if an administrator adds a new object to the Active Directory on a particular domain controller, that domain controller is responsible for sending that change to all other domain controllers. Without effective replication, an Active Directory environment would quickly fall apart since each domain controller would be unaware of changes made by other domain controllers.

Most of the replication problems involve poor directory information, which can be remedied with Active Directory Sites and Services. The result of these problems is undistributed new directory information, or service requests that are not handled in a timely manner. One way to help with poor directory information distribution is by designating a bridgehead server. A bridgehead server is the contact server for the exchange of directory information between sites. If a high level of directory information exchange is typical, a bridgehead server can ensure that these exchanges are handled promptly.

In this lab, you'll configure one of the bridgehead servers. By the end of this lab, you'll be able to

- Use Active Directory Sites and Services.
- Designate a preferred bridgehead server.

Lab Materials and Setup

For this lab exercise, you'll need

- A working computer
- Installed network card (NIC)

- Windows 2000 Server software (installed)
- TCP/IP installed
- Active Directory (AD) installed

Getting Down to Business

To designate a preferred bridgehead server, perform the following steps:

Step 1.   As administrator, log on to your domain. Access the Active Directory Sites and Services console. Expand the Sites folder until the server is visible.

Step 2.   Access the Properties window for the server. In the server's Properties window, select the IP transport protocol and click Add. The transport protocol will move from its original location to the area that designates the server as a preferred bridgehead server for the listed protocols.

Step 3.   Accept the settings and exit the Active Directory Sites and Services console.

LAB ANALYSIS TEST

1. What is the effect of delegating control of an OU?

   _____

   _____

2. What type of server is used to replicate the schema for a company's large network?

   _____

   _____

3. A network administrator may grant other users control of an OU or container. What purpose would this serve for the administrator?

   _____

   _____

4. Describe the structure and function of Active Directory?

   _____

   _____

5. What can cause replication problems, and what is one way to help prevent them?

   _____

   _____

KEY TERM QUIZ

Use the following vocabulary terms to complete the sentences below. Not all of the terms will be used. Definitions for these terms can be found in "Managing a Microsoft Windows 2000 Network Environment Study Guide."

> Bridgehead server
>
> Global Catalog server
>
> Site link bridge
>
> Site link
>
> Delegation of Control Wizard
>
> Active Directory replication
>
> Intersite replication
>
> Intrasite replication
>
> Replication
>
> Knowledge consistency checker

1. The replication traffic that occurs between two or more sites is known as _____.

2. Acting as a contact point for the exchange of directory information, the _____ is a preferred server that has appropriate bandwidth to transmit and receive information.

3. _____ is the replication traffic that occurs only within a site.

4. The _____ assigns permissions only at the OU level, and simplifies the process of assigning object permissions.

5. The _____ sets up controller replication connections within and between sites.

LAB SOLUTIONS FOR CHAPTER 9

In this section, you'll find solutions to the lab exercises, Lab Analysis Test, and Key Term Quiz.

Lab Solution 9.01

In this lab, you created an OU named Human Resources that contains three user accounts (for test purposes prior to adding the remaining users), and used the Delegation of Control Wizard to delegate control over the user objects in the OU to the director, Helen Packet. By the end of this lab, you were able to

■ Create an organizational unit (OU).

■ Delegate control of an OU to a user.

To create an OU and delegate control of the OU and the objects contained within, perform the following steps:

Step 1.   As administrator, log on to your domain. Click Start | Programs | Administrative Tools | Active Directory Users and Computers. Expand the console tree, right-click your domain, and open its context menu. From the context menu, choose New | Organizational Unit. Enter the name of the new OU, Human Resources, and click OK.

Step 2.   In the OU, create the three user objects using the information provided in the scenario. Right-click on the OU and select New | User. Create an object for each of the users, and enter the required passwords. Accept the defaults for all other settings. Provide the three users membership to the Print Operators group, which will allow them to log on locally to the domain controller.

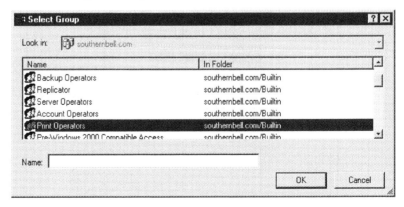

The newly created users of the Human Resources container are made members of the Print Operators group.

Step 3. Next, we'll view the default permissions of the users within the OU. Click View from the menu and select Advanced Features. The option lets you review and configure Active Directory permissions. Right-click the OU object and select Properties from the context menu.

Step 4. Click the Security tab. The newly created users need to be added in the Security window. Click the Add button and select the new users. Make note of the user accounts and their assigned permissions, as shown in Figure 9-1.

The sample user, Helen Packet, receives the Read permission in this container.

Step 5.   Lastly, we need to delegate control of the OU. Right-click the OU and select Delegate Control from the context menu, as shown next. This will activate the wizard.

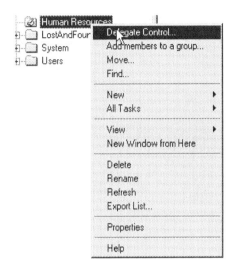

Step 6.   Click past the Welcome window. The wizard will bring you to the Users or Group window. Presently, there are no users or groups listed. Click Add to display the Select Users, Computers, or Groups window. Select the Helen Packet user object, click Add, and then click OK. The object is added to the Selected Users and Groups window, as shown in Figure 9-2.

Step 7.   Click Next. In this window of the wizard, Tasks to Delegate, you choose one or more common tasks from the list. You also have the option to customize what is delegated. Select Create, Delete, and Manage User Accounts; Create, Delete, and Manage Groups; and Reset Passwords on User Accounts, as shown in Figure 9-3.

Step 8.   Be sure that Delegate the Following Common Tasks is selected. Click Next. Review the summary page and click Finish. Exit the Active Directory Users and Computers console.

FIGURE 9-2

This step assigned the selected user to perform administrative tasks with the container.

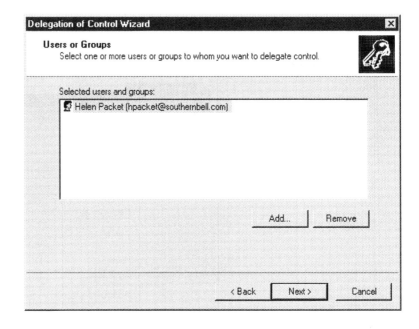

FIGURE 9-3

Common tasks are selected and assigned to the user, and will be performed on objects within the Human Resources container.

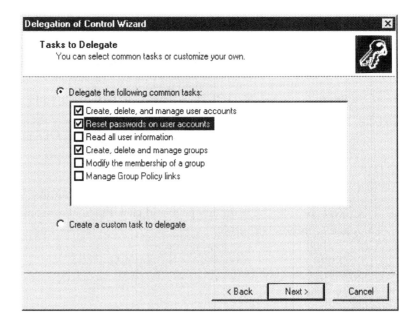

Lab Solution 9.02

A global catalog server is a domain controller that stores extra information. It ensures that the schema and configuration information is available to all the sites on the network. It also provides a method of locating objects in Active Directory.

In this lab, you configured a server to be a global catalog server. By the end of this lab, you were able to

■ Create a global catalog server.

To create a global catalog server, perform the following steps:

Step 1.   As administrator, log on to your domain. Click Start | Programs | Active Directory Sites and Services. Expand the Sites folder, through the Servers folder, until the server is visible.

Step 2.   Select the NTDS Settings object, as shown in Figure 9-4. Right-click the object and select Properties. Designate this server to be a global catalog server by verifying that global catalog is checked.

Step 3.   Click OK to accept the settings. Exit the Active Directory Sites and Services console. This will designate this domain controller as a global catalog server, providing essential information between domains.

FIGURE 9-4	
The NTDS Settings object is contained in the server object.	

Lab Solution 9.03

Most of the replication problems involve poor directory information, which can be remedied with Active Directory Sites and Services. One way to help with poor directory information distribution is by designating a bridgehead server. A bridgehead server is the contact server for the exchange of directory information between sites. It serves as the main server for intersite replication. A bridgehead server is configured for each site created for each of the intersite replication protocols. This allows an administrator to control which server in a site is used to replicate information to other servers.

In this lab, you configured one of two bridgehead servers. By the end of this lab, you were able to

- Use Active Directory Sites and Services.
- Designate a preferred bridgehead server.

To designate a preferred bridgehead server, perform the following steps:

Step 1. As administrator, log on to your domain. Click Start | Programs | Active Directory Sites and Services. Expand the Sites folder, through the Servers folder, until the server is visible.

Step 2. Right-click the server and select Properties. In the server's Transports Available for Intersite Transfer area, select the IP transport protocol for this bridgehead server. Click Add. The transport protocol will move from its original location to the area that designates the server as a preferred bridgehead server for the listed protocols, as shown in Figure 9-5.

Step 3. Click OK to accept the settings. Exit the Active Directory Sites and Services console.

FIGURE 9-5

Once the IP
protocol is
transferred, the
server becomes
the control
point for all
information
between
the sites.

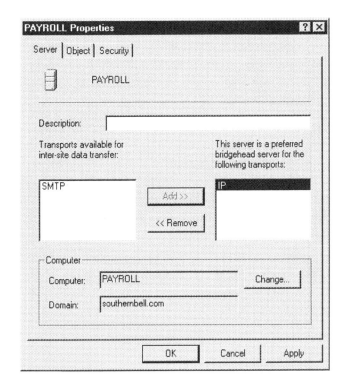

ANSWERS TO LAB ANALYSIS

1. When delegating control to a user or group of an organizational unit, you are granting permissions to that user or group to manage the objects within the OU.

2. Within a domain, the domain controller is responsible for the replication of objects that belong to that domain. The global catalog servers replicate the information about a multidomain (enterprise) network, including a list of all objects, the schema, and configuration information.

3. Delegating Active Directory duties to other users provides for a higher level of efficiency. On a large network, the number of objects to manage can be large; it makes administrative sense to make users who function as managers or supervisors of an OU directly responsible for creating and maintaining the objects that are their responsibility.

4. It supports a single unified view of all objects on a network with the ability to locate and manage resources. Active Directory service uses a structured data store as the basis for a logical, hierarchical organization of directory information. It allows for a central management and sharing of information relative to network resources and users while acting as the central authority for network security.

5. Most of the replication problems involve poor directory information, which can be remedied with Active Directory Sites and Services. The result of these problems is undistributed new directory information, or service requests that are not handled in a timely manner. One way to help with poor directory information distribution is by designating a bridgehead server. A bridgehead server is the contact server for the exchange of directory information between sites. If a high level of directory information exchange is typical, a bridgehead server can ensure that these exchanges are handled promptly.

ANSWERS TO KEY TERM QUIZ

1. Intersite replication

2. Bridgehead server

3. Intrasite replication

4. Delegation of Control Wizard

5. Knowledge consistency checker

MICROSOFT CERTIFIED SYSTEMS ASSOCIATE

10

Managing Data Storage

LAB EXERCISES

10.01   Configuring Disks and Volumes

10.02   Configuring and Enforcing
         Disk Quotas

10.03   Implementing Encrypting
         File System (EFS)

10.04   Implementing and Managing a
         Distributed File System (Dfs)

■   Lab Analysis Test

■   Key Term Quiz

■   Lab Solutions

W indows 2000 introduces many new features for managing data storage that provide more functionality and capabilities than in previous versions. Besides the addition of dynamic disk storage to the basic disk storage, Windows 2000 also introduces disk quotas, providing administrators with a way to track and limit the amount of disk space available to users.

Disk Management is a system utility for managing hard disks and the volumes, or partitions, which they contain. With Disk Management, you can initialize disks, create volumes, format volumes with the FAT, FAT32, or NTFS file systems, and create fault-tolerant disk systems. Disk Management enables you to perform most disk-related tasks without shutting down the system or interrupting users; most configuration changes take effect immediately.

Encrypting File System (EFS) allows users to store their on-disk data in encrypted format. It is the process of converting data into a format that cannot be read by another user. Once a user has encrypted a file, the file automatically remains encrypted whenever the file is stored on disk.

Microsoft Distributed File System (Dfs) is Windows 2000 Server software that makes it easier for you to find and manage data on your enterprise network. It provides mapping and a uniform naming convention for collections of servers, shares, and files. Dfs also adds the capability of organizing file servers and their shares into a logical hierarchy, making it considerably easier to manage and use information resources.

In this chapter, we will look at configuring disks and volumes by creating and mounting a volume, and configuring and enforcing disk quotas—the idea of allocating disk space to users so that the space is assigned equitably. We'll also look at encrypting, implementing, and managing the file system.

CERTIFICATION OBJECTIVE 10.01

Configuring Disks and Volumes

15 Minutes

Philip is a network administrator for the Lawn-MD Lawn and Shrub Fertilizer Company. He replaced the previous administrator four months ago, and has finally settled in to the position. The office has a Windows 2000 Server computer accessed by the 11 service agents that handle customer requests and scheduling. Today, he is attempting to create a volume on the disk using Disk Management so he can later create a mirrored volume, but the option is not available. While reviewing the configuration changes made by the previous administrator, he notices that when the system was upgraded to Windows 2000, the hard drive was kept as a basic disk. What does Philip need to do to the disk in order to create a mirrored volume?

Learning Objectives

In this lab, you'll convert a basic disk to dynamic. By the end of this lab, you'll be able to

- Use Disk Management.
- Upgrade a basic disk to a dynamic disk.
- Create a new simple volume.

Lab Materials and Setup

For this lab exercise, you'll need

- A working computer
- Installed network card (NIC)
- Windows 2000 Server software (installed)

lab
Warning   *To upgrade a disk to dynamic storage, it must contain at least 1MB of free space for the upgrade to succeed. Also, the file system needs to be NTFS.*

Getting Down to Business

To convert a basic disk to dynamic and create a volume, perform the following steps:

Step 1.   First, you'll convert a basic disk to dynamic. Open the Disk Manager and choose Upgrade to Dynamic Disk from the disk's context menu. When you're prompted with the disk number of the disk you want to upgrade, click OK.

Step 2.   In the Disks to Upgrade dialog box, upgrade the disk. The Disk Management dialog box appears, warning you that no other versions of Windows will boot to this disk anymore. Because dynamic disks are unique to Windows 2000, converting will render them unreadable by any other local-booting operating systems. Continue.

Step 3.   Confirm that you know Windows 2000 will reboot to complete the upgrade. This will happen only if the partitions on the disk are currently being used—like the boot partition.

Step 4. After restart, log on. When the Systems Settings Change dialog box appears, you will have to restart your server.

Step 5. Lastly, you need to create a simple volume. Launch the Computer Management console and open the Disk Manager. Select the free space you need to create the volume in and choose Create Volume from the menu that appears. Navigate past the Welcome to the Create Volume Wizard screen.

Step 6. At the Select Volume Type screen, select Simple Volume. At the Select Disks screen, keep the default size for the partition you need to create in the For Selected Disk text box under the heading Size.

Step 7. At the Assign Drive Letter or Path screen, keep the default drive letter you need to assign to this volume. The settings in the Format Volume screen will be NTFS for the file system, the default for the allocation unit size, and VOL1 for the volume name . Once the values have been entered, continue to complete the process.

Step 8. Once the process is complete, close out of the Computer Management console.

CERTIFICATION OBJECTIVE 10.02

Configuring and Enforcing Disk Quotas

15 Minutes

Larry is the network administrator for a company with two member servers and 100 users on a single LAN. Each of his servers has three volumes, one that stores the system/boot partitions, one that stores program files, and a third that stores user data. The divisions of sizes are 2GB, 5GB, and 20GB, respectively. Each volume is formatted with NTFS. An alert has just popped up on his computer telling him that the free space on one of his server's drives has fallen below ten percent. Upon closer examination, he sees that certain users have been copying a tremendous number of personal files onto the server to make space on their personal hard drives. Now he wants to cap the amount of storage each of the users has on the data volume of the server at 25MB. In addition, he would like to be able to configure the cap for himself at 50MB. How can this be done?

Learning Objectives

In this lab, you'll configure disk quotas. By the end of this lab, you'll be able to

- Limit disk space for all users.
- Configure an exemption to the allocated disk space.

Lab Materials and Setup

For this lab exercise, you'll need

- A working computer
- Installed network card (NIC)
- Windows 2000 Server software (installed)
- TCP/IP installed

Getting Down to Business

To configure disk quotas on your drive, perform the following steps:

Step 1.   Access the VOL1's Properties window for which you want to enable disk quotas. Select the Quota tab. On the Quota properties page, activate the Enable Quota Management check box, and then click OK.

Step 2.   Next, assign disk quota limits for all users by selecting the Deny Disk Space to Users Exceeding Quota Limit option. The disk space limit will be 25MB.

Step 3.   Set the warning level to 20MB. Activate both quota-logging options at the bottom of the dialog box. This will log the event when a user hits his or her quota and/or warning level.

Step 4.   Now, exclude the administrator from the disk space limitations. In the Quota Entries for Local Disk dialog box, using the Quota menu, Select and add Administrator. Click OK.

Step 5.   Set the Limit Disk Space To option to 50MB, and the Warning Level option to 45MB. Verify that Administrator is listed in the Quota Entries dialog box. Close and exit all windows.

Implementing Encrypting File System (EFS)

10 Minutes

Samuel is the network administrator for the Two-by-Two company, a biotechnology plant in Edinburgh. He wants to be able to encrypt some of his critical (and sensitive) data located in his folder—Sams Files, located in the shared folder named Clone Files on the server. What steps does Samuel need to take to secure his information?

Learning Objectives

In this lab, you'll learn how to secure data. By the end of this lab, you'll be able to

■ Encrypt a folder.

Lab Materials and Setup

For this lab exercise, you'll need

■ A working computer
■ Installed network card (NIC)
■ Windows 2000 Server software (installed)
■ Two folders: Clone Files (shared) and Sams Files

Getting Down to Business

To encrypt a folder and its contents, perform the following steps:

Step 1. Using Windows Explorer or My Computer, navigate to Sams Files folder. Open the folder's Properties window from the context menu.

Step 2. In the Advanced Attributes dialog box of the window, select the Encrypt Contents to Secure Data check box. Complete the procedure and exit the Properties dialog box.

CERTIFICATION OBJECTIVE 10.04

Implementing and Managing a Distributed File System (Dfs)

15 Minutes

Angela is the network administrator of a Windows 2000 network. She wants to set up a distributed file system so that users in the domain, containing four servers, can access the data. How is this accomplished?

Learning Objectives

In this lab, you'll learn implement Distributed File System (Dfs). By the end of this lab, you'll be able to

- Create a Dfs root.
- Create Dfs links.

Lab Materials and Setup

For this lab exercise, you'll need

- A working computer
- Installed network card (NIC)
- Windows 2000 Server software (installed)
- TCP/IP installed
- Domain Name System (DNS) installed
- Active Directory (AD) installed

Getting Down to Business

To create a new Dfs domain root and populate it with a link, perform the following steps:

Step 1. Launch the Distributed File System console. Create a Dfs root at the main Dfs screen using the Action menu. This will invoke the New Dfs Root Wizard.

Step 2. Choose Create a Domain Dfs Root at the Select the Dfs Root Type window. Click Next to continue.

lab
Warning *Be sure that you have Active Directory (AD) installed; otherwise, you can only create a stand-alone Dfs root.*

Step 3. Select the domain that you want to host the Dfs root, from the Trusting domains list (unless you have other domains active on your network, you'll only see your domain) in the Select the Host Domain for the Dfs Root window.

Step 4. Next, you need to specify the name of the server or click Browse to locate the server that you want to use to host the Dfs root in the Specify the Host Server for the Dfs Root window. Specify whether to use an existing share to create a new share in the Specify The Dfs Root Share window. In our case, we will use an existing share. Continue.

Step 5. Keep the default name for the new Dfs root in the Name the Dfs Root window. You also have the ability to include a content description for the share. Continue.

Step 6. Complete the procedure using the wizard. The new root appears in the scope pane of the Distributed File System console window.

Step 7. Now that you've created the Dfs root, you need to create a Dfs link to the root. From the context menu of the Dfs root object, select New Dfs Link.

Step 8. In the Link Name box, enter the name of the link—**Shared**. This is the name that users will see when they browse the Dfs root for available shares. Browse to locate the shared folder. You can enter a description name for the link in the comment box.

Step 9. Complete the process and close out of all windows.

LAB ANALYSIS TEST

1. What is the difference between a basic disk and a dynamic disk in Windows 2000?

   _____

   _____

2. What is a disk quota and how is it enforced?

   _____

   _____

3. How does the Encrypting File System work and why would you want to use it?

   _____

   _____

4. As a network administrator, you're trying to decide whether to implement a domain-based Dfs or a stand-alone Dfs. What advantage does one have over the other?

   _____

   _____

5. What three steps are required when installing a new basic disk in a Windows 2000 computer?

   _____

   _____

KEY TERM QUIZ

Use the following vocabulary terms to complete the sentences below. Not all of the terms will be used. Definitions for these terms can be found in "Managing a Microsoft Windows 2000 Network Environment Study Guide."

> Universal Naming Convention (UNC)
>
> Encrypting File System (EFS)
>
> Replication
>
> Distributed File System (Dfs)
>
> Basic disk
>
> Dynamic disk
>
> Disk quota
>
> Disk Management Tool
>
> Dfs replication

1. A service used to build a logical structure of file shares from separate computers presented in a single directory tree is named a _____.

2. _____ is the process of copying data from a file system to multiple computers in order to synchronize the data.

3. A new storage system supported by Windows 2000, _____ divides physical disk space into volumes.

4. The Windows 2000 file system that allows an administrator to encrypt files and folders on NTFS volumes for security's sake is named _____.

5. _____ is a way to monitor and control the amount of disk space available to users.

LAB SOLUTIONS FOR CHAPTER 10

In this section, you'll find solutions to the lab exercises, Lab Analysis Test, and Key Term Quiz.

Lab Solution 10.01

Philip is attempting to create a volume on the disk using Disk Management so he can later create a mirrored volume, but when he attempts to follow through with the task, the option is not available. When the system was upgraded to Windows 2000, the hard drive was kept as a basic disk. Before Philip can create a mirrored volume, he needs to convert the disk from basic to dynamic.

In this lab, you converted a basic disk to dynamic. By the end of this lab, you were able to

- Use Disk Management.
- Upgrade a basic disk to a dynamic disk.
- Create a new simple volume.

lab
Warning   *To upgrade a disk to dynamic storage, it must contain at least 1MB of free space for the upgrade to succeed.*

To create and mount a volume, perform the following steps:

Step 1.   First, you'll convert a basic disk to dynamic. Click Start | Programs | Administrative Tools, and select Computer Management. Open the Disk Manager folder. Right-click the disk indicator shown in the window and choose Upgrade to Dynamic Disk from the context menu, as shown in Figure 10-1. When you're prompted with the disk number of the disk you want to upgrade, click OK.

Step 2.   In the Disks to Upgrade dialog box, click Upgrade to upgrade the disk. The Disk Management dialog box shown next appears, warning you that no other versions of Windows will boot to this disk anymore.

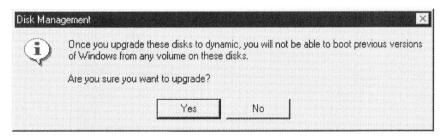

FIGURE 10-1 Right-click Disk 0 to begin the Conversion Wizard.

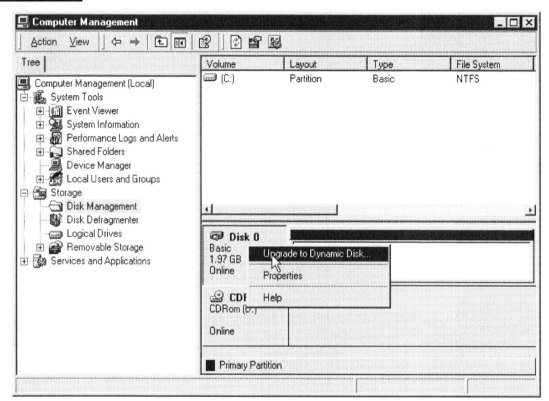

Step 3. In the Upgrade Disks dialog box, click Yes to continue. Click Yes to force the dismount of the upgraded disk. In the Confirm dialog box shown next, click OK to confirm that you know Windows 2000 will reboot to complete the upgrade. This will happen only if the partitions on the disk are currently being used—like the boot partition.

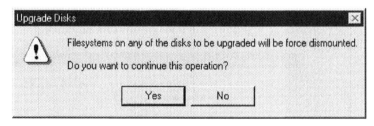

Step 4.   After restart, log on. When the Systems Settings Change dialog box appears, click Yes to restart your server. Note that dynamic disks are unique to Windows 2000, and converting will render them unreadable by any other local-booting operating systems.

Step 5.   Lastly, you need to create a simple volume. Click Start | Programs | Administrative Tools, and select Computer Management. Open the Disk Manager folder. Right-click the free space you want to create the volume in and choose Create Volume from the menu that appears. At the Welcome to the Create Volume Wizard screen, click Next to continue.

Step 6.   At the Select Volume Type screen, select Simple Volume, as shown in Figure 10-2. Click Next. At the Select Disks screen, keep the default size for the partition you need to create in the For Selected Disk text box under the heading Size. Click Next to continue.

FIGURE 10-2

A simple volume contains disk space from a single disk. It provides no fault tolerance.

Create Volume Wizard

Select Volume Type
What type of volume do you want to create?

Volume type
- ⦿ Simple volume
- ○ Spanned volume
- ○ Striped volume
- ○ Mirrored volume
- ○ RAID-5 volume

Description
A simple volume is made up of free space on a single dynamic disk. Create a simple volume if you have enough free disk space for your volume on one disk. You can extend a simple volume by adding free space from the same disk or another disk.

< Back | Next > | Cancel

Step 7. At the Assign Drive Letter or Path screen, keep the default drive letter you need to assign to this volume and click Next. At the Format Volume screen, choose the NTFS file system and default allocation unit size, as shown next. The volume label will be VOL1. Click Next to continue. At the Completing the Create Volume Wizard screen, click Finish.

Step 8. Notice that the newly created volume is listed on the right pane of the Console Management window. Before the volume is usable, it needs to be formatted to the NTFS file system, as shown in Figure 10-3.

FIGURE 10-3	

Notice that the new volume needs to be formatted prior to its use. Notice the format progress.

Lab Solution 10.02

Larry sees that certain users have been copying a tremendous number of personal files onto the server to make space on their personal hard drives. The result is that the server's hard drive space is below ten percent. To solve the issue, he needs to cap the amount of storage each user has on the data volume of the server at 25MB. In addition, he would like to be able to configure the cap for the power users at 50MB. He accomplishes all this by configuring a disk quota.

In this lab, you configured disk quotas. By the end of this lab, you were able to

- Limit disk space for all users.
- Configure an exemption to the allocated disk space.

To configure disk quotas on your drive, perform the following steps:

Step 1. To enable disk quotas, open My Computer. Right-click the disk volume for which you want to enable disk quotas and then click Properties. In the Properties dialog box, click the Quota tab, shown next. On the Quota properties page, click the Enable Quota Management check box and then click OK.

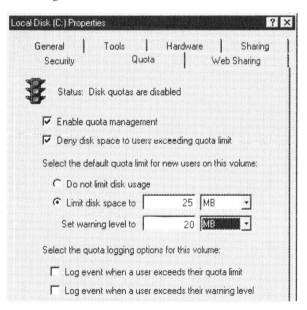

Step 2. Next, assign disk quota limits by selecting the Deny Disk Space to Users Exceeding Quota Limit option. In the text box next to Limit Disk Space To, type 25 and then choose MB from the drop-down menu.

Step 3.   In the text box next to Set Warning Level To, type **20** and then choose MB from the drop-down menu. Select the check box next to both Quota Logging options at the bottom of the dialog box. This will log the event when the quota and/or warning level is reached by the user.

Step 4.   Click the Quota Entries button. In the Quota Entries for Local Disk dialog box, open the Quota menu and select New Quota Entry. Select Administrator and click Add. Click OK.

Step 5.   Set the Limit disk space to 50MB. Set the warning level to 45MB. Click OK. Verify that Administrator is listed in the Quota Entries dialog box, as shown here:

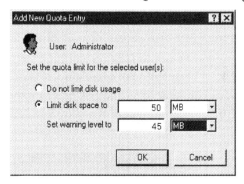

Close the window. The new quota window indicates the limits have been activated. Click OK twice and exit out of remaining windows.

Lab Solution 10.03

Samuel wants to encrypt some of his critical (and sensitive) data located in his folder—Sams Files—located in the shared folder named Clone Files on the server.

In this lab, you learned how to secure data. By the end of this lab, you were able to

■   Encrypt a folder.

To encrypt a folder and its contents, perform the following steps:

Step 1.   Using Windows Explorer or My Computer, navigate to the Sams Files folder located in the Clone Files. Right-click the object to be encrypted, Sams Files, and choose Properties from the context menu.

Step 2.   In the General tab box, click the Advanced button. In the Advanced Attributes dialog box, select the Encrypt Contents to Secure Data check box, as shown in Figure 10-4. Click OK twice to exit the Properties dialog box. The files are now secured from possible viewing by others accessing the Clone Files folder.

FIGURE 10-4

Encrypting data
will scramble the
data so only the
owner of the data
can read it. When
applied to a
folder, all files
contained in it
will be encrypted.

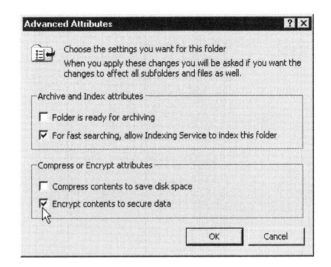

Lab Solution 10.04

In this lab, you learned to implement Distributed File System (Dfs). By the end of
this lab, you were able to

- Create a Dfs root.
- Create Dfs links.

To create a new Dfs domain root and populate it with a link, perform the
following steps:

Step 1.   Click Start | Programs | Administrative Tools and select Distributed File
System, which will launch the Distributed File System console. At the main Dfs
screen, create a Dfs root by selecting New Dfs Root from the Action menu. This
will invoke the new Dfs root.

Step 2.   At the Welcome to the New Dfs Root Wizard screen, click Next to
continue. At the Select the Dfs Root Type screen, choose Create a Domain Dfs
Root, as shown in Figure 10-5. Click Next to continue.

lab
ⓦarning

*Be sure that you have Active Directory (AD) installed; otherwise, you can only
create a stand-alone Dfs root.*

Step 3.   In the Select the Host Domain for the Dfs Root window, verify the
default domain that you want to host the Dfs, as shown in Figure 10-6.

Select to create a domain Dfs root so it can use Active Directory to store Dfs configuration information.

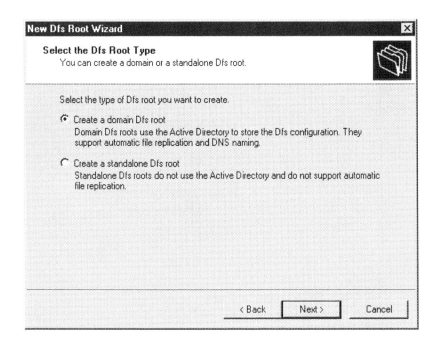

Unless you have other domains active on your network you'll only see your domain in the Domain Name window and Trusting Domains window.

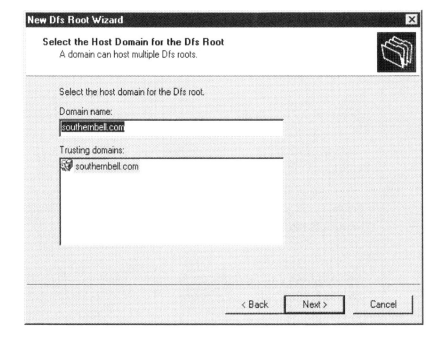

Step 4.   Next, you need to specify the name of the server, as shown next. You can also click Browse to locate the server that you want to use to host the Dfs root, in the Specify the Host Server for the Dfs Root window.

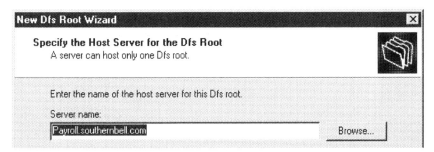

Click Next to continue. Here you can specify whether to use an existing share to create a new share in the Specify the Dfs Root Share window. Use the pull-down menu to select an existing share—Program Files (see Figure 10-7). Click to continue.

Step 5.   Keep the default name for the new Dfs root in the Name the Dfs Root window. You also have the ability to include a content description for the share. Click Next to continue.

FIGURE 10-7

Use the pull-down menu to select an existing share to become the Dfs root share.

Step 6. Now you can end the wizard by clicking Finish in the Completing the New Dfs Root window. The new root appears, now in the scope pane of the Distributed File System console window.

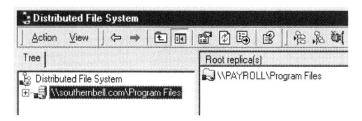

Step 7. Now that you've created the Dfs root, you need to create a Dfs link to the root. Right-click the Dfs root object. From the context menu, select New Dfs Link. This opens the Create a New Dfs Link window.

Step 8. In the Link Name box, enter the name of the link—**Shared**, as shown next. This is the name that users will see when they browse the Dfs root for available shares. In the Send the User to this Shared Folder box, browse to locate the share. You can also enter a description name for the link in the comment box.

Step 9. In the Clients Cache this Referral for *X* Seconds input box, the *X* designates the length of time for which clients cache a referral to a Dfs link. After the referral time expires, a client queries the Dfs server about the location of the link. Click OK to close the window and add the link to the Dfs root.

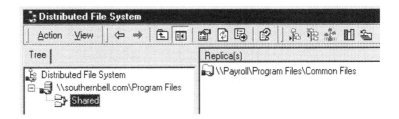

ANSWERS TO LAB ANALYSIS

1. The difference is that a dynamic disk supports volumes and can be configured with simple, spanned, mirrored, striped, or RAID-5 volumes. A basic disk supports only primary partitions and logical drives. It does not support fault-tolerant configurations or expandable volumes.

2. Disk quotas are storage limits set on NTFS partitions. A disk quota defines the amount of disk space a user can consume. The total amount of disk space used by a user is determined by the number of files the user owns.

3. The EFS allows a user to secure the contents of a file from being read and allows only the user to access the file. This would be implemented in an environment where a user works with mission-critical and sensitive information.

4. Domain-based Dfs has its configuration stored in the domain's Active Directory. When a client connects to a resource through the Dfs, the directory (Active Directory) is consulted to determine where it should go. You can configure multiple root servers so that if one goes down, clients will be redirected to another. This is not possible with stand-alone Dfs.

5. When installing a new hard disk drive in a Windows 2000 computer and configuring it as a basic disk, you need to initialize the disk, create a partition or partitions on the disk, and then format the partitions on the disk before you can store data on it.

ANSWERS TO KEY TERM QUIZ

1. Encrypting File System (EFS)

2. Distributed File System (Dfs)

3. Dynamic disk

4. Disk quota

5. Dfs replication

MICROSOFT CERTIFIED SYSTEMS ASSOCIATE

11

Configuring Internet Information Services (IIS)

LAB EXERCISES

11.01   Creating Web Sites

11.02   Creating FTP Sites

11.03   Securing Web and FTP Sites

11.04   IIS Maintenance and Troubleshooting

          Lab Analysis Test

          Key Term Quiz

          Lab Solutions

Microsoft Internet Information Server (IIS) can help you deploy Internet Explorer browser and other business applications, host and manage web sites, and publish and share information securely across a company intranet or the Internet. IIS can also help you manage the web sites where you distribute and maintain your custom browser packages and other related files and programs, generate dynamic web pages by using Active Server Page (.asp) files, customize web site content (including custom error messages and content expiration), and capture user information in log files, which enables you to collect and analyze valuable customer and usage data.

IIS management tools and flexible administration options can help you easily set up web sites to distribute the browser and manage your custom packages and other content. You can create HTML page templates by using Active Server Page (.asp) files, which enable you to build dynamic web pages for site information that is updated frequently.

You can require users to provide a valid Windows account name and password before accessing any information on your server. This identification process is commonly called *authentication*. Authentication, like many of the features in IIS, can be set at the web site, directory, or file level. IIS provides several web and FTP methods for controlling access to content on your server. The web methods are anonymous authentication, basic authentication, digest authentication, integrated windows authentication, and certificate authentication. The FTP methods are anonymous FTP authentication and basic FTP authentication.

Additionally, once IIS is installed and configured, the server still needs to be maintained and updated. This usually includes regular backups, starting and stopping IIS-related services, and applying updates.

In this chapter, we will look at creating web and FTP sites. We'll also look at ways to secure these sites and the implementation of a basic disaster recovery plan in case the site information becomes corrupt or is deleted.

CERTIFICATION OBJECTIVE 11.01

Creating Web Sites

20 Minutes

You are the network administrator for the Believe In Us consulting firm; a ten-person startup company that services clients in the stock market. You've been asked to create an intranet web site in order to provide customers with access to the company's information. Before you actually create the site and make it available, you want to test-drive the IIS server and a shared folder. What's the procedure to accomplish this task?

Learning Objectives

In this lab, you'll install IIS and share out a folder for web access. By the end of this lab, you'll be able to

Install IIS.

Use Web Sharing service.

Share out a folder for web access.

Lab Materials and Setup

For this lab exercise, you'll need

A working computer

Installed network card (NIC)

Windows 2000 Server software (installed)

TCP/IP installed

Domain Name System (DNS) installed

Certificate Services installed

Windows 2000 Server CD

Getting Down to Business

To install IIS and share a folder, perform the following steps:

Step 1.   First, you'll need to install Internet Information Services (IIS). Use the Add/Remove Programs utility.

Step 2.   From the Internet Information Services (IIS) dialog box, select the following components: Common Files, File Transfer Protocol (FTP) Server,

Internet Information Services Snap-in, World Wide Web Server, and Documentation and Internet Services Manager (HTML). When you're asked for the CD-ROM, insert it into the drive to complete the installation.

Step 3. Next, you want to share a web folder using the Web Sharing service. Select the folder (Share folder) you want to share and choose Sharing. In the Web Sharing tab, select the radio button labeled Share this Folder.

Step 4. When the Edit Alias dialog box appears, fill in an alias name (the name that a web user can reference this web share by—it does not have to be the same as the folder's real name) or keep the default name, Share folder. Then choose the Read access permission from the four security levels.

Step 5. Finally, choose Execute within the Application permissions box. Execute means that all programs in the folder can be run by browser clients.

Step 6. On an NTFS partition, you need to set NTFS permissions. From the Security tab, add local permissions for all the users you want to allow to access this folder over the Web. Add domain users and groups and add the IIS anonymous users. You will need to set as many NTFS permissions for any user as you have given access to in the previous step.

Step 7. If you gave out read and write access, you must also give out read and write NTFS permission; otherwise, the lesser of the access levels will prevail for your web users. Click OK when you are done.

CERTIFICATION OBJECTIVE 11.02

Creating FTP Sites

10 Minutes

Continuing with the same lab scenario, you also want to configure an FTP site on your web server. This will allow a user to download an application form to become a client of the consulting firm. You only want to allow read access for anonymous access. In addition, when the user logs in and exits the site, you want messages to appear on the screen. Since this is a test site, a simple "Welcome to my FTP site" and "Thank you for visiting my FTP site" are needed. What steps need to be taken to configure the site?

Learning Objectives

FTP is the file transfer protocol in the Internet's TCP/IP protocol suite. It's not really transferring files, but copying files from one computer to another.

When installing IIS, a default FTP site is created. This site responds to TCP/IP port 21 on all configured IP addresses of the server.

In this lab, you'll configure the default FTP site. By the end of this lab, you'll be able to

Use Internet Services Manager.

Allow for anonymous access to FTP site.

Lab Materials and Setup

For this lab exercise, you'll need

A working computer

Installed network card (NIC)

Windows 2000 Server software (installed)

TCP/IP installed

Internet Information Services (IIS) installed

Getting Down to Business

To configure the default FTP site to allow anonymous access, perform the following steps:

Step 1.   Launch Internet Services Manager. Open the Properties window of Default FTP Site. Verify that the Allow Anonymous Connects box is checked in the Security tab.

Step 2.   In the Welcome Text box, type **Welcome to my FTP Server**. In the Exit Text box, type **Thank you for visiting my FTP Server**. Click OK.

Step 3.   To test and verify that Welcome and Exit messages are working, access the FTP server using the anonymous account. Notice the Welcome message. Exit and close all windows. Now users will receive these messages when accessing the FTP Server.

lab
ⓗint   *Use a DOS session to perform step 3.*

CERTIFICATION OBJECTIVE 11.03

Securing Web and FTP Sites

20 Minutes

Harold is the network administrator of a Windows 2000–based web server at the Auto Parts Company in Houston, Texas. He has decided to implement Integrated Windows authentication for the 15 auto parts consultants at the store, in addition to anonymous access. What does Harold need to perform to accomplish this goal?

Learning Objectives

In this lab, you'll configure the user authentication method. By the end of this lab, you'll be able to

Use Internet Information Services console.

Configure a web site to use the digest authentication method.

cross
ⓡeference   *For further information, refer to securing web and FTP sites in Chapter 11 of "Managing a Windows 2000 Network Environment Study Guide."*

Lab Materials and Setup

For this lab exercise, you'll need

A working computer

Installed network card (NIC)

Windows 2000 Server software (installed)

TCP/IP installed

Domain Name System (DNS) installed

Certificate Services installed

Internet Information Services (IIS) installed

Getting Down to Business

To configure a web site to use Integrated Windows authentication, perform the following steps:

Step 1. Launch Internet Services Manager. When you see your web site in the tree under the name of your server, open the Properties window.

Step 2. In the Directory Security tab, edit Anonymous Access and Authentication Control. From the Authentication Methods dialog box, enable Integrated Windows authentication. Select the appropriate check boxes. Update the web site's properties. Attempt to access the web site with the Anonymous account and with the Administrator account.

CERTIFICATION OBJECTIVE 11.04

IIS Maintenance and Troubleshooting

10 Minutes

Jan has just installed an IIS server for her company. It has been tested and configured and "tweaked" over the past two months. Before she makes the site "live," she wants to perform a test backup and restore the configuration settings of the IIS server. She will be using a folder named Docs to test the backup and restore procedure. What steps does she take to perform her test?

Learning Objectives

Backing up your web site data, or any data on your system, is one of the most important things that you do in your position as an administrator. (You never seem to miss something until it is gone.)

In this lab, you'll learn how to back up and restore your IIS configuration. By the end of this lab, you'll be able to

Use Internet Services Manager.

Use the Backup/Restore Configuration utility.

Backup and restore IIS configuration.

Lab Materials and Setup

For this lab exercise, you'll need

A working computer

Installed network card (NIC)

Windows 2000 Server software (installed)

TCP/IP installed

A virtual directory named Docs

Internet Information Services installed

Getting Down to Business

To back up and restore the IIS configuration, perform the following steps:

Step 1. Launch Internet Services Manager. Select Backup/Restore Configuration for your server, and Create Backup. In the Configuration Backup Name text box, type *<today's date>* **backup**. Complete the backup process.

Step 2. Now, we'll delete some directories and verify that the backup session will restore them. Delete the Docs virtual directory.

Step 3. Select the Backup/Restore Configuration option for your server. Restore today's date backup entry. Complete the process and close the Configuration Backup/Restore window.

Step 4. Verify that the Docs virtual directory is restored in the Internet Information Services console and verify its presence using Internet Explorer. Close out of the Console window.

LAB ANALYSIS TEST

1. What is the default authentication method for an IIS server, and what changes are made to your Windows 2000 security during the original installation process to allow this access?

   _____

   _____

2. What are the three maintenance tasks performed on an IIS server?

   _____

   _____

3. How would you describe a virtual directory?

   _____

   _____

4. Of the four authentication methods available that allow users to access web and FTP sites, which two require users to have Windows 2000 user accounts?

   _____

   _____

5. Which utility would you use to back up IIS server configuration settings?

   _____

   _____

KEY TERM QUIZ

Use the following vocabulary terms to complete the sentences below. Not all of the terms will be used. Definitions for these terms can be found in "Managing a Microsoft Windows 2000 Network Environment Study Guide."

> File Transfer Protocol (FTP)
>
> Integrated Windows authentication
>
> Virtual directory
>
> Basic authentication
>
> Secure Socket Layer (SSL)
>
> Digest authentication
>
> Anonymous access
>
> Internet Services Manager
>
> Host header
>
> Internet Information Services (IIS)

1. The administrative tool used to manage the Internet Information Services server components is named _____.

2. _____ is used to transfer files and perform basic file management tasks between computers using the TCP/IP protocol.

3. An authentication method that prompts users for a username and password in order to access web resources, and prevents hackers from obtaining information, is named

   _____.

4. _____ is a Windows 2000 component that provides web-related services. It also supports web site creation, configuration, and management.

5. _____ is a mapping to a physical directory containing content, web or FTP, that's included on a site.

LAB SOLUTIONS FOR CHAPTER 11

In this section, you'll find solutions to the lab exercises, Lab Analysis Test, and Key Term Quiz.

Lab Solution 11.01

The easiest way to create IIS web or FTP sites is to have all the sites' files located in the home directories or subdirectories. However, IIS allows an administrator to add files from other locations to the site without moving them. These are called virtual directories.

In this lab, you installed IIS and shared out a folder for web access. By the end of this lab, you were able to

Install IIS.

Use Web Sharing Services.

Share out a folder for web access.

To install IIS and share out a folder, perform the following steps:

Step 1.   First, you'll need to install Internet Information Services (IIS). From the Control Panel, double-click the Add/Remove Programs icon. In the Add/Remove Programs dialog box, click Add/Remove Windows Components.

Step 2.   In the Windows Components Wizard dialog box, click on Internet Information Services (IIS) and then click the Details button.

Step 3.   From the Internet Information Services (IIS) dialog box, as shown in Figure 11-1, select the following components: Common Files, File Transfer Protocol (FTP) Server, Internet Information Services Snap-in, and World Wide Web Server. Optionally, you can also select Documentation and Internet Services Manager (HTML). HTML allows you to administer most aspects of your IIS server from a browser. When you finish, click OK.

Step 4.   Then, click Next in the Windows Components dialog box. At this point, configuration begins. When you're asked for the CD-ROM, insert it into the drive to complete the installation. When installation is complete, exit the Components Wizard and the Add/Remove Programs dialog box.

FIGURE 11-1

Select the
required IIS
program files to
create complete
web and
FTP sites.

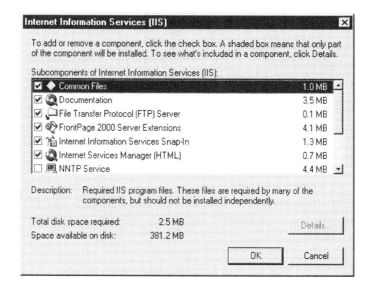

Step 5. Next, you want to share a web folder using the Web Sharing service. Right-click the folder you want to share (Share folder) and choose Sharing from the menu that appears. In the Folder Properties dialog box, select the Web Sharing tab, as shown here:

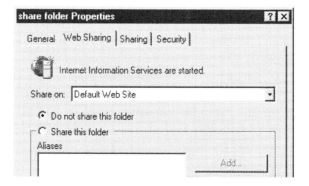

Step 6. In the Share On field, choose the site you want to share this folder on—Default Web Site. All the virtual sites you have configured on your web server will appear in the pull-down list. Select the radio button labeled Share this Folder.

Step 7. When the Edit Alias dialog box appears, as shown next, confirm the alias name (the name that a web user can reference this web share by—it does not have to be the same as the folder's real name)—Share folder. Then, choose the Read access permission from the four security levels. Read means that users can look at content. Write means that users can upload into the folder. Script source access means that users can view the source of script files in the folder. Directory browsing means that users can browse the folder's contents and its subfolders. Generally, only read access is given to publicly accessed folders.

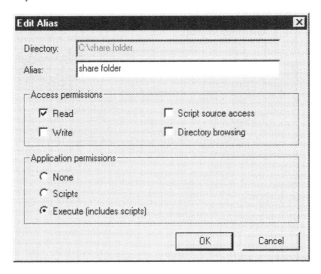

Step 8.   Finally, choose the Execute application permission. None means that no scripts or applications present in the folder can be run by a browser client. Scripts means that script files can be executed. Execute means that all programs in the folder can be run by browser clients. If you select Write access and Scripts application permissions, a dialog box will appear, indicating that you are allowing users to upload scripts they can then run (a potentially dangerous situation).

Step 9.   If the folder is on an NTFS partition, you need to set NTFS permissions. Click the Security tab at the top of the Properties dialog box. From the Security tab, add local permissions for the domain users and Anonymous to allow access to this folder over the Web by clicking the Add button and adding them to the list. You can add users and groups as you normally would. However, to allow anonymous users to access the data, you must either explicitly add the IIS anonymous users or implicitly add these users by adding the local group Guests, as shown next. You will need to set as many NTFS permissions for any user as you have given access to in previous steps.

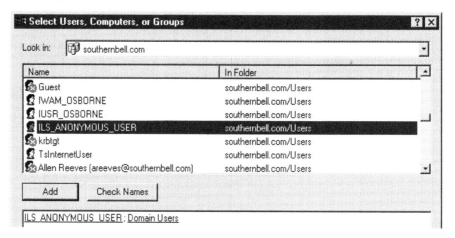

Step 10. If you gave out read and write access, you must also give out read and write NTFS permission; otherwise, the lesser of the access levels will prevail for your web users. Click OK when you are done.

Lab Solution 11.02

Copying a file from one computer to another is a pretty basic task, and copying those files over a network sure beats using floppies! How much access you have to files and folders on FTP servers depends on whether you gain access to the servers through a CERN proxy server or directly. When installing IIS, a default FTP site is created. This site responds to TCP/IP port 21 on all configured IP addresses of the server.

In this lab, you configured a default FTP site. By the end of this lab, you were able to

Use Internet Services Manager.

Allow for Anonymous access to FTP site.

To configure the default FTP site to allow anonymous access, perform the following steps:

Step 1. Click Start | Programs | Administrative Tools, and select Internet Services Manager. Double-click your server to expand the tree on the web server. Right-click Default FTP Site and select Properties from the context menu.

Step 2.   Now, select the Security Accounts tab and verify that the Allow Anonymous Connections box is checked, as shown next. Click the Messages tab.

```
Default FTP Site Properties                                    ? X

FTP Site  Security Accounts | Messages | Home Directory | Directory Security |

    ┌─ ☑ Allow Anonymous Connections ───────────────────────────────┐
    │                                                                 │
    │   Select the Windows User Account to use for anonymous access to this resource │
    │                                                                 │
    │   Username:   │UTHERNBELL\ILS_ANONYMOUS_USER│    │ Browse.. │   │
    │                                                                 │
    │   Password:   │                             │                   │
    │                                                                 │
    │               ☐ Allow only anonymous connections                │
    │               ☐ Allow IIS to control password                   │
    └─────────────────────────────────────────────────────────────────┘
```

Step 3.   In the Welcome text box, type **Welcome to my FTP Server.**, and in the Exit text box, type **Thank you for visiting my FTP Server.**, as shown next. Click OK.

```
Default FTP Site Properties                                    ? X

FTP Site | Security Accounts | Messages | Home Directory | Directory Security |

    ┌─ FTP Site Messages ──────────────────────────────────────────┐
    │                                                                │
    │   Welcome:                                                     │
    │   │Welcome to my FTP Server.                              │    │
    │                                                                │
    │   Exit:                                                        │
    │   │Thank you for visiting my FTP Server.                  │    │
    └────────────────────────────────────────────────────────────────┘
```

Step 4.   To test and verify that Welcome and Exit messages are working, open a DOS session and type **ftp**<*servername*>, where <*servername*> is the name of the server (payroll)—ftp payroll. Type **anonymous** for the user, and then press ENTER at the password prompt. Notice the Welcome message shown here:

```
C:\NTSRVR\System32\cmd.exe                              _ □ X
Microsoft Windows 2000 [Version 5.00.2195]
(C) Copyright 1985-1999 Microsoft Corp.

C:\Documents and Settings\Administrator.PAYROLL.000>ftp payroll
Connected to Payroll.southernbell.com.
220 Payroll Microsoft FTP Service (Version 5.0).
User (Payroll.southernbell.com:(none)): anonymous
331 Anonymous access allowed, send identity (e-mail name) as password.
Password:
230-Welcome to my FTP Server.
230 Anonymous user logged in.
ftp> bye
221  Thank you for visiting my FTP Server.

C:\Documents and Settings\Administrator.PAYROLL.000>
```

Step 5.   To exit, type **Bye** and close all windows. Now users will receive these messages when accessing the FTP Server.

Lab Solution 11.03

Internet Information Services (IIS) has available a variety of methods to prevent unauthorized access by users to web and FTP sites. This includes authentication, port assignments, IP address and domain name restrictions, and security protocols such as Secure Socket Layer (SSL).

In this lab, you configured a user authentication method. By the end of this lab, you were able to

Use Internet Information Services console.

Configure a web site to use the digest authentication method.

To configure a web site to use digest authentication, perform the following steps:

Step 1. From the Start menu, choose Programs | Administrative Tools | Internet Services Manager. In the IIS Console window, you can locate your web site by expanding the Console Root, Internet Information Services, and your server. When you see your default web site in the tree under the name of your server, right-click it and choose Properties from the menu that appears.

Step 2. In the Web Site Properties window, on the Directory Security tab, click the Edit button in the section labeled Anonymous Access and Authentication Control, as shown here:

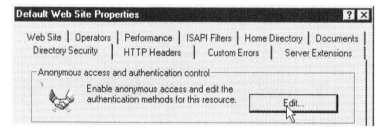

Step 3. From the Authentication Methods dialog box, choose which authentication method you wish to incorporate.

Step 4. You've decided to enable Integrated Windows authentication, so you'll use the Authentication Methods box, shown in Figure 11-2. Select the appropriate

FIGURE 11-2

Enabling
Integrated
Windows
authentication

check boxes. Click OK to update the web site's properties. Note that username and password are required when logging in as other than anonymous.

Step 5. Attempt to access the web site as anonymous and as Administrator, using a browser.

Lab Solution 11.04
Backing up your web site data, or any data on your system, is one of the most important things that you do in your position as an administrator. (You never seem to miss something until it is gone.)

In this lab, you'll learn how to back up and restore your IIS configuration. By the end of this lab, you'll be able to

Use Internet Services Manager.

Use the Backup/Restore Configuration utility.

Back up and restore IIS configuration.

To back up and restore the IIS configuration, perform the following steps:

Step 1. Click Start | Programs | Administrative Tools and select Internet Services Manager. Double-click your server to expand the tree on the web server. Right-click the server name and select Backup/Restore Configuration from the context menu. Then select Create Backup.

Step 2. In the Configuration Backup Name text box, type *<today's date>* backup. Click OK and close the window. You've just made a backup of the web server's contents. Note that the backup file is listed in the Previous Backups window, as shown here:

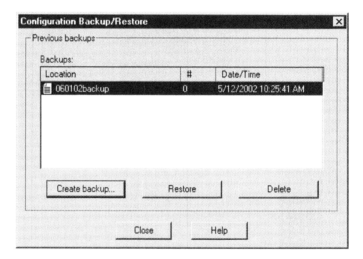

Step 3. Now, we'll delete some directories and verify that the backup session will restore them. Click the + sign next to Default Web Site and delete the Docs virtual directory.

Step 4. Right-click the server name and select the Backup/Restore Configuration option from the context menu. Select today's date backup entry and then click the Restore button. Click Yes at the prompt. You'll see this warning:

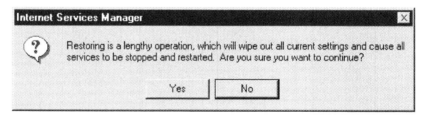

Step 5. Once the procedure is complete, click OK at the Operation Completed Successfully message. Close the Configuration Backup/Restore Window.

Step 6. Verify that the Docs virtual directory is restored by expanding Default Web Site in the Internet Information Services console. Close out of the Console window.

ANSWERS TO LAB ANALYSIS

1. By default, an IIS server is configured to enable anonymous users to access the web site without being prompted for a password. To identify an anonymous user, a special local account is created—IUSER_SERVERNAME. Any user connecting to the server is automatically assigned the rights this user has to the web site.

2. Regular IIS maintenance tasks include backing up the IIS configuration, starting or stopping services, and installing hot fixes or service packs.

3. A virtual directory is a term used to describe web server directories that appear to be located below a web server's home directory, but could actually be located in any location accessible to the web server. IIS uses an alias to describe the virtual directory so that web browser users are unaware of the directory's physical location and path.

4. Both digest authentication and integrated Windows authentication require users to have a valid user account.

5. The easiest way to back up IIS configuration settings is to use the Backup/Restore Configuration utility found within the IIS console.

ANSWERS TO KEY TERM QUIZ

1. Internet Services Manager

2. File Transfer Protocol (FTP)

3. Digest authentication

4. Internet Information Services (IIS)

5. Virtual directory

MICROSOFT CERTIFIED SYSTEMS ASSOCIATE

12

Implementing and Analyzing Security

LAB EXERCISES

12.01   Configuring and Auditing Security

12.02   Administering Security Templates

12.03   Analyzing Security Settings

       Lab Analysis Test

       Key Term Quiz

       Lab Solutions

A feature of Windows 2000 that monitors various security-related events is security auditing. Monitoring system events is necessary to detect intruders and to detect attempts to compromise data on the system. For example, an event that would indicate possible system intrusions, which can be audited, is a failed logon attempt. The most common types of events audited are access to objects, such as files and folders, management of user and group accounts, and when users log on to and log off of the system. In addition to auditing security-related events, Windows 2000 generates a security log and provides a way for you to view the security events reported in the log. Finally, the Windows 2000 auditing feature generates an audit trail to help you keep track of all security administration events that occur on the system.

Establishing an audit trail is an important facet of security. Monitoring the creation or modification of objects gives you a way to track potential security problems, helps to ensure user accountability, and provides evidence in the event of a security breach.

In order to track an event, you must first turn on the categories of events you wish to audit. Second, you must set the size and behavior of the security log. Lastly, if you have selected either the Audit directory service access category or the Audit object access category, you must determine which objects you want to monitor access to and modify their security descriptors accordingly.

Security settings define the security-relevant behavior of the system. Through the use of Group Policy objects in the Active Directory, administrators can centrally apply the security levels required to protect enterprise systems. A security template is a physical representation of a security configuration—a file where a group of security settings may be stored. Windows 2000 includes a set of security templates, each based on the role of a computer—from security settings for low security domain clients to highly secure domain controllers. These templates can be used as-is, modified to fit a particular need, or serve as a basis for creating custom security templates.

In this chapter, we will look at how to configure and audit security on files and folders, administer a security template by modifying an existing security template, and analyze security settings using the Security Configuration and Analysis utility.

CERTIFICATION OBJECTIVE 12.01

10 Minutes

Configuring and Auditing Security

You are the network administrator for Oncology/Infusion Services, Inc. The company provides outpatient services for oncology patients. Patients are scheduled on a daily basis and the nine oncology nurses that staff the unit need access to patient information stored in a shared folder. At the same time, the 12 nursing assistants are not required to access those records. How would you set permissions to the folder and track possible unauthorized access by the nursing assistants? The nurses have been placed in a group named Users, and the nursing assistants have been placed in a Guest group.

Learning Objectives

Security auditing policy is a component of security policy that allows you to configure which security related events you wish to monitor. The function of auditing is to track user and operating system activities, or events, on a computer. The audited events are configured in an audit policy, which again is a component of security policy. An audit policy can be configured one of two ways: through the Security Settings of Group Policy or by using Security Configuration and Analysis.

When configuring auditing on files and folders, you are doing so on an NTFS file system only. And, when specifying auditing, there are several concepts to address: auditing failed events for Read operations on critical or sensitive files, auditing the success or failure of Delete operations on confidential files, auditing success or failed operations for Change Permissions and Take Ownership permission usage for confidential or personal files, auditing the success or failure of all events performed by members of the Guest group (if such group is active), and auditing file and folder access on all computers containing shared data.

In this lab, you'll specify auditing on a particular folder and files on an NTFS partition. By the end of this lab, you'll be able to

Configure auditing on a folder and files.

Enable object access auditing (success or failure).

Lab Materials and Setup

For this lab exercise, you'll need

A working computer

Installed network card (NIC)

Windows 2000 Server software (installed)

TCP/IP installed

Active Directory (AD) installed

Getting Down to Business

To configure auditing on a folder and files, perform the following steps:

Step 1. Launch Windows Explorer. Locate the Share folder on your NTFS partition. Open the Properties window of the folder.

Step 2. In the Properties window, select the Security tab to display the current permissions. Open the Advanced Security Configuration window and select the Audit tab. This displays the current configured audit settings for the folder.

Step 3. Add the Users group for whom we want to monitor activity on this folder. Once the selection is made, the Auditing Entry window for the Users group will be displayed. Here you will select the events you need to audit successful or failed access.

Step 4. In the Audit Onto drop-down menu, select the item that will apply these audit settings to this folder and its children.

Step 5. Since this is a confidential folder and files, we want to track the successful and failed attempt for Read Attributes, List Folder / Read Data, Change Permissions, and Take Ownership.

Step 6. After making the choices, apply and save the settings. Exit Windows Explorer.

CERTIFICATION OBJECTIVE 12.02

Administering Security Templates

15 Minutes

Pam is the network administrator for the Gold Coast Insurance Company. There are 250 agents that handle customer claims throughout the United States. She's been in this position for six months, replacing the previous network administrator who left for another opportunity. She's noticed that the security policies are very liberal, especially when it comes to password settings. Pam wants to ensure that all users on the Windows 2000 domain change their passwords every 45 days, and that they use the password for at least 14 days before they can change it. Additionally, the password must meet complexity requirements—that it does not contain all or part of the user's account name, that it is at least six characters in length, and that it be an alphanumeric entry. How can Pam satisfy these requirements for the users?

Learning Objectives

In Windows 2000, there are two primary ways of implementing security polices: using security templates or using group policy. Templates make it easier to reapply similar settings to many systems once the template has been created.

A security template is a text file with an .INF extension. The file includes security settings applicable to a single computer using the Security Configuration and Analysis Microsoft Management Console (MMC) snap-in. These settings can also be imported into Group Policy and be applied to a site, domain, or organizational unit (OU) level. The four levels of security templates are Basic, Compatible, Secure, Highly Secure, and Dedicated Domain Controller.

In most security situations, it may not be necessary to create an original security template. You can take an existing template and use it as a basis for creating a new, modified template. The main advantage of using an existing template is the fact that a template may already contain most of the security settings you wish to apply. Making modifications to include a few more will not take as long as adding settings to a new template. It is important, no matter which method is chosen, to always be aware of the security content of the template and verify, through testing, that the changes made to the template will result in the security behavior that you expect.

In this lab, you'll modify an existing security template. By the end of this lab, you'll be able to

Use Security Templates MMC snap-in.

Modify settings in the template.

For further information, refer to the section on security templates in Chapter 12 of "Managing a Microsoft Windows 2000 Network Environment Study Guide."

Lab Materials and Setup

For this lab excrcise, you'll need

A working computer

Installed network card (NIC)

Windows 2000 Server software (installed)

TCP/IP installed

Active Directory (AD) installed

Security Templates added to the MMC

Getting Down to Business

To modify an existing security template, perform the following steps:

Step 1.   Be sure you're logged on to the server as Administrator, or as a user with administrative rights. Access the Microsoft Management Console.

Step 2.   Expand Security Templates in the MMC. We need to expand into the Password Policy template. Click the Password Policy template to reveal the settings that can be changed.

Step 3.   Change the Maximum Password Age value to 45, change the Minimum Password Age value to 14, and enable the Passwords Must Meet Complexity Requirements value.

Step 4.   Once all the changes have been made, close the MMC. These new policy settings will take effect.

CERTIFICATION OBJECTIVE 12.03

Analyzing Security Settings

15 Minutes

You are the administrator of a large multinational food distributor responsible for the network in the North East. During the past eight months, you and your team have upgraded domain and application servers to a Windows 2000 platform. Security policies on all levels of the organization have been added, deleted, and modified. At this final stage of the process, you want to compare these changes to a security standard set by Windows 2000. What tool would you use to determine the overall security health of the network?

Learning Objectives

Security Configuration and Analysis is a tool for analyzing and configuring local system security. Since the state of the operating system and applications on a computer is dynamic, security levels may be required to change temporarily to enable immediate resolution of an administration or network issue; this change can often go unreversed. This means that a computer may no longer meet the requirements for enterprise security.

Periodic security analysis allows an administrator to track and ensure an appropriate level of security on each computer as part of an overall, company-wide risk management program. Analysis is highly specified—information about all system aspects related to security is provided in the results. This enables an administrator to tune the security levels and, most importantly, detect any security flaws that may occur in the system over time.

In this lab, you'll learn how to analyze security settings. By the end of this lab, you'll be able to

Use the Security Configuration and Analysis MMC snap-in.

Configure a database for analyzing a computer.

Analyze a computer's security settings.

Use a security template as a comparison tool.

Lab Materials and Setup

For this lab exercise, you'll need

A working computer

Installed network card (NIC)

Windows 2000 Server software (installed)

TCP/IP installed

Active Directory (AD) installed

Security Configuration and Analysis snap-in added to the MMC

Getting Down to Business

To analyze a computer's security, perform the following steps:

Step 1. Be sure you're logged on to the server as Administrator, or as a user with administrative rights. Access the Microsoft Management Console.

Step 2. First, we need to configure a database for analyzing our computer. Display the database requirements by selecting the Security Configuration and Analysis object.

Step 3.   To create a database, follow the instructions that are displayed in the window. Access the context menu and select Open Database. In the Open Database File Name field, type the name of the database file we wish to create, **Comparison**. Click Open.

The default location of the database file being created is in your user profile in a folder called Security/Database.

Step 4.   Next, you're presented with a dialog window and asked to import a security template that will be used to compare the computer's security settings against those in the template. Select securedc. Click Open.

Step 5.   Now that we have configured the computer to compare its settings against a security standard, we need to perform the analysis. Refer to the directions on the right side of the console window and perform the required steps.

Step 6.   When prompted to select the location of the error log file, keep the default path. Make a note of it before clicking OK.

Step 7.   The analysis will begin and a progress bar will be displayed. Once the analysis is complete, the console will display all the areas included in the comparison process.

Step 8.   Select View Log File from the Security Configuration and Analysis context menu to view the contents of the file. Review the contents to obtain a complete picture of how close the system resembles the template and which settings need to be changed. When finished, close the MMC.

LAB ANALYSIS TEST

1. For what purpose would you use Security Configuration and Analysis?

   _____

   _____

2. You wish to track unauthorized access to a color printer whose use is limited to the Graphic Arts department. How would you accomplish this?

   _____

   _____

3. What is the default extension of the database files created by Security Configuration and Analysis?

   _____

   _____

4. Where does Windows 2000 keep information gathered during the auditing process?

   _____

   _____

5. What is the command-line version of the Security Configuration and Analysis snap-in that allows security analysis and configuration used to refresh the audit policy?

   _____

   _____

KEY TERM QUIZ

Use the following vocabulary terms to complete the sentences below. Not all of the terms will be used. Definitions for these terms can be found in "Managing a Microsoft Windows 2000 Network Environment Study Guide."

MMC snap-in

auditing

Security Configuration and Analysis

Active Directory

Group Policies

Scope

Audit policy

securedc

Organizational unit (OU)

Security Templates

1. _____ are text files that contain rules used to enforce security settings for users and computers.

2. Default security settings for the domain controller are contained in a template named _____.

3. A portion of security policy, _____ lets you configure which security-related event to monitor.

4. The process of tracking execution of user rights, file access, or other security elements on a computer is named _____.

5. An MMC snap-in, _____, is primarily designed to analyze local system security settings and apply security templates to a local computer.

LAB SOLUTIONS FOR CHAPTER 12

In this section, you'll find solutions to the lab exercises, Lab Analysis Test, and Key Term Quiz.

Lab Solution 12.01

Only the oncology nurses are allowed to view patient schedules and information. They, therefore, need access to those files. The 12 nursing assistants should not have access to those records. The nurses are in a group named users, and the nursing assistants have been placed in a Guest group.

Security auditing policy is a component of security policy whose function is to track user and operating system activities, or events, on a computer. An audit policy can be configured one of two ways: through the Security Settings of Group Policy or by using Security Configuration and Analysis.

In this lab, you specified auditing on a particular folder and files on an NTFS partition. By the end of this lab, you were able to

Configure auditing on a folder and files.

Enable object access auditing (success or failure).

To configure auditing on a folder and files, perform the following steps:

Step 1.   Be sure you're logged on to the server as Administrator, or as a user with administrative rights. Launch Windows Explorer using the My Computer icon. Locate the Share folder on your NTFS partition. Right-click the folder and select Properties.

Step 2.   In the Properties window, select the Security tab to display the current permissions, as shown in Figure 12-1. Open the Advanced Security Configuration window and select the Auditing tab. This displays the current configured audit settings for the folder, as shown in Figure 12-2.

Step 3.   Click the Add button and select the Users group for whom we want to monitor activity on this folder. Once the selection is made, click OK. The Auditing Entry window for the Users group will be displayed.

Step 4.   In the Audit onto drop-down menu, select This Folder, Subfolders, and Files. Since this is a confidential folder and files, we want to track the successful and failed attempts for Read Attributes, List Folder / Read Data, Change Permissions, and Take Ownership. Click the Successful and Failed boxes for each item, as shown in Figure 12-3.

FIGURE 12-1

Folder
permissions for
assigned users
and groups are
displayed in the
Security window.

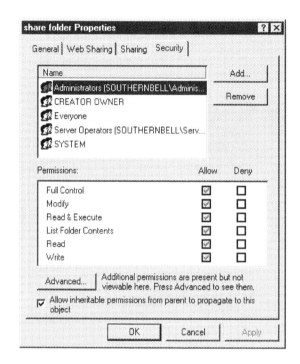

Step 5. After making the choices, click OK twice to apply and save the settings.
Exit Windows Explorer.

FIGURE 12-2

Tracking (that is,
auditing user
permissions) is
entered here in
the Access
Control Settings
window.

FIGURE 12-3

Here you will select the events needed to audit successful or failed access for a selected user or group.

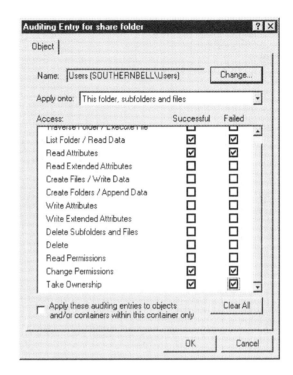

Lab Solution 12.02

Pam's task here is to ensure that all users on the Windows 2000 domain have a less liberal password security environment. The easiest way for her to apply this policy is through the use of a security template.

Templates make it easy to apply similar settings to many systems once the template has been created. The file includes security settings applicable to a single computer using the Security Configuration and Analysis MMC snap-in. The main advantage of using an existing template is the fact that a template may already contain most of the security settings you wish to apply.

In this lab, you modified an existing security template. By the end of this lab, you were able to

Use the Security Templates MMC snap-in.

Modify settings in the template.

cross
Reference

For further information, refer to the section on security templates in Chapter 12 of "Managing a Microsoft Windows 2000 Network Environment Study Guide."

To modify an existing security template, perform the following steps:

Step 1. Be sure you're logged on to the server as Administrator, or as a user with administrative rights. Access the Microsoft Management Console, click Start | Run, and type **MMC**.

Step 2. Expand Security Templates in the MMC. Expand the basicdc folder to display a list of areas where settings may be changed. Expand the Account Policy folder and click the Password Policy template, as shown in Figure 12-4.

Step 3. Double-click Maximum Password Age and change the value to 45. Notice that, by default, the minimum password setting is set to 30. Click Minimum Password Age and change the value to 14. Then, click Passwords Must Meet Complexity Requirements and enable this setting, as shown here.

FIGURE 12-4　Selecting Password Policy reveals the settings that can be changed in the right pane of the window.

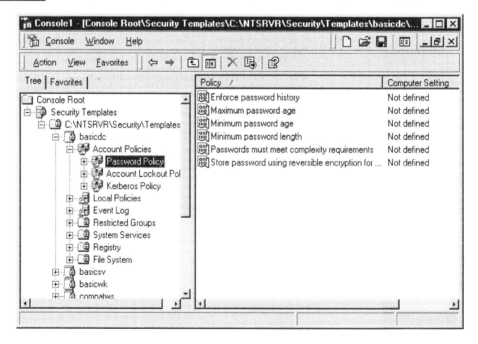

Step 4.   Once all the changes have been made, close the MMC. These new policy settings will take effect.

Lab Solution 12.03

In this scenario, security policies on all levels of the organization have been added, deleted, and modified. Making security changes without verification may compromise the network. And because there have been many changes made, it's not feasible to visually, and individually, verify each policy. A more comprehensive process is required here.

Security Configuration and Analysis is a tool for analyzing and configuring local system security. Periodic security analysis allows an administrator to track and ensure an appropriate level of security on each computer as part of an overall, company-wide risk management program.

In this lab, you learned how to analyze security settings. By the end of this lab, you were able to

Use the Security Configuration and Analysis MMC snap-in.

Configure a database for analyzing a computer.

Analyze a computer's security settings.

Use a security template as a comparison tool.

To analyze a computer's security, perform the following steps:

Step 1.   Be sure you're logged on to the server as Administrator, or as a user with administrative rights. Access the Microsoft Management Console by clicking Start | Run and typing **MMC**.

Step 2.   First, we need to configure a database for analyzing our computer. Click Security Configuration and Analysis to display the database creation steps in the right pane of the window.

Step 3.   To create a database, follow the instructions that are displayed in the window, as shown in Figure 12-5. Right-click Security Configuration and Analysis. In the context menu, select Open Database. In the Open Database File Name field, enter the name of the database file we wish to create, **comparison**, as shown here. Click Open.

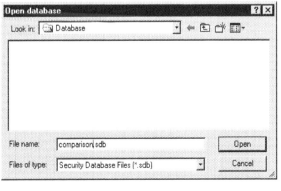

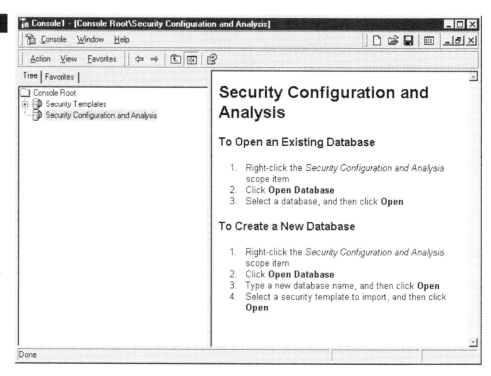

FIGURE 12-5

Simple instructions for using an existing database or creating a new database are provided in the window.

lab
Hint   *The default location of the database file being created is in your user profile in a folder called Security/Database.*

Step 4.   Next, you're presented with a dialog window and asked to import a security template that will be used to compare the computer's security settings against those in the template. Select securedc, as shown in Figure 12-6. Click Open.

Step 5.   Now that we have configured the computer to compare its settings against a security standard, we need to perform the analysis. Refer to the directions on the right side of the console window and perform the required steps.

Step 6.   Right-click Security Configuration and Analysis. In the context menu, select Analyze Computer Now. When prompted to select the location of the error log file, keep the default path, as shown here. Make a note of it before clicking OK.

FIGURE 12-6

Select an existing template that will be used as a benchmark against our security settings for the domain.

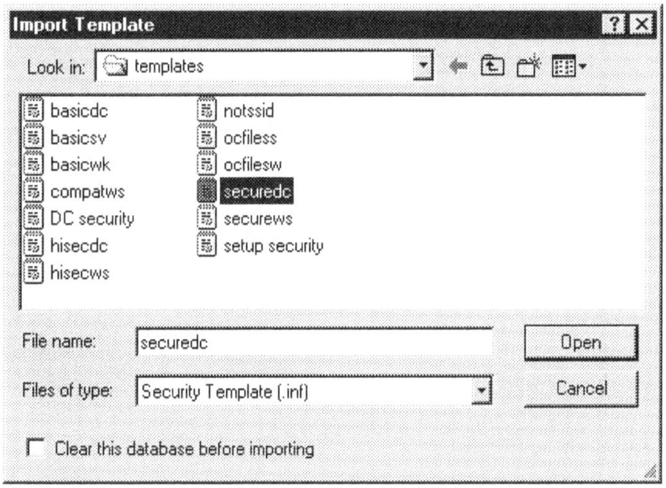

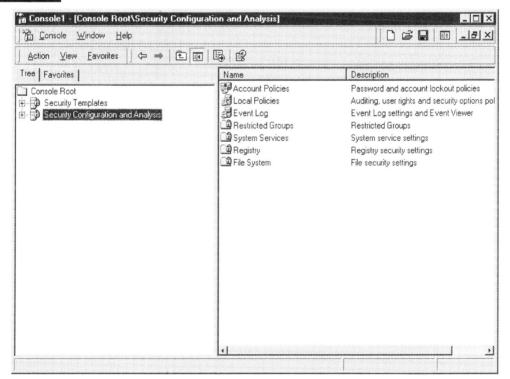

Step 7.   The analysis will begin and a progress bar will be displayed. Once the analysis is complete, the console will display all the areas included in the comparison process, as shown in Figure 12-7.

FIGURE 12-7   The security areas in need of review are displayed in the right pane of the window.

Step 8. Select View Log File from the Security Configuration and Analysis context menu to view the contents of the file. Review the contents to obtain a complete picture of how close the system resembles the template and which settings need to be changed. When finished, close the MMC. You may be prompted to save the log for archive purposes.

ANSWERS TO LAB ANALYSIS

1. Security Configuration and Analysis can be used to analyze system security by creating a security database and comparing the settings to a security template. It can also be used to configure system security by applying template settings to the computer.

2. You would assign appropriate permissions to the shared printer to ensure that only members of the Graphics Arts department have access. You would enable access auditing on the Windows 2000 computer where the printer is defined.

3. The default extension for the security database files created by Security Configuration and Analysis is .SDB.

4. Auditing information is stored in the security log on the computer where the event occurred.

5. Secedit.exe.

ANSWERS TO KEY TERM QUIZ

1. Security Templates

2. securedc

3. Audit policy

4. Auditing

5. Security Configuration and Analysis

MICROSOFT CERTIFIED SYSTEMS ASSOCIATE

13

Configuring Remote Access and VPN Connections

LAB EXERCISES

13.01   Configuring a Routing and Remote Access Service (RRAS) Virtual Private Network (VPN) Server

13.02   Configuring a Remote Access Policy

13.03   Configuring a Virtual Private Network (VPN) Using a PPTP Connection

13.04   Managing Existing Server-to-Server PPTP Connections Using Remote Access Security

13.05   Configuring and Verifying the Security of a VPN Connection

■   Lab Analysis Test

■   Key Term Quiz

■   Lab Solutions

The Routing and Remote Access service for Windows 2000 Server provides multiprotocol routing and remote access services for the Microsoft Windows platform. Some of the features include Layer Two Tunneling Protocol (L2TP), improved administration, and management tools. The graphical user interface program is the Routing and Remote Access administrative utility, a Microsoft Management Console (MMC) snap-in.

Combined features of the Windows 2000 Routing and Remote Access service make a Windows 2000 Server–based computer function as a multiprotocol router, a demand-dial router, and a remote access server. The combination of routing and remote access services on the same computer creates a Windows 2000 remote access router.

An advantage of the Routing and Remote Access service is its integration with the Windows 2000 Server operating system. The Routing and Remote Access service works with a wide variety of hardware platforms and hundreds of network adapters. IT's implementation results in a lower-cost solution than many midrange dedicated router or remote access server products.

In this chapter, we will look at how to configure an RRAS to act as a VPN server for remote connection, how to configure a VPN with a PPTP connection over a public network, managing configuration settings for existing connections, and verifying authentication and encryption settings to provide a high level of security during remote connections.

CERTIFICATION OBJECTIVE 13.01

Configuring a Routing and Remote Access Service (RRAS) Virtual Private Network (VPN) Server

10 Minutes

Tony Autostrada started his auto parts store 40 years ago in a storefront in Olneyville. Today, Autostrada Auto Parts Co. has 35 stores in three states in New England. As the network engineer, you need to set up private connections to your inventory database server for each store manager to access. Since all of the stores have Internet connections, you can provide access using the existing public connection by configuring a virtual private network (VPN). How do you configure the RRAS to act as a VPN server?

Learning Objectives

A virtual private network (VPN) has the ability to exchange data between two computers—a client and a server—across an interconnected network in a fashion that makes the user believe that the user is connected directly, securely, and privately, while using a public connection such as the Internet. It is a cost-effective solution for users that travel and need to connect from various locations.

For virtual private network access across the Internet, the server typically has a permanent connection to the Internet. A nonpermanent connection to the Internet is possible if the Internet service provider (ISP) supports demand-dial connections. The connection is created when traffic is delivered to the VPN server. However, this is not a common configuration. If the VPN server provides access to a network, you must install and connect a separate network adapter to provide access.

In this lab exercise, you'll create a virtual private network (VPN) connection. By the end of this lab, you'll be able to

- Configure RRAS to function as a VPN server.

For further information, refer to the VPN section of Chapter 13 in "Managing a Windows 2000 Network Environment Study Guide."

Lab Materials and Setup

For this lab exercise, you'll need

- A working computer
- Installed network card (NIC)
- Windows 2000 Server software (installed)
- TCP/IP installed
- Domain Name System (DNS) installed
- Active Directory (AD) installed
- Routing and Remote Access Service installed

Getting Down to Business

To configure RRAS as a VPN server, perform the following steps:

Step 1.   Launch the Routing and Remote Access console. Select the server's Properties window and launch the Routing and Remote Access Server Setup Wizard.

Step 2. Configure the connection type to be a Virtual Private Network (VPN) Server. Verify that TCP/IP appears in the Protocols list and that the Yes, All of the Available Protocols Are On This List option is selected. Continue on to the Internet Connection window.

Step 3. In the Internet Connections list, select <No Internet Connection>, verify that the Automatically option for No, I Don't Want to Set Up This Server to Use RADIUS Now is selected.

Step 4. Complete the configuration process, close the wizard, and start the RRAS server if it doesn't start on its own.

CERTIFICATION OBJECTIVE 13.02

Configuring a Remote Access Policy

15 Minutes

The Ocean State Beverage Company has grown over the past few years. In doing so, their network has also grown. They've gone from one server hosting a relational database to a Windows 2000 domain server, an application server, and a database server. Due to the increased number of sales representatives, you've installed a Routing and Remote Access service and added a bank of modems to the domain server. Now you need to perform additional configurations by applying a set of parameters by which regional directors and sales representatives dialing into the network can access the resources on the network. They need the ability to check available stock and place orders.

Learning Objectives

In Windows 2000, remote access connections are accepted based on the dial-in properties of a user account and remote access policies. A remote access policy is a set of conditions and connection parameters that define the characteristics of the incoming connection and the set of constraints imposed on it. Remote access policies can be used to specify allowable connections that are conditioned by the time of day and day of the week, the Windows 2000 group to which the dial-in user belongs, the type of remote access client (dial-up or VPN), and so on. Remote access policies can be used to impose connection parameters such as maximum session time, idle disconnect time, required secure authentication methods, required encryption, and so on.

In this lab, you'll configure a remote access policy. By the end of this lab, you'll be able to

- Select groups for remote access permissions.
- Set up access constraints.
- Make IP address assignments.
- Configure IP Packet Filters.
- Configure Remote Access Server encryption.

Lab Materials and Setup

For this lab exercise, you'll need

- A working computer
- Installed network card (NIC)
- Windows 2000 Server software (installed)
- TCP/IP installed
- Domain Name System (DNS) installed
- Active Directory (AD) installed
- Routing and Remote Access Service installed

Getting Down to Business

To create and configure a remote access policy, perform the following steps:

Step 1. Launch the Routing and Remote Access console. Select Remote Access Policy and create a New Remote Access Policy.

Step 2. Enter a user-friendly name, **Remote Access**, and click Next to continue. Add a condition in the Add Remote Access Policy Conditions dialog window. Select Windows-Groups. Using the Windows-Groups attribute allows you to enable remote access by user groups, as defined in the Users and Groups console.

Step 3. Continue to the Groups dialog window. Select the Domain users group for the rule. Return to the Groups dialog box and add the Windows-Groups condition to the policy.

Step 4. Open the Add Remote Access Policy window. You can either grant or deny remote access permission by selecting the appropriate option. Select the Grant Remote Access Permission option and click Next.

Step 5. The Edit Dial-in Profile dialog box that opens allows you to access the dial-in profile for the users affected by this policy. Click Finish to complete the creation of the profile.

CERTIFICATION OBJECTIVE 13.03

Configuring a Virtual Private Network (VPN) Using a PPTP Connection

10 Minutes

In the first lab scenario of this chapter, your task was to configure RRAS as a VPN for Autostrada Auto Parts. Now you need to configure the VPN service to fit the needs of the users using the Point-to-Point Tunneling Protocol (PPTP) for encryption. How do you accomplish this task?

Learning Objectives

The Point-to-Point Tunneling Protocol (PPTP) is a de facto industry standard tunneling protocol first supported in Windows NT 4.0. PPTP is an extension of the Point-to-Point Protocol (PPP) and leverages the authentication, compression, and encryption mechanisms of PPP. PPTP is installed with the Routing and Remote Access service. By default, PPTP is configured for five PPTP ports. You can enable PPTP ports for inbound remote access and demand-dial routing connections by using the Routing and Remote Access Wizard.

In this lab exercise, you'll configure a virtual private network (VPN). By the end of this lab, you'll be able to

- Configure ports for VPN use.
- Configure a port using Point-to-Point Tunneling Protocol (PPTP).

Lab Materials and Setup

For this lab exercise, you'll need

- A working computer
- Installed network card (NIC)

- Windows 2000 Server software (installed)
- TCP/IP installed
- Domain Name System (DNS) installed
- Active Directory (AD) installed
- Routing and Remote Access Services installed

Getting Down to Business

To configure a VPN service, perform the following steps:

Step 1. Launch the Routing and Remote Access console. Display the Ports entry under the server. Notice that the initial number of ports is ten—five PPTP ports and five L2TP/IPSec ports. This is because the server has five user licenses configured when the Routing and Remote Access Service is installed.

Step 2. Configure the PPTP ports through the Ports Properties window. You can see each of the protocols listed.

Step 3. Select and configure the first PPTP protocol port that you will modify. Set the direction of the interface (inbound only or inbound and outbound) to Inbound Only, and set the number of ports to 5. Complete the process and close all windows.

CERTIFICATION OBJECTIVE 13.04

Managing Existing Server-to-Server PPTP Connections Using Remote Access Security

5 Minutes

The Che Bella Cosa Importing Company had you, the network administrator, install a new Windows 2000 Routing and Remote Access server. The marketing agents overseas connect to the network via a VPN. Your U.S. regional sales representatives access the network using point-to-point connections. What is the most secure way to ensure that the sales representatives have a secure VPN access?

Learning Objectives

The Point-to-Point Tunneling Protocol (PPTP) is a great solution to the tunneling needs of clients. It is relatively simple to set up when compared to L2TP/IPSec, and it provides good security when used with a username/strong password method. PPTP is an industry standard protocol that was first supported in Windows NT 4.0. The protocol uses the authentication, compression, and encryption of the PPP. PPTP is still in wide use on networks today. PPTP encapsulates Point-to-Point Protocol (PPP) frames into IP datagrams for transmission over an IP-based internetwork, such as the Internet or a private intranet. Compare this to sending an envelope addressed to an individual and placing it in an interoffice envelope for delivery addressed to that individual. The interoffice envelope is the standard transport for the company.

Authentication that occurs during the creation of a PPTP-based VPN connection uses the same mechanisms as PPP connections, such as Extensible Authentication Protocol (EAP), Microsoft Challenge-Handshake Authentication Protocol (MS-CHAP), CHAP, Shiva Password Authentication Protocol (SPAP), and Password Authentication Protocol (PAP). For Windows 2000, either EAP-Transport Level Security (EAP-TLS) or MS-CHAP must be used in order for the PPP data to be encrypted using Microsoft Point-to-Point Encryption (MPPE).

In this lab exercise, you'll verify settings for a secure method of user authentication when connecting via the Remote Access Server. By the end of this lab, you'll be able to

- Configure Remote Access Security.

Lab Materials and Setup

For this lab exercise, you'll need

- A working computer
- Installed network card (NIC)
- Windows 2000 Server software (installed)
- TCP/IP installed
- Domain Name System (DNS) installed
- Active Directory (AD) installed
- Routing and Remote Access Services installed

Getting Down to Business

To verify security for a specific group of settings for a Remote Access Security policy, perform the following steps:

Step 1. Launch the Routing and Remote Access console. Open the server's Properties windows.

Step 2. In the Security tab, confirm that the authentication provider is set to Windows Authentication. The Accounting provider should also be set to Windows Accounting. A log of connection requests and sessions is kept by Windows.

CERTIFICATION OBJECTIVE 13.05

Configuring and Verifying the Security of a VPN Connection

10 Minutes

In part two of the previous lab scenario, you need to apply additional secure user authentication. This is important since the client and server are two continents apart. What additional encryption protocols can be applied to the present configuration?

Learning Objectives

In today's climate, the authentication and encryption of remote access clients is an important security concern. Windows 2000 supports a number of authentication and encryption protocols.

In this lab, you'll verify security protocols for remote access. By the end of this lab, you'll be able to

- Use Routing and Remote Access console.
- Configure authentication protocols MS-CHAP and MS-CHAP v2.
- Set a strong level of encryption.

Lab Materials and Setup

For this lab exercise, you'll need

- A working computer
- Installed network card (NIC)

- Windows 2000 Server software (installed)
- TCP/IP installed
- Domain Name System (DNS) installed
- Active Directory (AD) installed
- Routing and Remote Access Services installed

Getting Down to Business

To verify authentication and encryption protocols for remote access, perform the following steps:

Step 1. First, you configure the authentication protocols. Launch the Routing and Remote Access console. Right-click the server and select Properties. Open the server's Properties windows. Select the Security tab and open the Authentication Methods window.

Step 2. Verify that the MS-CHAP and MS-CHAP v2 protocols for a connection are selected. Return to the Routing and Remote Access console.

Step 3. Now, you need to configure the encryption protocol level. Select Remote Access Policies from the tree view. Open the Properties window, and the Edit Profile window from Policy Properties. Set the encryption level to Strong. Complete the process and close out of all windows.

LAB ANALYSIS TEST

1. What are the four authentication protocols supported by Windows 2000 RAS?

   _____

   _____

2. As part of your network, you maintain a Windows 2000 Routing and Remote Access server to provide remote access services as part of VPN. Which VPN protocols will the server support?

   _____

   _____

3. How does a VPN reduce the cost of supporting remote access clients?

   _____

   _____

4. When troubleshooting connectivity problems, which four common problems would you check first?

   _____

   _____

5. What is the purpose of encryption protocols when configured in an RRAS server?

   _____

   _____

KEY TERM QUIZ

Use the following vocabulary terms to complete the sentences below. Not all of the terms will be used. Definitions for these terms can be found in "Managing a Microsoft Windows 2000 Network Environment Study Guide."

> Authentication
>
> Encryption
>
> Routing and Remote Access Service (RRAS)
>
> Virtual private network (VPN)
>
> Point-to-Point Tunneling Protocol (PPTP)
>
> Remote Authentication Dial-In User Service (RADIUS)
>
> Extensible Authentication Protocol (EAP)
>
> Microsoft-created Challenge Handshake Authentication Protocol (MS_CHAP v2)
>
> Data Encryption Standard (DES)
>
> Layer Two Tunneling Protocol (L2TP)

1. A mechanism for securing data, encrypting data, and translating it into a secret code, and read only with the correct key to translate the secret code back to the original data is named _____.

2. _____ allows a client and an RRAS server to negotiate the exact authentication scheme.

3. A VPN protocol _____ is used to establish a secure tunnel between two endpoints over an unsecure network.

4. _____ uses a LAN protocol such as TCP/IP encapsulated within a WAN protocol sending data securely over a public network.

5. _____ determines whether a user has a valid user account with the proper permissions to access a resource.

LAB SOLUTIONS FOR CHAPTER 13

In this section, you'll find solutions to the lab exercises, Lab Analysis Test, and Key Term Quiz.

Lab Solution 13.01

Tony wants to provide network access using the existing public connection by configuring a virtual private network (VPN) for all users to connect by.

A virtual private network (VPN) is the ability to exchange data between two computers—a client and a server—across an interconnected network in a fashion that makes the user believe that that user is connected directly, securely, and privately, while using a public connection such as the Internet. It is a cost-effective solution for users that travel and need to connect from various locations.

In this lab exercise, you configured a VPN. By the end of this lab, you were able to

■ Configure RRAS to function as a VPN server.

cross
Reference

For further information, refer to the VPN section of Chapter 13 in "Managing a Windows 2000 Network Environment Study Guide."

To create, share, and publish a shared folder, perform the following steps:

Step 1. Click Start | Programs | Administrative Tools and select the Routing and Remote Access console. Right-click the server object in the tree and select Configure and Enable Route and Remote Access from the context menu, as shown next. This will launch the Routing and Remote Access Server Setup Wizard.

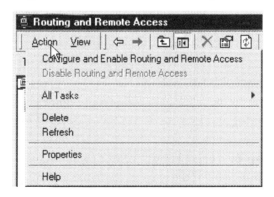

Step 2. Bypass the Welcome window and proceed to the Common Configurations window. Select Virtual Private Network (VPN) Server and click Next to proceed to the Remote Client Protocols page.

Step 3. Verify that TCP/IP appears in the Protocols list and that the Yes, All of the Available Protocols Are On This List option is selected, as shown next. Click Next to continue on to the Internet Connection window.

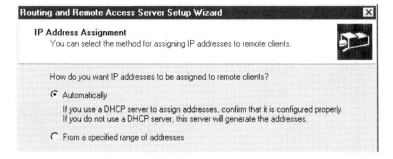

Step 4. In the Internet Connections list, select <No Internet Connection> and proceed to the IP Address Assignment window. Verify that the Automatically option is selected, as shown next. Proceed to the Managing Multiple Remote Access Servers window.

Step 5. Make sure the No, I Don't Want to Set Up This Server to Use RADIUS Now option is selected, a shown in Figure 13-1. Proceed to the Completing the Routing and Remote Access Server Setup Wizard window.

Step 6. Click Finish. A Routing and Remote Access message box will appear warning you of the need to configure a DHCP relay agent to support the relaying of DHCP messages from remote access clients.

Step 7. Complete the configuration process, close the wizard, and start the RRAS server if it doesn't start on its own.

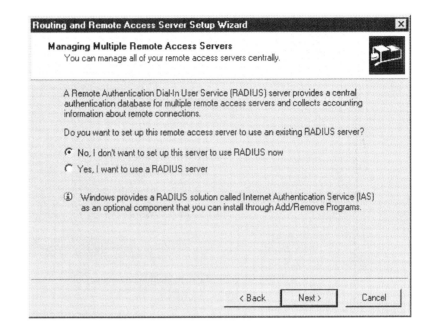

FIGURE 13-1

A RADIUS server is only used when multiple RRAS servers are configured on a network. It allows for centralized administration of accounts.

Lab Solution 13.02

In this lab scenario, you need to apply a set of parameters by which regional directors and sales representatives dialing into the network can access the resources on the network. They need the ability to check available stock and place orders.

Remote access policies can be used to impose connection parameters such as maximum session time, idle disconnect time, required secure authentication methods, required encryption, and so on.

In this lab, you configured a remote access policy. By the end of this lab, you were able to

- Select groups for remote access permissions.
- Set up access constraints.
- Make IP address assignments.
- Configure IP Packet Filters.
- Configure Remote Access Server encryption.

To create and configure a remote access policy, perform the following steps:

Step 1.   Open the Routing and Remote Access console by going to Start | Programs | Administrative Tools and selecting Routing and Remote Access. Expand the application tree in the left pane by double-clicking the server. Right-click Remote

Access Policy and select New Remote Access Policy from the context menu, as shown here. The Add Remote Access Policy window opens.

Step 2. Enter a user-friendly name, **Remote Access**, as shown here, and click Next to continue. The Add Remote Access Policy Conditions dialog box opens.

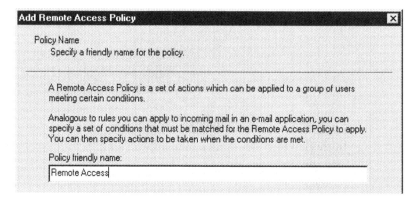

Click Add to add a condition. Select one attribute from the list of attributes. Each attribute will create a slightly different process, and you will need to configure the attribute appropriately. For this example, select Windows-Groups, as shown in Figure 13-2.

Step 3. Click Add to go to the Groups dialog box. Then click Add to open the Select Groups window and select the Domain Users group for the rule. Click OK to return to the Groups dialog box. Click OK to add the Windows-Groups condition to the policy, as shown next. If you were to add an additional condition, users would need to meet both conditions to have the policy applied (a logical AND operation).

FIGURE 13-2

Using the
Windows-Groups
attribute allows
you to enable
remote access
by user groups.

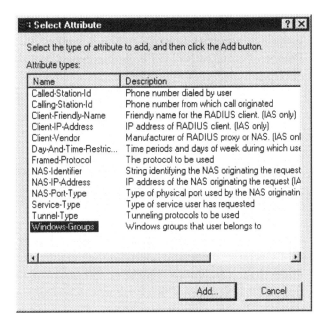

Step 4. Click Next to open the Add Remote Access Policy window. You can either grant or deny remote access permission by selecting the appropriate option. Select the Grant Remote Access Permission option, as shown next, and click Next.

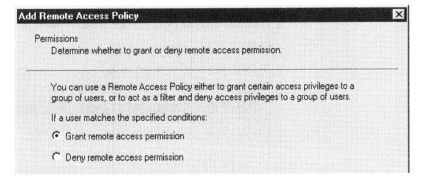

Step 5. The Edit Dial-in Profile dialog box that opens allows you to access the dial-in profile for the users affected by this policy. Click OK to return to the User Profile screen. Click Finish to complete the creation of the profile.

Lab Solution 13.03

In part two of the first lab scenario, you need to configure the VPN service to fit the needs of the users using the Point-to-Point Tunneling Protocol (PPTP) for encryption.

The Point-to-Point Tunneling Protocol (PPTP) is a de facto industry standard tunneling protocol first supported in Windows NT 4.0. It is an extension of the Point-to-Point Protocol (PPP) and leverages the authentication, compression, and encryption mechanisms of PPP.

In this lab exercise, you configured a virtual private network (VPN). By the end of this lab, you were able to

■ Configure ports for VPN use.

■ Configure a port using Point-to-Point Tunneling Protocol (PPTP).

To configure a VPN service, perform the following steps:

Step 1. Open the Routing and Remote Access by going to Start | Programs | Administrative Tools and select Routing and Remote Access. Click the Ports entry under the server. Notice that the sample configuration shows five PPTP ports and five L2TP/IPSec ports. This is because the server had five user licenses configured when the Routing and Remote Access Service was installed.

Step 2. To configure the ports, select Ports in the left pane and right-click. From the context menu, select Properties. The Ports Properties dialog box opens, as shown here:

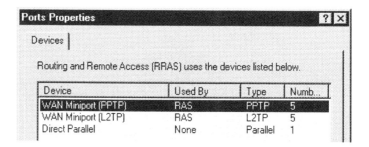

Step 3. Select the PPTP protocol you need to modify and click Configure. The Configure Device dialog box opens, as shown next. This screen allows you to set the direction of the interface (inbound only or inbound and outbound) as well as the number of ports. You've decided on inbound only. You can also set the phone number of the device, although this is of limited use with a VPN implementation. Close out of both windows and return to the RRAS console.

```
Configure Device - WAN Miniport (PPTP)                            [?] [X]

You can use this device for remote access requests or demand-dial
connections.

[✓] Remote access connections (inbound only)

[ ] Demand-dial routing connections (inbound and outbound)

Phone number for this device:         [                    ]

You can set a maximum port limit for a device that supports multiple ports.

Maximum ports:        [5    ] [▲▼]


                                      [   OK   ]   [ Cancel ]
```

Lab Solution 13.04

In this lab scenario, you needed to provide the most secure way for the sales representatives to access the network. The Che Bella Cosa Importing Company had you, the network administrator, install a new Windows 2000 Routing and Remote Access server. The marketing agents overseas connect to the network via a VPN. Your U.S. regional sales representatives access the network using point-to-point connections. What is the most secure way to ensure that the sales representatives have a secure VPN access?

PPTP is a great solution to the tunneling needs of clients. It is relatively simple to set up when compared to L2TP/IPSec, and it provides good security when used with a username/strong password method. PPTP is an industry standard protocol that was first supported in Windows NT 4.0. This protocol uses the authentication, compression, and encryption of the PPP. PPTP is still in wide use on networks today.

In this lab exercise, you verified a secure method of user authentication when connecting via the Remote Access Server. By the end of this lab, you were able to

■   Configure Remote Access Security.

To configure security for a specific group of settings for a Remote Access Security policy, perform the following steps:

Step 1.   Open the Routing and Remote Access by going to Start | Programs | Administrative Tools and selecting Routing and Remote Access. Right-click the server and select Properties. This opens the server properties.

Step 2.   Select the Security tab, which is shown next. By default, the Authentication Provider is Windows Authentication, as shown next. The

Accounting Provider should also be set to Windows Accounting. A log of connection requests and sessions is kept by Windows.

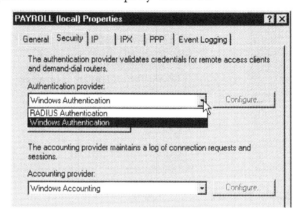

Lab Solution 13.05

In part two of the previous lab scenario, you need to verify additional secure user authentication. Windows 2000 supports a number of authentication and encryption protocols.

In this lab, you verified addition protocols for secure remote access. By the end of this lab, you were able to

- Use Routing and Remote Access console.
- Configure authentication protocols MS-CHAP and MS-CHAP v2.
- Set a strong level of encryption.

To configure authentication and encryption protocols for remote access, perform the following steps:

Step 1.   First, you need to confirm the authentication protocols. Open the Routing and Remote Access by going to Start | Programs | Administrative Tools and selecting Routing and Remote Access. Right-click the server and select Properties. This opens the server properties. Select the Security tab and click Configure.

Step 2.   The Authentication Methods window opens, as shown in Figure 13-3. Verify that the MS-CHAP and MS-CHAP v2 protocol for a connection is checked off. Click OK. Click OK to return to the Routing and Remote Access console.

Step 3.   Now, configure the encryption protocol level. Select Remote Access Policies from the tree view. In the right pane, right-click the Remote Access policy you want to set the encryption level for and select Properties. From the Policy Properties dialog box, click Edit Profile.

Several
authentication
protocols are
available for
remote
connections.

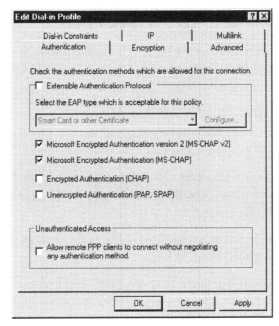

Step 4. Click the Encryption tab. Set the encryption level to Strong, as shown in Figure 13-4. You can set the encryption levels to No Encryption, Basic, Strong, or any combination of the three. Click OK to apply the setting and exit out of remaining windows.

Select the Strong
encryption level
for this remote
access connection.

ANSWERS TO LAB ANALYSIS

1. The four authentication protocols are Extensible Authentication Protocol (EAP), Microsoft Challenge Handshake Authentication Protocol (MS-CHAP), Challenge Handshake Authentication Protocol (CHAP), and Shiva Password Authentication Protocol (SPAP).

2. The Windows 2000 Routing and Remote Access Service will support IPSec, a suite of cryptographic-based protection services and security protocols; PPTP, Microsoft's legacy protocol for VPN support; and L2TP, a combination of PPP and L2F tunneling protocols.

3. A VPN reduces remote access costs by doing away with the need for long-distance dial-up connection for remote users. By connecting to the Internet using a local ISP, telephone charges are kept to a minimum.

4. The four most common connection problems are no answer errors, not enough available ports, authentication errors, and L2TP connectivity errors.

5. Encryption protocols are used to encrypt data sent between a client and a RRAS server. This ensures that the data passed between a client and server is secure. In cases such as VPN, encryption should always be required if data is being sent across a public network.

ANSWERS TO KEY TERM QUIZ

1. Encryption

2. Extensible Authentication Protocol (EAP)

3. Point-to-Point Tunneling Protocol (PPTP)

4. Virtual private network (VPN)

5. Authentication

MICROSOFT CERTIFIED SYSTEMS ASSOCIATE

14

Implementing Security Policies

LAB EXERCISES

14.01   Configuring Routing and Remote
Access Service (RRAS) to Use
Internet Authentication Service (IAS)

14.02   Configuring Authentication and
Encryption Protocol for Demand
Dial Routers

14.03   Troubleshooting a Remote
Access Policy

     ▥   Lab Analysis Test

     ▥   Key Term Quiz

     ▥   Lab Solutions

T oday, many companies are giving users remote access to their global network. This is due to the evolution of the on-site office, which is morphing into a virtual office, accessible from anywhere that there is dial-up or VPN connection. In some cases, providing remote access may be rather simple, giving employees access to a single network resource—their e-mail. Access to the company's network from home may be limited to a small group of executives and only when they dial into the company's remote access server (RAS).

In other cases, it may be more complicated, where a large number of employees are required to access network resources remotely because they spend most of their time outside of the office, or work from home. An example of this may be a mobile sales group, or traveling sales representatives. In view of today's global economy, they may require access from almost anywhere in the world. Whether it be from a laptop computer or a kiosk at an airport, almost universal access is required to a variety of resources, which not only include e-mail but also the company's web server, a database server, and possibly files on the file server.

Keeping security at the forefront of network administration, not only in-house but also for remote access, must include policies to protect the network from a potential breach of security. Remote access, for a majority of companies, is the only place other than their Internet firewall where the network is directly accessible from the outside world. The remote user gains access from an open access point through a dial-up connection or a virtual private network (VPN) connection. Therefore, it is imperative that these access points are made as secure as possible.

In this chapter, we look at the process of implementing Remote Access Service (RAS) in conjunction with Internet Authentication Service (IAS). We also address the requirements surrounding Remote Access policies and profiles that are put in place. In addition, we include an exercise on the selection of appropriate encryption and authentication protocols that will provide for a secure connection. Lastly, we look at troubleshooting problems that relate to security.

Configuring Remote Access Service (RAS) to Use Internet Authentication Service (IAS)

25 Minutes

You are the network administrator for Coast-to-Coast Bounty Hunters, Inc. You have users connecting to regional remote access points throughout the country. Managing the authentication process for each region is a monumental task. The solution is to configure and enable Microsoft's Internet Authentication Service to be the central point of authority that each RAS server will use to authenticate remote users. How would you incorporate this into your system?

Learning Objectives

Supporting a large number of remote access users that may be connecting to multiple RAS servers can be difficult to administer even if you're using remote access policies. What makes this complicated is the possibility that clients may be connecting from different landline sites, or through a virtual private network (VPN). Additionally, the RAS servers may be located in different locations, maybe worldwide. Windows 2000 includes IAS to support this environment.

Remote Authentication Dial-In User Service (RADIUS) is an industry standard protocol for providing centralized authentication, authorization, and accounting services for distributed dial-up networking. A RADIUS server typically used by an Internet service provider (ISP) receives user and connection information from multiple dial-up servers, then authenticates and authorizes the requests.

Internet Authentication Service (IAS) is a RADIUS server. IAS enables you to centrally manage user authentication, authorization, and accounting, and you can use it to authenticate users in databases on your Windows NT 4.0 or Windows 2000 domain controller. It supports a variety of network access servers (NAS), including Routing and Remote Access.

In this lab, you'll configure RAS to use IAS. By the end of this lab, you'll be able to

■ Install and configure IAS as a RADIUS server.

■ Configure RAS to use IAS to authenticate users.

Lab Materials and Setup

For this lab exercise, you'll need

■ A working computer

■ An installed network card (NIC)

■ Windows 2000 Server software (installed)

■ TCP/IP installed

■ Active Directory (AD) installed

Getting Down to Business

To configure IAS and RAS, perform the following steps:

Step 1.   First, we need to install IAS since it is not installed by default in Windows 2000 server. Use the Add/Remove Wizard to perform the installation.

Step 2.   Next, we need to configure the IAS server in order to meet our security requirements and allow connections from other RADIUS clients. Access the IAS console and open the Properties dialog window for the local service. Configure the settings for the Service tab by entering the server name, **IAS**.

Step 3.   On the RADIUS tab, configure the port numbers for authentication and account requests. Next, register the IAS server in Active Directory using the context menu of the Internet Authentication Service object.

Step 4. Configure the RRAS server to use IAS for authentication and remote access policy by adding the RRAS server as an IAS client. To carry this out, you need to create a new client. In the dialog window, type a name for the RRAS server. It need not be the same as the actual computer name.

Step 5. In the next dialog window, enter the IP address or DNS name for the IAS client and configure the Client-Vendor field as RADIUS Standard. Enter and confirm a password that will be used as the primary security mechanism.

Step 6. The last step is to configure the RRAS server to use IAS for authenticating users. Access the Routing and Remote Access console. Open the Properties dialog window of the server and select the Security tab. Configure the Authentication Provider field and the Accounting Provider field with the appropriate option from the pull-down menu.

Step 7. Open the Configuration dialog window and add the IAS server information. Enter the server name and configure the secret to be the same as the IAS server. The rest of the settings will be accepted as defaults. Accept your settings.

lab
Warning

Once the settings have been accepted, you will receive a warning that the RRAS server will need to be restarted. Be sure to stop and start the service in order for your settings to take effect.

CERTIFICATION OBJECTIVE 14.02

Configuring Authentication and Encryption Protocol for Demand-Dial Routers

20 Minutes

You are the network administrator for Broken Wing Travel Agency, a six-location agency in the greater New York state area. You have just upgraded your system to include a remote access server for dialing-in to the main office, which contains the client database. The last steps for the installation are to apply authentication and encryption protocols for the dial-up service. What necessary steps must you take to enable this level of security?

Learning Objectives

An important security concern of remote access clients is the authentication protocol that is negotiated during the connection establishment process to provide for a secure connection. The various protocols are Extensible Authentication Protocol (EAP), which is an arbitrary authentication mechanism that validates a remote access connection; Microsoft Challenge Handshake Authentication Protocol (MS-CHAP), which is a nonreversible, encrypted password authentication protocol; and MS-CHAP v2, which provides two-way, mutual authentication. The remote access client receives verification that the remote access server that is being dialed has access to the user's password. With MS-CHAP v2, the cryptographic key is always based on the user's password and an arbitrary challenge string. Each time the user connects with the same password, a different cryptographic key is used: The Shiva Password Authentication Protocol (SPAP) is a reversible encryption mechanism employed by Shiva (a remote access server produced by LanRover); Password Authentication Protocol (PAP) uses plaintext passwords and is the least sophisticated authentication protocol; and Windows 2000 supports unauthenticated access, which means that user credentials (a username and password) are not required by the caller.

Additionally, for dial-up connections, Windows 2000 implements an Internet Protocol Security (IPSec) standard that uses Data Encryption Standard (DES) encryption and Triple DES (3DES). DES uses a 56-bit encryption key, which is considered barely adequate for business use, and 3DES takes the 56-bit encryption concept and triples it, making it a 168-bit encryption key. This encryption standard provides data integrity during a remote connection, keeping the data and the client identity safe from possible deciphering.

cross
Reference

For further information, refer to the section on remote access encryption and authentication in "Managing a Microsoft Windows 2000 Network Environment Study Guide."

In this lab, you'll configure remote access security. By the end of this lab, you'll be able to

- Configure an authentication protocol.
- Apply an encryption protocol.

Lab Materials and Setup

For this lab exercise, you will need

- A working computer
- An installed network card (NIC)
- Windows 2000 Server software (installed)
- TCP/IP installed
- Active Directory (AD) installed

Getting Down to Business

To configure an authentication protocol and apply an encryption level, perform the following steps:

Step 1. First, we need to configure the authentication protocol for the server. Access the Routing and Remote Access console. Open the Properties dialog window of the server.

Step 2. Within the Security tab of Properties, access the Authentication Methods dialog window. There are several authentication options that can be chosen. Enable authentication for Microsoft's Challenge Handshake Authentication Protocol (MS-CHAP) and for version 2. Click OK to apply the settings.

Step 3. Next, we need to apply encryption settings for remote access. Expand the Remote Access Policies folder and select the <blank> policy that we will edit. Open the Properties window and edit the Dial-in Profile. We have decided to apply strong encryption on the profile. Click OK to apply your choice. Exit the Routing and Remote Access console.

CERTIFICATION OBJECTIVE 14.03

Troubleshooting a Remote Access Policy

15 Minutes

You manage a newly installed Windows 2000 Remote Access Server used for remote dial-in access. The consulting firm that built the server suggested that on a regular basis you review the login reports that the server generates. The reports identify the users that have logged in—their day and time—and you also scan the report for any errors. You notice that there have been several occurrences where a user is showing up on the report logging in after normal hours. You had made it clear that day and time restrictions were to be implemented to prevent users from dialing in during unauthorized times. What configuration settings could be allowing this user to log in without permission?

Learning Objectives

A common problem with remote access policies is that an open-ended connection policy has been implemented, allowing for dial-in access at any time, any day. Troubleshooting open-ended connections can be very time-consuming when there are multiple remote access policies in place.

A remote access policy is a fancy term to identify a set of rules that govern connections. There can be multiple policies, which may apply to, and execute for, a particular user. Routing and Remote Access Service is added to the host and a default remote access policy is created, allowing access when dial-in permission is enabled.

With multiple remote access policies, different sets of conditions can be applied to different remote access clients or different requirements can be applied to the same remote access client based on the parameters of the connection attempt. For example, multiple remote access policies can be used to allow or deny connections if the user account belongs to a specific group, or define different days and times for different user accounts based on group membership. You can also configure different authentication methods for dial-up and VPN remote access clients; configure different authentication or encryption settings for Point-to-Point Tunneling Protocol (PPTP) or Layer Two Tunneling Protocol (L2TP) connections, or configure different maximum session times for different user accounts based on group membership.

The trick is to put some thought into the design of a policy and how it affects other policies that may be in place.

In this lab, you'll resolve a configuration issue that involves a remote access policy. By the end of this lab, you'll be able to

■ Troubleshoot a remote access policy.

Lab Materials and Setup

For this lab exercise, you will need

■ A working computer

■ An installed network card (NIC)

■ Windows 2000 Server software (installed)

■ TCP/IP installed

■ Active Directory (AD) installed

Getting Down to Business

To review and troubleshoot policy settings, perform the following steps:

Step 1. Access the Routing and Remote Access console. Expand the tree into the Remote Access Policy folder. Select the policy we wish to review and resolve—Allow Access if Dial-in Permission Is Enabled.

Step 2. Display the Properties dialog window for the policy. There are three sections to this window: the Policy Name box, which allows you to create one or more policies with unique names; a Conditions box, which allows you to set day and time restrictions; and another Conditions section, which lets you either grant or deny permission for a dial-in session. We notice the problem, which is allowing the user to login after hours. Make the appropriate setting adjustments. Apply and save your settings.

LAB ANALYSIS TEST

1. You are a junior network administrator studying for your certification exam. One of the objectives requires you to know the five authentication protocols used by your Remote Access Service. List and briefly explain the five protocols.

   _____

   _____

2. Explain why IPSec would be a valuable framework for a dial-up connection environment.

   _____

   _____

3. Briefly explain what Remote Authentication Dial-In User Service (RADIUS) is, and in which environment you would use it.

   _____

   _____

4. You manage a Windows 2000 Remote Access server used for remote dial-in access. Certain users belong to more than one group and would require specialized access parameters. How would multiple remote access policies be helpful?

   _____

   _____

5. If you have Windows 2000 Professional clients dialing into a Remote Access server, which of the authentication protocols would you enable, and why?

   _____

   _____

KEY TERM QUIZ

Use the following vocabulary terms to complete the sentences below. Not all of the terms will be used. Definitions for these terms can be found in "Managing a Microsoft Windows 2000 Network Environment Study Guide."

Remote Access Service (RAS)

Internet Authentication Service (IAS)

Virtual private network (VPN)

Remote Access Dial-in User Service (RADIUS)

Encryption Protocol

Authentication Protocol

Challenge Handshake Authentication Protocol (MS-CHAP)

Layer Two Tunneling Protocol (L2TP)

Point-to-Point Tunneling Protocol (PPTP)

Extensible Authentication Protocol (EAP)

1. _____ is an industry standard protocol for providing centralized authentication, authorization, and accounting services for distributed dial-up networking.

2. The nonreversible, encrypted password authentication protocol is known as _____.

3. _____ is considered to be a RADIUS server implemented by Microsoft.

4. The service used to give remote access clients access to a network via a dial-up connection is known as _____.

5. An important security concern of remote access clients is the _____, which is negotiated during the connection establishment process to provide for a secure connection.

LAB SOLUTIONS FOR CHAPTER 14

In this section, you'll find solutions to the lab exercises, Lab Analysis Test, and Key Term Quiz.

Lab Solution 14.01

Using Remote Authentication Dial-In User Service (RADIUS) provides a centralized authentication, authorization, and accounting service for a large distributed dial-up networking. Internet Authentication Service (IAS) is a RADIUS server that enables you to centrally manage user authentication, authorization, and accounting.

In this lab, you configured RAS to use IAS. By the end of this lab, you were able to

- Install and configure IAS as a RADIUS server.
- Configure RAS to use IAS to authenticate users.

To configure IAS and RAS, perform the following steps:

Step 1. First, we need to install IAS since it is not installed by default in Windows 2000 server. Click Start | Settings | Control Panel and then click the Add/Remove Programs icon. Click the Add/Remove Windows Components button on the left side of the window frame. This opens the Windows Components Wizard, as shown in Figure 14-1.

Step 2. Click the Networking Services entry and click Details. Notice that the check box next to Networking Services is grayed. This indicates that not all services have been installed. From the Networking Services window, select and check Internet Authentication Service, as shown in Figure 14-2. Click OK to install the service.

FIGURE 14-1

This wizard lets you add or remove Windows 2000 components.

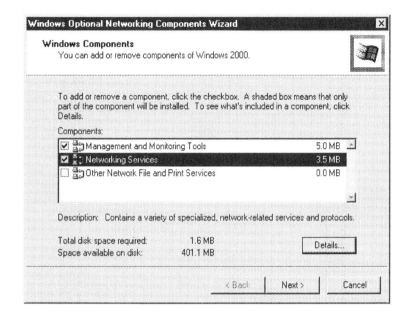

FIGURE 14-2

Select IAS, the subcomponent of Networking Services.

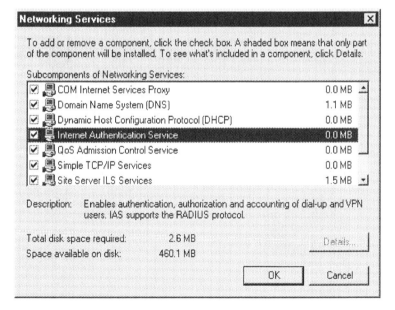

Step 3. Next, we need to configure the IAS server in order to meet our security requirements and allow connections from other RADIUS clients. Click Start | Programs | Administrative Tools | Internet Authentication Service. Right-click the Internet Authentication Service (Local) object and select Properties, as shown here.

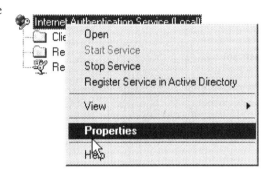

You can change the Description field to something other than IAS, as shown here:

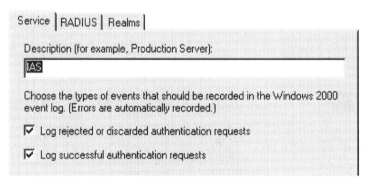

Step 4 On the RADIUS tab, take note of the port numbers used for authentication and account requests. Click OK to save any changes. Next, we need to register the IAS server in Active Directory if we want the IAS server to check Active Directory for user information. Right-click the Internet Authentication Service object and select Register Service in Active Directory in the context menu, as shown here.

Step 5.   Since our objective is to manage a large pool of RAS servers, we need to configure the RRAS servers to use IAS for authentication and remote access policy by adding the RRAS server as an IAS client. To carry this out, you need to create a new client. Right-click the Clients folder in Internet Authentication Service and select New Client. In the dialog window, type a name for the RRAS server—**southernbell**, as shown next. We use the same name as the computer to avoid any confusion. Click Next.

Step 6.   In the next dialog window, enter the IP address or DNS name for the IAS client and configure the Client-Vendor field as RADIUS Standard, as shown in Figure 14-3. Enter and confirm a password that will be used as the primary security mechanism. This password will be used by all IAS clients and is the primary security mechanism. The goal is to make it as complex as possible, preferably alphanumeric. For our purpose, we will use *password*. Click Finish to complete the process. Close out of the Internet Authentication Service console.

Step 7.   The last step is to configure the RRAS server to use IAS for authenticating users. Access the Routing and Remote Access console by Clicking Start | Programs | Administrative Tools | Routing and Remote Access. Right-click the server object and select Properties. Within the dialog window, select the Security

FIGURE 14-3

Configure the
RADIUS with a
DNS server, a
client-vendor
type, and a
shared secret.

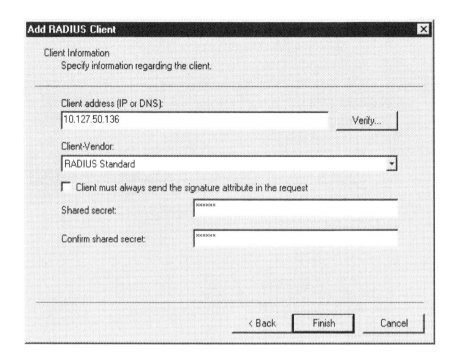

tab. Configure the Authentication Provider field and the Accounting Provider field
to use RADIUS Authentication, as shown here:

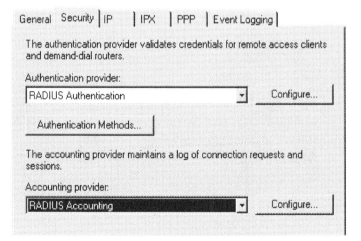

Step 8. Click Configure to add the IAS server information. Enter the server name, **southernbell**, as shown next. Enter the same secret (password) we used for the IAS server. The rest of the settings will be accepted as defaults. Click OK to accept the settings. A message warning you to stop and restart the RRAS service will appear. Click OK.

Lab Solution 14.02

An important security concern of remote access clients is the authentication protocol that is negotiated during the connection establishment process to provide for a secure connection. Additionally, for dial-up connections, Windows 2000 implements an Internet Protocol Security (IPSec) standard that uses Data Encryption Standard (DES) encryption and Triple DES (3DES).

In this lab, you configured remote access security. By the end of this lab, you were able to

■ Configure an authentication protocol and apply an encryption protocol.

lab

Warning

Before you can successfully perform this lab, you need to return the authentication provider and the accounting provider assigned in the previous lab back to Windows authentication and Windows accounting, respectively. Otherwise, the remote access policies will not appear within the Routing and Remote Access console tree.

To configure an authentication protocol and apply an encryption level, perform the following steps:

Step 1. First, we need to configure the authentication protocol for the server. Access the Routing and Remote Access console by Clicking Start | Programs | Administrative Tools | Routing and Remote Access. Right-click the server and select Properties to open the Properties dialog window.

Step 2. Select the Security tab and click Authentication Methods to open the dialog window, as shown in Figure 14-4. There are several authentication options that we can choose. Verify that the authentication methods for Microsoft's Challenge Handshake Authentication Protocol (MS-CHAP), and for version 2, are checked. Click OK to apply the settings and return to the Routing and Remote Access console.

Step 3. Next, we need to apply encryption settings for remote access. Expand the Remote Access Policies folder in the right pane of the console. The left pane will

Remote Access security is configured in this dialog window.

Authentication Methods

The server authenticates remote systems by using the selected methods in the order shown below.

☐ Extensible authentication protocol (EAP)

    EAP Methods...

☑ Microsoft encrypted authentication version 2 (MS-CHAP v2)
☑ Microsoft encrypted authentication (MS-CHAP)
☐ Encrypted authentication (CHAP)
☐ Shiva Password Authentication Protocol (SPAP)
☐ Unencrypted password (PAP)

Unauthenticated access
    ☐ Allow remote systems to connect without authentication

OK   Cancel

display policies that have been added. Select and right-click Remote Access Policies, as shown next, and select Properties.

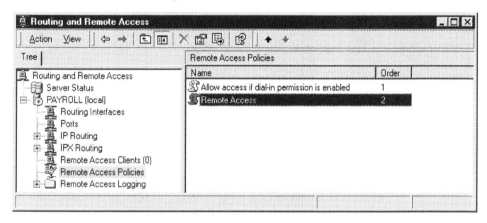

Step 4. Within the Properties window, click Edit Profiles. Select the Encryption dialog window, where we have decided to apply strong encryption on the profile, as shown next. Be sure the other levels are unchecked. Click OK twice to apply your choice. Exit the Routing and Remote Access console.

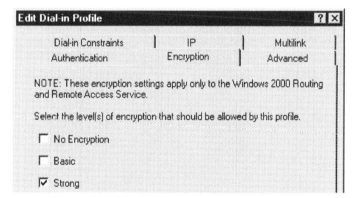

Lab Solution 14.03

A common problem with remote access policies is that a connection has liberal policies—in fact, no time restrictions have been placed. Troubleshooting where the lack of restriction is located can be very time-consuming when there are multiple remote access policies in place.

In this lab, you resolved a configuration issue that involves a remote access policy. By the end of this lab, you were be able to

■ Troubleshoot a remote access policy.

To review and troubleshoot policy settings, perform the following steps:

Step 1. Access the Routing and Remote Access console by Clicking Start | Programs | Administrative Tools | Routing and Remote Access. Expand the tree into the Remote Access Policy folder. Right-click Allow Access if Dial-in Permission Is Enabled and select Properties.

Step 2. There are three sections within this window: the Policy Name box, which allows you to create one or more policies with unique names; a Conditions box, which allows you to set day and time restrictions; and another Conditions section, which lets you either grant or deny permission for a dial-in session. These elements are shown in Figure 14-5. The error, which is causing the remote user's ability to dial in at any time, is the date and time policy. We need to restrict the dial-in times only to regular work hours. Make the appropriate setting adjustments, as shown in Figure 14-6. Click OK to apply and save your settings. Exit the Routing and Remote Access console.

LAB SOLUTIONS FOR CHAPTER 14

The date and time settings have no dial-in restrictions.

FIGURE 14-5

The date and
time settings
have no dial-in
restrictions.

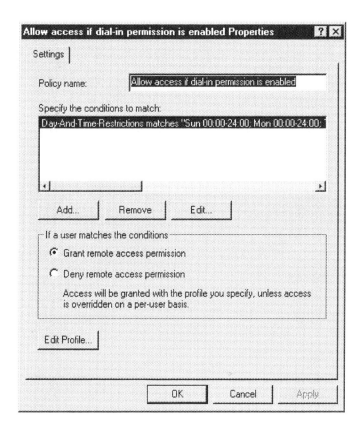

FIGURE 14-6

Allow dial-in
ability only
during weekday
hours of 8 am
to 6 pm.

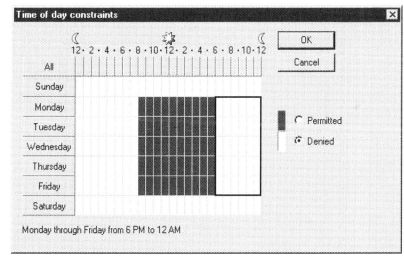

ANSWERS TO LAB ANALYSIS

1. The five authentication protocols are Extensible Authentication Protocol (EAP), which uses an arbitrary authentication mechanism to validate a remote access connection; Microsoft Challenge Handshake Authentication Protocol (MS-CHAP), which is a nonreversible, encrypted password authentication protocol; MS-CHAP v2, which provides two-way, mutual authentication. the Shiva Password Authentication Protocol (SPAP), which is a reversible encryption mechanism employed by Shiva (a remote access server produced by LanRover); and Password Authentication Protocol (PAP), the least sophisticated protocol, which uses plaintext passwords.

2. Internet Protocol Security (IPSec) standard uses Data Encryption Standard (DES) encryption and Triple DES (3DES), which provide a 56-bit encryption key and a 168-bit encryption key, respectively. This encryption standard provides data integrity during a remote connection, keeping the data and the client identity safe from possible deciphering.

3. Remote Authentication Dial-In User Service (RADIUS) is an industry standard protocol for providing centralized authentication, authorization, and accounting services for distributed dial-up networking. A RADIUS server typically used by an Internet service provider (ISP) receives user and connection information from multiple dial-up servers, then authenticates and authorizes the requests.

4. With multiple remote access policies, different sets of conditions can be applied to different remote access clients, or different requirements can be applied to the same remote access client based on the parameters of the connection attempt. You can also configure different authentication methods for dial-up and VPN remote access clients.

5. MS-CHAP v2 provides two-way, mutual authentication. It is considered to be the most secure protocol. The remote access client receives verification that the remote access server that is being dialed has access to the user's password. With MS-CHAP v2, the cryptographic key is always based on the user's password and an arbitrary challenge string. Each time the user connects with the same password, a different cryptographic key is used.

ANSWERS TO KEY TERM QUIZ

1. Remote Authentication Dial-In User Service (RADIUS)

2. Microsoft Challenge Handshake Authentication Protocol (MS-CHAP)

3. Internet Authentication Service (IAS)

4. Remote Access Service (RAS)

5. Authentication Protocol

MICROSOFT CERTIFIED SYSTEMS ASSOCIATE

15

Implementing Terminal Services for Remote Access

LAB EXERCISES

15.01   Configuring Terminal Services for
         Remote Administration

15.02   Configuring Terminal Services
         Licensing Server

15.03   Configuring Remote Access Security

■   Lab Analysis Test

■   Key Term Quiz

■   Lab Solutions

Terminal Services provides remote access to a server through what is called "thin client" software. This thin client software serves as a terminal emulator by transmitting only the user interface of the program to the client in what can be considered as screen slices. The client keyboard and mouse clicks are sent to the server to be processed. And, each user logs on and sees only their individual session, managed transparently by the server operating system and independent of any other client session. Third-party software companies provided such products prior to Terminal Services—PCAnywhere, and CarbonCopy, just to name two.

Client software is hardware and software independent. Only Macintosh computers or UNIX-based workstations require additional third-party software.

Terminal Services can be deployed on the server in either application server mode, which delivers the Windows 2000 desktop along with the most current Windows-based applications to computers that might not normally be able to run Windows, or remote administration mode, which provides remote access for administering your server from virtually anywhere on your network. It's as if the administrator, and user, has hyperextendible arms that can reach the Windows 2000 server from a distance.

In this chapter, we'll look at how an administrator can remotely log on to and manage Windows 2000 systems from anywhere on the network, which includes a local area network (LAN), a wide area network (WAN), and even a dial-up connection. We'll see how Terminal Services licensing is used to register and track licenses for Terminal Services clients. The licensing service simplifies the task of license management for the system administrator and helps determine how many additional licenses may need to be purchased. Lastly, we'll investigate the security aspect of Terminal Services. Terminal Services has a built-in Remote Desktop Protocol (RDP) encryption feature that allows administrators to encrypt all or some of the RDP data sent between the Windows 2000 Server and Terminal Services Clients at three different levels (low, medium, or high), depending on security needs. The default encryption level is medium, providing bidirectional encryption between the server and the client. Administrators can also limit the number of user logon attempts to prevent hackers from attacking a server, as well as the connection time of any individual user or groups of users. Administrators can provide security restrictions either for individual users or an entire server. This even includes limiting the ability to redirect to local devices.

cross Reference *For further information about Terminal Services, refer to Chapter 15 of "Managing a Microsoft Windows 2000 Network Environment Study Guide."*

CERTIFICATION OBJECTIVE 15.01

Configuring Terminal Services for Remote Administration

10 Minutes

Nathan is a network administrator for the Sentimental Greeting Card Company. Three new Windows 2000 Server computer have been included on the network, one for each of the three departments. The servers are situated in various parts of the building, which is two stories tall. He has his domain controller in his office, so there is no problem administering it. But, he wants to manage the other three servers also from his office. What does Nathan need to install on each server?

Learning Objectives

Remote Administration is a powerful tool for an administrator to remotely administer any Windows 2000 Server computer on a network using a TCP/IP connection. You can administer file and print sharing, edit the registry from another computer on the network, or perform any task as if you were sitting at the console.

Remote Administration mode only installs the remote access components of Terminal Services. It does not install application-sharing components. This means you can use Remote Administration with very little overhead on mission-critical servers. Terminal Services allows a maximum of two concurrent Remote Administration connections. No additional licensing is required for those connections, and you do not need a license server.

In this lab, you'll install and configure Terminal Services in the remote Administration mode. By the end of this lab, you'll be able to

- Install Terminal Services on a Windows 2000 server.
- Configure Terminal Services for Remote Administration.

Lab Materials and Setup

For this lab exercise, you'll need

- A working computer
- Installed network card (NIC)
- Windows 2000 Server software (installed)
- TCP/IP installed
- Active Directory (AD) installed
- Windows 2000 Server CD

Getting Down to Business

To install and set up Terminal Services, perform the following steps:

Step 1. Start the Windows Component Wizard through the Add/Remove Programs utility. From the Components list, select Terminal Services and begin the installation.

Step 2. In the setup page, you have a choice of specifying the Application Server mode or the Remote Administration mode. Select the latter and continue.

Step 3. The wizard will copy the files needed to install Terminal Services. After the file copying, the installation process is complete. Once completed, the system will need to be rebooted.

CERTIFICATION OBJECTIVE 15.02

10 Minutes

Configuring Terminal Services Licensing Server

Joshua is the Terminal Services administrator for a small manufacturing company. He has a number of thin network clients, and on March 23, 2000, he configured a terminal server in Application mode to host their applications. Initially, everything ran very smoothly. However, on June 21, 2000, all the clients received messages that there were not enough client licenses, and their applications failed to run. How could Joshua have prevented this problem?

Learning Objectives

Terminal Services has its own method for licensing clients that log on to terminal servers, separate from the licensing method for Windows 2000 Server clients. Before a client is allowed to log on to a Terminal Services server in application mode, the client must receive a valid license issued by a license server. When using Terminal Services in remote administration mode, two concurrent connections are automatically allowed to log on and a license server is not required.

In application server mode, Terminal Services requires an activated license server installed on the network. Once activated, the license server provides a secure way to install client licenses and issue them to Terminal Services clients. When a client attempts to log on to a terminal server for the first time, the server will contact the license server to request a license for the client. This license is in addition to the license for a Windows 2000 server. There is a grace period of 90 days provided for the use of applications hosted on a Terminal Services server. If licenses have not been purchased by the end of 90 days, the clients will no longer be able to connect.

In this lab, we'll enable Terminal Services Licensing to avoid future connectivity and licensing problems. By the end of this lab, you'll be able to

■ Deploy Terminal Services Licensing in Application Server mode.

lab

ⓦarning *In a production system, licenses will need to be purchased from Microsoft to allow permanent access to applications on the terminal server.*

Lab Materials and Setup

For this lab exercise, you will need

■ A working computer

■ Installed network card (NIC)

■ Windows 2000 Server software (installed)

- TCP/IP installed
- Active Directory (AD) installed

Getting Down to Business

To install and set up Terminal Services Licensing, perform the following steps:

Step 1.   Start the Windows Component Wizard through the Add/Remove Windows Components utility. From the Components list, select Terminal Services Licensing and begin the installation.

Step 2.   Proceed to the Terminal Services Setup window after selecting the component. In this window, be sure to select Application Server Mode. Continue on to the Terminal Services Licensing Setup window.

Step 3.   This window presents you with a choice of license servers: Domain License Server and Enterprise License Server. Select Domain License Server since the terminal server is a domain within a geographical location in a Windows 2000 domain. Continue to the Configuring Components window and complete the installation.

CERTIFICATION OBJECTIVE 15.03

Configuring Remote Access Security

15 Minutes

Sarah is the manager for your company's tax division. During tax time, she hires temporary professionals to help with tax preparation for the previous year. Most of these individuals access the database remotely from their own offices. She needs to add and configure these users to provide access to the company's database. How can you give Sarah the appropriate permissions to manage these users without compromising the network's level of security?

Learning Objectives

Since Terminal Services is a powerful tool, it's important to secure access to the terminal server. Without proper permissions granted appropriately to the user, the user may be able to delete files on the server, change settings, or possibly shut the server down. Two security issues that may need to be addressed are Remote Access Security and Transmission Security.

If Terminal Services is installed in Remote Administration mode, only members of the Administrator group are able to connect to the terminal server. A case or two may arise where users other than administrators need to log into the terminal server. For example, you may grant a user permission to reset passwords in their container, and you need the user to log into the terminal server to perform such a task.

The other issue is the security of the information transmitted between a user and the terminal server. Remote Desktop Protocol (RDP) is used to carry communication between a server and a user. Although the data is encrypted, you can adjust the level of the encryption to meet certain security requirements. Enable encryption whenever there is a risk of unauthorized transmission interception on the link between server and user. Terminal Services provides multilevel encryption support. Before setting the level of encryption for a connection, determine the appropriate level of security.

In this lab, we'll look at these two security issues. By the end of this lab, you'll be able to

- Implement Remote Access Security.
- Implement Transmission Security.

Lab Materials and Setup

For this lab exercise, you will need

- A working computer
- Installed network card (NIC)
- Windows 2000 Server software (installed)
- TCP/IP installed
- Active Directory (AD) installed

Getting Down to Business

To configure Remote Access Security and Transmission Security, perform the following steps:

Step 1. First, we need to set Remote Access Security. Click Start | Administrative Tools | Terminal Services Configuration. Right-click on the RDP-Tcp connection and select Properties from the context menu. Click the Permissions tab and add the Terminal Server User group. The three permissions available are Full Control, User Access, and Guest Access. Full Control allows complete control of a session, including administering other sessions, remote control, and sending messages. User Access allows for user logon, sending messages, and querying information about other sessions. Guest Access allows for session logon only.

Select Full Control of remote sessions, which includes the ability to administer other sessions.

Step 2. Next, we need to set the encryption level to meet our security requirements. Low secures all data sent from the client to the server by using a 56-bit key between a Windows 2000 Terminal server and a Windows 2000 client. Medium secures data sent in both directions by using a 56-bit key between a Windows 2000 Terminal server and a Windows 2000 client. High secures data sent in both directions using the 128-bit key encryption. This level of encryption is available only in the United States or Canada. It is not exportable. Select the General tab window.

Step 3. Adjust the Encryption level option to High. This level of encryption will provide secure transmission between a client and the server. Click OK to apply and close the window. Exit the Terminal Services Configuration window.

LAB ANALYSIS TEST

1. Briefly explain the two methods that you can use to deploy Terminal Services.

   _____

   _____

2. You have successfully deployed Terminal Services in the Application Server mode for your company. One of the end users wishes to understand how the remote connection works. Briefly explain how the process works.

   _____

   _____

3. You have just explained the Terminal Services deployment, including licensing needs, to members of the IT department representing hardware, networking, and software support. The software team manager would like you to further explain the need for licensing when the company already has software, Windows 2000 Professional, and Windows 2000 Server user licenses.

   _____

   _____

4. Another team member, from the hardware group, wishes to understand what the additional permissions for Terminal Services provides and what purposes they serve.

   _____

   _____

5. List and explain the three encryption levels provided by Transmission Security.

   _____

   _____

KEY TERM QUIZ

Use the following vocabulary terms to complete the sentences below. Not all of the terms will be used. Definitions for these terms can be found in "Managing a Microsoft Windows 2000 Network Environment Study Guide."

Remote Desktop Protocol (RDP)

Terminal Services Licensing

Application Server mode

Remote Administration mode

Domain license server

Enterprise license server

Thin client

Terminal emulator

Bidirectional encryption

Secure transmission

1. _____ is used to register and track licenses for Terminal Services clients.

2. Terminal Services has a built-in _____ encryption feature that allows administrators to encrypt data sent between the Windows 2000 Server and Terminal Services clients.

3. _____ is a powerful tool for an administrator to remotely administer any Windows 2000 Server computer on a network using a TCP/IP connection.

4. _____ provides remote access to a server through what is called "thin client" software.

5. The process of scrambling information that is transmitted between two points on the network to ensure confidentiality is known as _____.

LAB SOLUTIONS FOR CHAPTER 15

In this section, you'll find solutions to the lab exercises, Lab Analysis Test, and Key Term Quiz.

Lab Solution 15.01

Nathan needs to install Terminal Services on each computer so he can view and manage each Windows 2000 Server computer.

In this lab, you installed and configured Terminal Services in the Remote Administration mode. By the end of this lab, you were able to

■ Install Terminal Services on a Windows 2000 server.

■ Configure Terminal Services for Remote Administration.

To install and set up Terminal Services, perform the following steps:

Step 1.　Click Start | Settings | Control Panel. Double-click the Add/Remove Windows Components icon to start the Windows Component Wizard. From the Components list, check off Terminal Services and click Next to open the Terminal Services Setup window, as shown in Figure 15-1.

Step 2.　In the setup page, you have a choice of specifying the Application Server Mode or the Remote Administration Mode. Select Remote Administration Mode, as shown in Figure 15-2, and click Next.

FIGURE 15-1

Add or remove
components
using the
Windows
Components
Wizard.

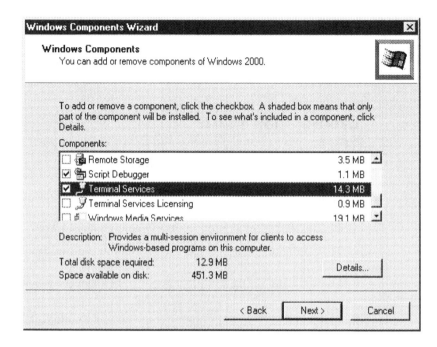

FIGURE 15-2

Remote
administration
mode allows
for two
administrators
to remotely
manage the
terminal server.

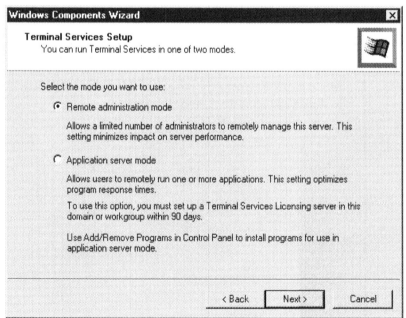

Step 3. The wizard will copy the files needed to install Terminal Services. After the file copying is complete, click Finish. You will be prompted to reboot the computer. Once installed, additional administration tools will be added to the Administrative Tools program group, including Terminal Services Manager, Terminal Services Configuration, and Terminal Services Client Creator, as shown here.

- Active Directory Sites and Services
- Active Directory Users and Computers
- Certification Authority
- Component Services
- Computer Management
- Configure Your Server
- Connection Manager Administration Kit
- Console1
- DHCP
- DNS
- Internet Authentication Service
- Internet Services Manager
- Local Security Policy
- Network Monitor
- Performance
- Routing and Remote Access
- Server Extensions Administrator
- Services
- Terminal Services Client Creator
- Terminal Services Configuration
- Terminal Services Manager
- WINS

Lab Solution 15.02

On March 23, 2000, Joshua configured a terminal server in Application mode to host applications. Then, on June 21, 2000, all the clients received messages that there were not enough client licenses, and their applications failed to run. Because Terminal Services has its own method for licensing clients that log on to terminal servers, before a client is allowed to log on to a Terminal Services server in application mode the client must receive a valid license issued by a license server. There is a grace period of 90 days provided for the use of applications hosted on a Terminal Services server. If licenses have not been purchased by the end of 90 days, the clients will no longer be able to connect.

In this lab, you enabled Terminal Services Licensing to avoid future connectivity and licensing problems. By the end of this lab, you were able to

■ Deploy Terminal Services Licensing in Application Server mode.

lab
Warning

In a production system, licenses will need to be purchased from Microsoft to allow permanent access to applications on the terminal server.

To install and set up Terminal Services Licensing, perform the following steps:

Step 1. Click Start | Settings | Control Panel. Double-click the Add/Remove Programs icon to start the Windows Component Wizard. From the Components list, check off Terminal Services Licensing, as shown here, and click Next.

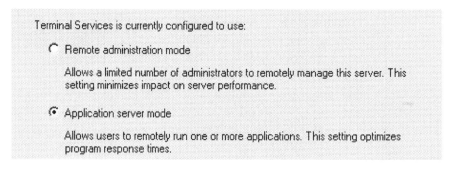

Step 2. In the Terminal Services Setup window, after selecting the component, be sure to select Application Server Mode, as shown here:

When Terminal Services is in remote administration mode, you do not need to enable Terminal Services Licensing. Click Next to move to the Windows Compatibility window. Check the radio button next to Permissions Compatible with Windows 2000 Users, as shown next. Click Next twice to move to the Terminal Services Licensing Setup window.

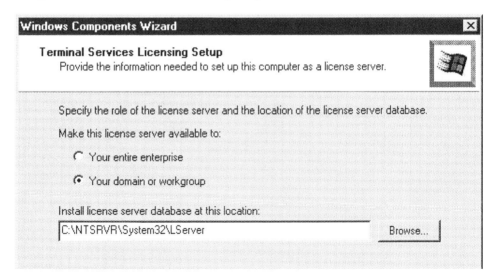

⊙ Permissions compatible with Windows 2000 Users

Select this option to provide the most secure environment in which to run applications. By default, Terminal Server Users will have the same permissions as members of the Users group and thus may not be able to run many legacy applications.

○ Permissions compatible with Terminal Server 4.0 Users

Select this option to provide an environment that is compatible with most legacy applications.

Step 3. In the Terminal Services Licensing Setup window, you select which type of license server is required—either a domain license server or an enterprise license server. By default, a license server is installed as a domain license server, which is appropriate if you want to maintain a separate license server for each domain. An enterprise license server is appropriate if your network includes several domains. Select Your Domain or Workgroup license server, as shown next, since the terminal server is in a domain within a geographical location in a Windows 2000 domain. Click Next to move to the Configuring Components window. Click Finish to complete the installation. You will be prompted to reboot.

Lab Solution 15.03

Since Terminal Services is a powerful tool, it's important to secure access to the terminal server. Without proper permissions granted appropriately to the user, the user may be able to delete files on the server, change settings, or possibly shut the server down.

If Terminal Services is installed in Remote Administration mode, only members of the Administrator group are able to connect to the terminal server. In our case, we have a user other than an administrator that needs to log into the terminal server to manage a group of users. We also want to secure information transmitted between Sarah and the terminal server.

In this lab, you looked at these two security issues. By the end of this lab, you were able to

- Implement Remote Access Security.
- Implement Transmission Security.

To configure Remote Access Security and Transmission Security, perform the following steps:

Step 1. First, we need to set Remote Access Security. Launch the Terminal Services Configuration program. Right-click the RDP-Tcp connection icon on the right side of the window and select Properties, as shown here:

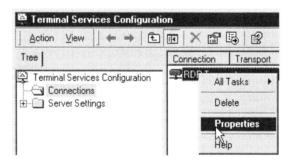

Click the Permission tab. Click the Add button to access the Select Users, Computers, or Groups window. Scroll through the objects, then select and add the Terminal Server User group, as shown next. Click OK to accept.

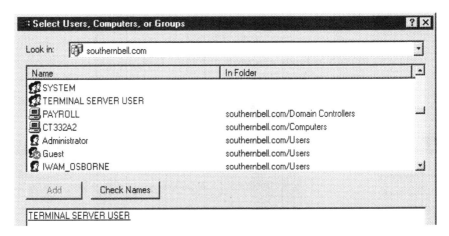

Step 2.   Give Full Control permission to the Terminal Server User group in the Permissions tab window, as shown in Figure 15-3. This allows for full control of remote sessions, including the ability to administer other sessions.

FIGURE 15-3

The Terminal Server User group will consist of users trusted to help administer remote sessions.

Step 3. Next, we need to set the encryption level to meet our security requirements. Select the General tab window and adjust the Encryption Level option to High, as shown in Figure 15-4. This level of encryption will provide secure transmission between a client and the server. Click OK to apply the settings and exit the Properties window. Exit the Terminal Services Configuration window.

A high encryption level will ensure data security between client and server during a remote session.

RDP-Tcp Properties

Remote Control | Client Settings | Network Adapter | Permissions
General | Logon Settings | Sessions | Environment

RDP-Tcp

Type: Microsoft RDP 5.0

Transport: tcp

Comment:

Encryption

Encryption level: High

All data sent between the client and the server is protected by encryption based on the server's maximum key strength.

☐ Use standard Windows authentication

OK | Cancel | Apply

ANSWERS TO LAB ANALYSIS

1. Terminal Services can be deployed on the server in either application server mode, which delivers the Windows 2000 desktop along with the most current Windows-based applications to computers that might not normally be able to run Windows, or remote administration mode, which provides remote access for administering a server from virtually anywhere on a network.

2. Terminal Services provides remote access to a server known as "thin client" software. This thin client software serves as a terminal emulator by transmitting only the user interface of the program to the client in what can be considered as screen slices. The client keyboard and mouse clicks are sent to the server to be processed. Each user logs on and sees only their individual session, managed transparently by the server operating system functioning independently of any other client session.

3. Terminal Services licenses client logons independently from Windows product licensing. The Terminal Services Licensing service obtains and manages license tokens for devices that connect to a Windows 2000 terminal server—for example, Terminal Services configured in application server mode. In this mode, licenses are required only for those users that are connected to the terminal server obtaining applications from the server. When using Terminal Services in remote administration mode, two concurrent sessions are allowed to log on to the server without requiring a license server.

4. The three permissions available are Full Control, User Access, and Guest Access. Full control allows complete control of a session, including administering other sessions, remote control, and sending messages. User Access allows for user logon, sending messages, and querying information about other sessions. Guest Access allows for session logon only.

5. There are three encryption levels to meet terminal service security needs. Low encryption level secures all data sent from the client to the server by using a 56-bit key between a Windows 2000 Terminal server and a Windows 2000 client. Medium encryption level secures data sent in both directions by using a 56-bit key between a Windows 2000 Terminal server and a Windows 2000 client. High encryption level secures data sent in both directions using the 128-bit key encryption. This level of encryption is available only in the United States or Canada.

ANSWERS TO KEY TERM QUIZ

1. Terminal Services Licensing

2. Remote Desktop Protocol

3. Remote Administration

4. Terminal Services

5. Encryption

16

Configuring Network Address Translation (NAT) and Internet Connection Sharing

LAB EXERCISES

16.01   Installing and Configuring Internet
        Connection Sharing

16.02   Troubleshooting Internet Connection
        Sharing Problems

16.03   Configuring Routing and Remote
        Access to Perform NAT

■   Lab Analysis Test

■   Key Term Quiz

■   Lab Solutions

I nternet connection sharing (ICS) provides an easy way of connecting computers in a home network or small office network to the Internet using a single Internet connection. By enabling ICS, network address translation, addressing, and name resolution services are provided for all computers on a small office/home office (SOHO) network. Once ICS is enabled, users in a SOHO environment can use browser and e-mail applications as if they were already connected to an Internet service provider (ISP). The ICS computer makes a connection to the ISP so users reach the specified web address or resource. To use the Internet connection-sharing feature on the internal private network, TCP/IP is configured through the local area connection to obtain an IP address automatically. The public side can be configured for static or dynamic IP addressing.

Windows 2000 Network Address Translation (NAT) allows computers in a SOHO environment to share a single Internet connection. The computer on which Internet connection sharing (ICS) is installed can act as a network address translator (*also* NAT), a simplified DHCP server, a DNS proxy, and a WINS proxy. This is the protocol that provides the vehicle for sharing a single connection. Private addresses are assigned within the network to individual computers. Each private address is then translated, or assigned to, a public address. The public address is the gateway out to the Internet.

In this chapter, we will look at ICS and NAT, and the services they provide for the small office. We'll first install and configure ICS, and see how it can provide a quick and easy way to connect to the Internet. Then, we'll look at how PING and IPconfig can help with troubleshooting ICS problems by checking that there is a live connection from a computer and by releasing and reassigning DHCP addresses. Lastly, we'll look at how NAT ties in with Routing and Remote Access Services—how NAT is used together with an Internet connection to provide security and address preservation.

CERTIFICATION OBJECTIVE 16.01

Installing and Configuring Internet Connection Sharing

15 Minutes

You are the network administrator of the Wild West Tour Company specializing in Grand Canyon, Las Vegas, and Hoover Dam tours. The office in Arizona that manages the Grand Canyon tours has a Window 2000 server connected to the

Internet and six computers connected to the network. You need to install ICS on the server in order to connect the six computers to the Internet. How would you enable this feature?

Learning Objectives

In this lab, you'll enable the ICS feature on a Windows 2000 server. By the end of this lab, you'll be able to

■ Install and configure ICS.

Lab Materials and Setup

For this lab exercise, you'll need

■ A working computer

■ Installed network card (NIC)

■ Windows 2000 Server software (installed)

■ TCP/IP installed

■ Network connection

lab
⚠arning   *To complete this lab, a network connection via a network or dial-up is required.*

Getting Down to Business

To install and configure ICS, perform the following steps:

Step 1.   Access the Properties window of My Network Places on the desktop. This will open the Network and Dial-up Connections window.

Step 2.   Open the Properties window of the Dial-up Connection icon that represents your Internet connection. This opens the Dial-up Connection Properties window.

Step 3.   Through the Sharing tab, select the Enable Internet Connection Sharing for This Connection option. The Enable On-Demand Dialing option is enabled by default.

Step 4.   Click OK. A warning appears stating that the IP address of the adaptor will change if you continue. Click Yes to complete the installation.

CERTIFICATION OBJECTIVE 16.02

Troubleshooting Internet Connection Sharing Problems

15 Minutes

As a network administrator, you periodically have to attend conferences and vendor shows that apply to networking, software, and hardware issues and innovations. You're leaving tomorrow for a four-day conference. You've just completed an ICS configuration on your Windows 2000 server. You want to make sure that in your absence, your junior administrator can easily troubleshoot any issues that may arise with ICS. You need to put together a list of troubleshooting tools and steps that he can follow if he needs to resolve any connectivity issues. Which two major tools would you suggest, and how would your junior administrator use them?

Learning Objectives

In this lab, you'll provide information on these two tools and how they would be used when troubleshooting a connectivity issue. By the end of this lab, you'll be able to

■ Understand PING and IPconfig.

Lab Materials and Setup

For this lab exercise, you'll need

■ Pencil and paper

Getting Down to Business

To explain PING and IPconfig, perform the following steps:

Step 1.   Explain the use of PING to determine that a computer is connected.

_____

_____

Step 2.   Explain the use of IPconfig to determine that TCP/IP settings have been applied to a computer.

_____

_____

For further information, refer to the PING and IPconfig section of Chapter 16 in "Managing a Microsoft Windows 2000 Network Environment Study Guide."

CERTIFICATION OBJECTIVE 16.03

Configuring Routing and Remote Access to Perform NAT

20 Minutes

You are the network administrator for Artisan city's fine arts museum's ticket reservation service. You've just installed a Windows 2000 server on a network with ten computers to connect the network to the Internet. The museum was able to purchase only one IP address for Internet access by the museum. What is the most cost-effective item or component to add to the server to let the users simultaneously connect to the Internet?

Learning Objectives

In this lab exercise, you'll install and configure NAT on your Windows 2000 server. By the end of this lab, you'll be able to

- Install NAT on the Windows 2000 server.
- Configure NAT for the network.

Lab Materials and Setup

This lab will require the following:

- A working computer
- Installed network card (NIC)
- Windows 2000 Server software (installed)
- TCP/IP installed
- Network Connection

Getting Down to Business

To install and configure NAT on the Windows 2000 server, perform the following steps:

Step 1. Launch the Routing and Remote Access Console. Expand the IP Routing icon and right-click on General. Select New Routing Protocol.

Step 2. Select Network Address Translation and click OK. Right-click the newly created Network Address Translation icon and select Properties. In the General tab, select Log Errors and Warnings if it's not already selected.

Step 3. Select the Address Assignment tab. Select Automatically Assign IP Address by Using DHCP. This tab lets you configure the private IP addresses and configure the DHCP service used in conjunction with NAT. Verify that the IP address is equal to 192.168.0.0 and the subnet mask is equal to 255.255.255.0.

Step 4. Click OK to complete the process and return to the RRAS console. Now, you need to configure the NAT interface.

Step 5. Select New Interface using the NAT icon. Select Remote Router as the interface to be used as the LAN interface and click OK. The dialog box for that connection opens. You will set this interface as an external connection. Now, select Public Connection to the Internet.

Step 6. Click OK to complete this process. Repeat the above steps for the Private Connection to the Internet.

LAB ANALYSIS TEST

1. As the network administrator of a small frozen meat delivery company, you are asked to connect to the Internet for the first time. The company wants to provide access to 12 employees, but wants to keep expenses to a minimum. What service should you install to ensure that the employees can successfully connect to the Internet and comply with the company's request?

   _____

   _____

2. Your surgical supply company, Precision Cuts, with a 100-user network, has had you install a Windows 2000 server to connect the network to the Internet. None of your users are able to connect to the Internet, even though the server does connect. What do you think may be the problem?

   _____

   _____

3. You're the administrator of the Up-Tick Investment Agency's Windows 2000 server. You're considering setting up ICS so the agents can connect to the Internet. What benefit would ICS provide?

   _____

   _____

4. Small Hands Toy Co. has recently installed several Windows 2000 Server systems and upgraded some clients to Windows 2000 Professional. Other computers on the system include Windows NT and Windows 98. The network needs Internet access, so the company has leased a dedicated 256MB fiber-optic connection. Which additional cost-effective services need to be enabled on a Windows 2000 server to allow users to connect to the Internet?

   _____

   _____

5. What are the three components of ICS?

   _____

   _____

KEY TERM QUIZ

Use the following vocabulary terms to complete the sentences below. Not all of the terms will be used. Definitions for these terms can be found in "Managing a Microsoft Windows 2000 Network Environment Study Guide."

> Internet Connection Sharing (ICS)
>
> Network Address Translation (NAT)
>
> Request for Comments
>
> Internet service provider
>
> Loopback address
>
> PING
>
> IPconfig
>
> Public IP addresses
>
> Private IP addresses
>
> Routing and Remote Access Server

1. Designated as a range of non-Internet connected IP addresses, _____ are used for internal network use only.

2. _____ are a range of IP addresses that are required to be registered with the Internet Assigned Numbers Authority.

3. A Windows 2000 service used to allow a SOHO to share a dial-up Internet connection is named _____.

4. Used for a diagnostic procedure, 127.0.0.1 is a _____, in which a signal is transmitted and returned to verify that a network device is functional.

5. _____ is an Internet standard that enables a Windows 2000 Server to use one set of IP addresses on an internal network and a different IP address on the external network.

LAB SOLUTIONS FOR CHAPTER 16

In this section, you'll find solutions to the lab exercises, Lab Analysis Test, and Key Term Quiz.

Lab Solution 16.01

You need to install ICS on a Windows 2000 server in order to connect six computers at the Grand Canyon office to the Internet.

In this lab, you enabled the ICS feature on the Windows 2000 server. By the end of this lab, you were able to

■ Install and configure ICS.

lab

⚠ Warning *To complete this lab, a network connection via a network or dial-up is required.*

To install and configure Internet Connection Sharing, perform the following steps:

Step 1. Right-click My Network Places on the desktop and select Properties. This will open the Network and Dial-up Connections window. You can also open Properties through the Control Panel and select Network and Dial-up Connections.

Step 2. Right-click the Dial-up Connection icon that represents your Internet connection and select Properties from the context menu. This opens the Dial-up Connection Properties window.

Step 3. Click the Sharing tab, which will allow other computers on the network to share this connection. Select the Enable Internet Connection Sharing for this Connection option, as shown in Figure 16-1. The Enable On-Demand Dialing option is enabled by default.

Step 4. Click OK. A warning appears stating that the IP address of the adaptor will change if you continue:

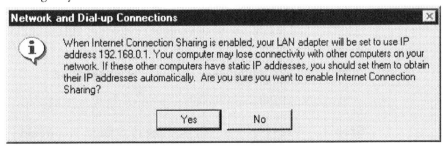

Click Yes to complete the installation.

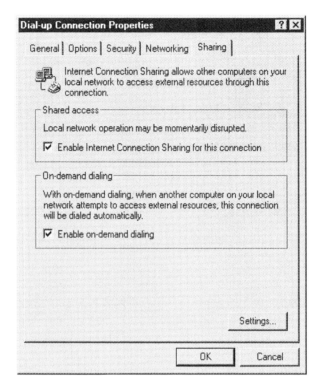

Lab Solution 16.02

In this lab, you needed to put together a list of troubleshooting tools and steps that your junior administrator could follow if he needed to resolve any connectivity issues. You suggested two utilities, and how he would be able to use them.

Situations may arise where, although ICS is configured on a Windows 2000 server and all is checked out between the server and clients, there may be clients who connected one day but could not connect the next. To help solve these types of issues, we can employ two rather simple and widely used command-line utilities: PING and IPconfig.

In this lab, you provided information on these two tools and how they would be used when troubleshooting a connectivity issue. By the end of this lab, you were able to

■ Understand PING and IPconfig.

To explain PING and IPconfig, perform the following steps:

Step 1. Since PING is your first line of defense, you would PING the loopback IP address—127.0.0.1. The syntax is ping 127.0.0.1. This will indicate that the network card is seated in the slot and working properly. If it passes this test, you want to PING the server's IP address. If this fails, you know there is a problem with the assigned IP address to the computer. If it passes, there is a problem at the server side.

Step 2.   If the PING fails, you need to use IPconfig to view the IP address assigned to the computer. Further, you may need to release and renew the assignable IP address for that computer. There are three steps involved, each with a particular switch:

- **ipconfig /all**   This command switch displays the computer's IP address, subnet mask, and default gateway information.
- **ipconfig /release**   This command switch releases the IP address for the network adaptor.
- **ipconfig / renew**   This command switch refreshes the IP address for the network adaptor.

This screen displays the results of the ipconfig /all command:

```
Command Prompt                                                    _ □ ×

C:\>ipconfig /all

Windows 2000 IP Configuration

        Host Name . . . . . . . . . . . . : Payroll
        Primary DNS Suffix . . . . . . . : southernbell.com
        Node Type . . . . . . . . . . . : Hybrid
        IP Routing Enabled. . . . . . . . : No
        WINS Proxy Enabled. . . . . . . . : No
        DNS Suffix Search List. . . . . . : southernbell.com

Ethernet adapter Local Area Connection 3:

        Connection-specific DNS Suffix  . :
        Description . . . . . . . . . . . : 3Com EtherLink XL 10/100 PCI For Com
plete PC Management NIC (3C905C-TX) #2
        Physical Address. . . . . . . . . : 00-01-02-69-2C-FF
        DHCP Enabled. . . . . . . . . . . : No
        IP Address. . . . . . . . . . . . : 192.168.142.1
        Subnet Mask . . . . . . . . . . . : 255.255.0.0
        Default Gateway . . . . . . . . . : 192.168.100.1
        DNS Servers . . . . . . . . . . . : 10.127.69.69

C:\>_
```

lab Hint   **These two switches are normally used together. You would not want to use *ipconfig /release* without invoking *ipconfig /renew*.**

cross Reference   **For further information, refer to the PING and IPconfig section of Chapter 16 in "Managing a Microsoft Windows 2000 Network Environment Study Guide."**

Lab Solution 16.03

In this scenario, you've just installed a Windows 2000 server on a network with ten computers to connect the network to the Internet. Because the museum was able to purchase only one IP address to connect to the Internet, you need to add NAT.

In this lab exercise, you'll install and configure NAT on your Windows 2000 server. By the end of this lab, you'll be able to

- Install NAT on the Windows 2000 server.
- Configure NAT for the network.

Step 1.   Click Start | Programs | Administrative Tools | Routing and Remote Access Console.
Expand the IP Routing icon in the left window pane and right-click on General.

Step 3.   Select New Routing Protocol to open the dialog box. Select Network Address Translation, as shown next, and click OK. The Network Address Translation icon will show as an icon under IP Routing.

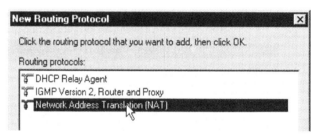

Step 5.   Right-click the newly created Network Address Translation icon and select Properties. In the General tab, select Log Errors and Warnings if it's not already selected, as shown next.

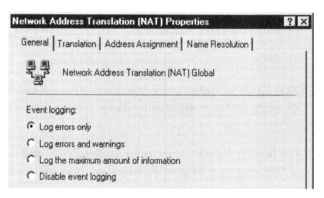

lab
Warning   *It's important to periodically check the Event Viewer for any errors or warnings that pertain to NAT.*

Step 6. Select the Address Assignment tab. Select Automatically Assign IP Address by Using DHCP, as shown next. This tab lets you configure the private IP addresses and configure the DHCP service used in conjunction with NAT. Verify that the IP address is equal to 192.168.0.0 and that the subnet mask is equal to 255.255.255.0.

Network Address Translation (NAT) Properties

General | Translation | Address Assignment | Name Resolution |

The network access translator can automatically assign IP addresses to computers on the private network by using Dynamic Host Configuration Protocol (DHCP).

☑ Automatically assign IP addresses by using DHCP

IP address: 192 . 168 . 0 . 0

Mask: 255 . 255 . 255 . 0

Exclude...

Step 7. Click OK to complete the process and return to the RRAS console. Now we need to configure the NAT interface.

Step 8. Right-click the NAT icon again and select New Interface. The New Interface for NAT dialog box opens. Select Remote Router as the interface to be used as the LAN interface and click OK, as shown here.

New Interface for Network Address Translation (NAT)

This routing protocol runs on the interface that you select below.

Interfaces:

Remote Router

Step 9. The dialog box for that connection opens. You will set this interface as an external connection. Therefore, select Public Interface Connected to the Internet. Also select Translate TCP/UDP Headers. Selecting this option designates this computer as the interface of data transmission. Both are shown here.

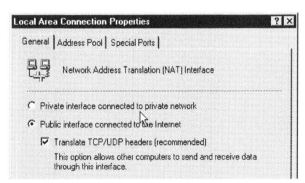

Local Area Connection Properties

General | Address Pool | Special Ports |

Network Address Translation (NAT) Interface

○ Private interface connected to private network

● Public interface connected to the Internet

☑ Translate TCP/UDP headers (recommended)

This option allows other computers to send and receive data through this interface.

lab

ⓗint *Since you are using a single public IP address allocated by your ISP, no other IP address configuration is needed.*

Step 10.   Click OK to complete this process. The above steps have configured NAT as an external connection to the Internet using the assigned IP address. The following steps will configure another interface for the local connection.

Step 11.   Right-click NAT again and select New Interface. The New Interface for NAT dialog box opens. Select Local Area Connection as the interface to be used as the LAN interface and click OK, as shown here.

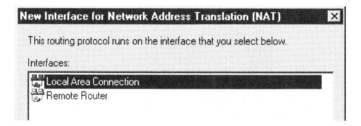

Step 12.   The dialog box for that connection opens. You will set this interface as an internal connection. Therefore, select Private Interface Connected to the Private Network, as shown next. This window identifies the NAT interface as connected to a private network. Click OK to complete this process.

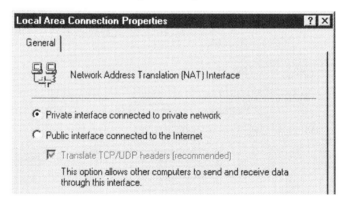

ANSWERS TO LAB ANALYSIS

1. The perfect solution for a small company is to implement ICS, which also bundles the services necessary to make the connection work.

2. You need to install ICS for the connection to work. ICS uses NAT to allow the company to use private addresses on its internal network and translate them to a single public address for Internet connection.

3. There are two reasons for using NAT. First, it provides a level of security when your network is connected to the Internet. It hides the internal addresses of the network and restricts the services that can access the internal network. It also lets you conserve public IP addresses.

4. You've purchased one public IP address from the ISP along with the dedicated line. One way your users can connect is to assign internal IP addresses to those computers. Another includes using a multi-homed server and a firewall/gateway hardware device. The Windows 2000 server needs to have Routing and Remote Access enabled and configured as an Internet Connection Server to connect to the Internet link.

5. Translation component, which acts as a network address translator (NAT), translating the IP addresses and TCP/UDP port numbers of packets that are forwarded between the private network and the Internet; and addressing component, which provides IP address configuration information to the other computers on SOHO network. It is a simplified DHCP server that allocates an IP address, a subnet mask, a default gateway, and the IP address of a DNS server; and a name-resolution component, which provides name-to-IP-address resolution for the other computers on the office or home network.

ANSWERS TO KEY TERM QUIZ

1. Private IP addresses

2. Public IP addresses

3. Internet Connection Sharing

4. Loopback address

5. Network Address Translation

17

Installing and Configuring Server and Client Hardware

LAB EXERCISES

17.01   Verifying Hardware Compatibility

17.02   Configuring Driver Signing Options

17.03   Verifying Digital Signatures

17.04   Configuring Operating System Support for Legacy Hardware Devices

■   Lab Analysis Test

■   Key Term Quiz

■   Lab Solutions

T he ability to configure server hardware is essential to a smooth-running operating system. Windows 2000 makes the configuration of hardware components easier through the implementation of the Plug and Play utility. This utility ensures that PnP components are automatically detected and that their drivers are installed. Non-PnP components can still be installed, but the drivers need to be manually configured. Either way, all devices must be on the Windows 2000 hardware compatibility list (hcl), or a verified driver supplied by the vendor. Digitally signing a file is the process guaranteeing a particular file comes from the source it claims to come from—that it's not "bootleg."

In this chapter, we will look at how we can verify hardware compatibility and obtain updates from the hardware compatibility list (hcl) database on Microsoft's web site. We'll also see how verified and digitally signed driver files play an important role with regard to system compatibility issues. And lastly, we'll look at how to troubleshoot the nonfunctioning legacy piece of hardware that is not recognized by Windows 2000.

CERTIFICATION OBJECTIVE 17.01

Verifying Hardware Compatibility

20 Minutes

Approximately a month ago you purchased a new Windows 2000 Server computer to join your existing domain of four servers. Before you bring it online, you want to ensure that the latest device drivers are installed on the computer. What is the most efficient way of obtaining driver updates?

Learning Objectives

In this lab, you'll perform Windows update for your server. By the end of this lab, you'll be able to

- Use the Windows Update web site.
- Search for Windows 2000 Server hardware and software updates.

Lab Materials and Setup

For this lab exercise, you'll need

- A working computer
- Installed network card (NIC)

- Windows 2000 Server software (installed)
- TCP/IP installed
- Network, or Internet, connection

Getting Down to Business

To look for and install the latest Windows 2000 Server updates, perform the following steps:

Step 1. Log on to Microsoft's Windows Update web site and scan for the latest operating system updates.

Step 2. Browse through the available updates in each category, select the update of your choice, and add it to the collection of updates you want to install. A full description of each update is provided.

Step 3. Once you have selected all the updates you want, complete the installation process and exit the browser. Depending on the update, you may be required to reboot the server.

CERTIFICATION OBJECTIVE 17.02

Configuring Driver Signing Options

15 Minutes

Marcia is trying to install a driver for an older network card. When she does, a dialog box appears telling her she is not allowed to install unsigned drivers on her Windows 2000 Server. The installation fails. What must she do to get around this message and install the driver?

Learning Objectives

In this lab, you'll configure driver signing options for hardware devices installed on the server. By the end of this lab, you'll be able to

- Use driver signing option configuration.
- Configure driver signing options.

Lab Materials and Setup

For this lab exercise, you'll need

- A working computer
- Installed network card (NIC)
- Windows 2000 Server software (installed)
- TCP/IP installed

Getting Down to Business

To configure driver signing options, perform the following steps:

Step 1.   Access the Properties window of the My Computer icon from the context menu. Select the Hardware tab. Now, select the Driver Signing button in the Device Manager area.

Step 2.   You wish to have the system warn you anytime an unsigned driver is installed. This provides you with the option to either accept or decline the installation. You also want to make this the system default option, not to be overridden by other users. Click OK to apply and save the settings. This will make it possible for Maria to get around the install warning.

CERTIFICATION OBJECTIVE 17.03

Verifying Digital Signatures

15 Minutes

You are an IT specialist for a small engineering firm. Through the course of the year, you have added new applications to your Windows 2000 server, have upgraded the memory to support the new applications, and have upgraded hardware components. During the last three hardware upgrades, you received a message stating that at least one of the services did not start. With so many changes made to the server, you feel you need to verify that the installed drivers are signed by Microsoft, are authentic, and are trouble free. What utility can you use to generate a log of driver files, listing their status as signed or unsigned?

Learning Objectives

In this lab exercise, you will verify driver file signatures. By the end of this lab, you'll be able to

- Use the Sigverif.exe utility.
- Monitor and troubleshoot driver signing.

Lab Materials and Setup

For this lab exercise, you'll need

- A working computer
- Installed network card (NIC)
- Windows 2000 Server software (installed)
- TCP/IP installed

Getting Down to Business

To monitor and troubleshoot driver signing on the file server, perform the following steps:

Step 1. Launch the Sigverif.exe utility. Move to the Advanced window in the File Signature dialog window.

Step 2. You wish to maintain the default setting of notifying the administrator if any system files are not digitally signed. A log file named Sigverif.txt will be created in your %Windir% Administrator home directory folder.

Step 3. Exit the Advanced window and start the utility. When the utility completes its discovery process, review the result list of files that are not signed. A decision needs to be made as to whether to keep or remove the files. Unwanted files can be moved to a folder created to hold these unsigned files. Close the File Signature Verification utility.

lab
Warning

Removing any digitally unsigned files may result in hardware problems. Only do this if you have installed hardware that is not working properly.

CERTIFICATION OBJECTIVE 17.04

Configuring Operating System Support for Legacy Hardware Devices

15 Minutes

Marcia is the network administrator in charge of maintaining a Windows 2000 file server. The network card just failed, and in the middle of the night she must repair the problem. She replaced the failed NIC with a card out of an old machine from the office. When she restarted Windows 2000, the card was not recognized by the Plug and Play administrator. What should she do to get this card working?

Learning Objectives

In this lab, you'll learn how to troubleshoot a non-PnP device. By the end of this lab, you'll be able to

■   Use the Add/Remove Hardware Wizard.

■   Troubleshoot a network card.

Lab Materials and Setup

For this lab exercise, you'll need

■   A working computer

■   Windows 2000 Server software (installed)

■   Installed network card (NIC)

■   TCP/IP installed

■   Deactivated network card (NIC)

cross
Reference

To deactivate a network component, refer to Chapter 17 of "Managing a Microsoft Windows 2000 Network Environment Study Guide."

Getting Down to Business

To troubleshoot a nonfunctioning network card, perform the following steps:

Step 1.   Open the Control Panel window and launch the Add/Remove Hardware utility. In the next window, activate the utility's Troubleshooting Wizard. The wizard will check for any new hardware.

Step 2.   Scroll through the subsequent list of testable devices; troubleshoot the nonfunctioning network card. Take note of the results and exit the wizard.

LAB ANALYSIS TEST

1. You want to replace an older SCSI adapter with a newer one. What tool will allow you to uninstall the old adapter?

   _____

   _____

2. What is the name of the software that allows the operating system to communicate with a hardware device?

   _____

   _____

3. How does Plug and Play automate the installation process?

   _____

   _____

4. What are the three file signature verification settings you can use to configure driver signing?

   _____

   _____

5. You change the resources your non-PnP video adapter uses in Device Manager, and the system does not boot correctly. What could be the problem?

   _____

   _____

KEY TERM QUIZ

Use the following vocabulary terms to complete the sentences below. Not all of the terms will be used. Definitions for these terms can be found in "Managing a Microsoft Windows 2000 Network Environment Study Guide."

> Driver
>
> Plug and Play (PnP)
>
> Driver signing
>
> Legacy hardware
>
> sigverif
>
> Digital signature
>
> Small Computer System Interface (SCSI)
>
> Device Manager
>
> Hardware compatibility list (HCL)
>
> Interrupt Requests (IRQs)

1. The _____ guarantees the driver to work with Windows 2000 and that it is corruption-free.

2. _____ is the ability of added, or installed, hardware to identify itself to the operating system for installation.

3. The _____ utility searches for unsigned or illegitimate files that may not be compatible with Windows 2000.

4. A digital signature incorporated into driver and system files, _____, is a way to verify their compatibility with Windows 2000.

5. _____ is a list of computer hardware tested by Microsoft and determined to be compatible with Windows 2000.

LAB SOLUTIONS FOR CHAPTER 17

In this section, you'll find solutions to the lab exercises, Lab Analysis Test, and Key Term Quiz.

Lab Solution 17.01

In this lab, you performed Windows update for your server. By the end of this lab, you were able to

- Use the Windows Update web site.
- Search for Windows 2000 Server hardware and software updates.

To look for and install the latest Windows 2000 Server updates, perform the following steps:

Step 1.   Log on to Microsoft's Windows Update web site: http://www.microsoft.com/hcl. Scan for the latest operating system updates by clicking the Windows Update button, as shown in Figure 17-1. In the Welcome page, click Product Updates to allow the site to discover software upgrades. A Please Wait pop-up window will appear while scanning for available updates.

FIGURE 17-1

Click the Windows Update logo to search for product updates on your system.

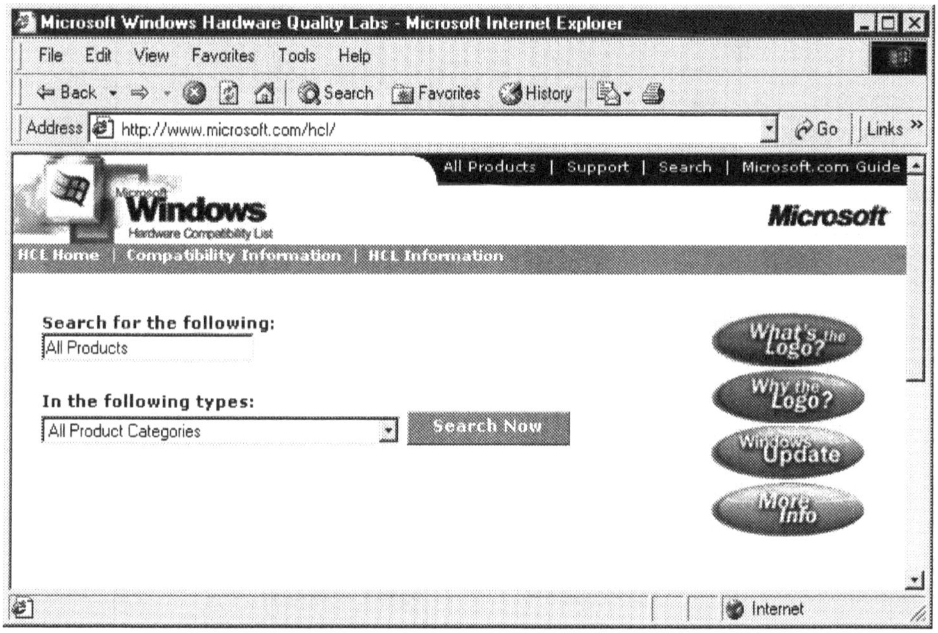

Step 2. As you browse through the available updates in each category, check the box next to the update of your choice and add it to the collection of updates you want to install. Periodically, a critical update will present itself as an update, as shown next. You can also read a full description of each item by clicking the Read More link.

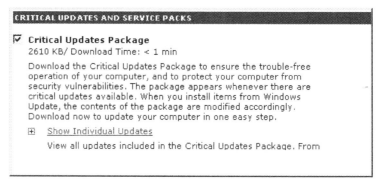

Step 3. Once you have selected all the updates you want, complete the installation process by clicking Start Download, as shown in Figure 17-2. Then click the Download button. Depending on the update, you may be required to reboot the server. After the download and installation is complete, exit the browser.

FIGURE 17-2

This screen provides for one last review opportunity before the download process.

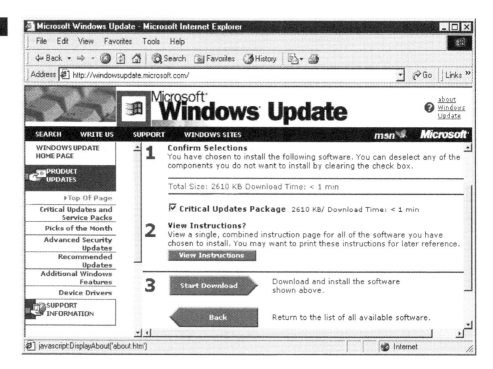

Lab Solution 17.02

In this lab, you configured driver signing options for hardware devices installed on the server. By the end of this lab, you were able to

- Use driver signing option configuration.
- Configure driver signing options.

To configure driver signing options, perform the following steps:

Step 1. Access the Properties window of the My Computer icon by right-clicking My Computer. Choose Properties from the context menu. Select the Hardware tab. Now select the Driver Signing button in the Device Manager area of the window. This opens the Driver Signing Options window, as shown in Figure 17-3.

Step 2. You wish to have the system warn the administrator anytime an unsigned driver is installed. In the Driver Signing Options dialog box, click the Warn - Display a Message Before Installing an Unsigned File radio button. This provides us with the option to either accept or decline the installation.

Step 3. You also want to make this the system default option, not to be overridden by other users. Select Apply Setting as SystemDefault in the Administrator area of the window. Click OK to apply and save the settings.

FIGURE 17-3

Configure your verification settings to determine system response when unsigned files are about to be installed.

Driver Signing Options

To ensure their integrity, all files on the Windows 2000 CD are digitally signed by Microsoft and are automatically verified during Setup.

When you install new software, the following verification settings will be used.

File signature verification
- ○ Ignore - Install all files, regardless of file signature
- ⦿ Warn - Display a message before installing an unsigned file
- ○ Block - Prevent installation of unsigned files

Administrator option
- ☑ Apply setting as system default

OK   Cancel

Lab Solution 17.03

As mentioned in the previous lab, all drivers included with Windows 2000 use digital signatures to verify that they have been tested by the Windows Hardware Quality Labs (WHQL). To help search for these unsigned or illegitimate files, Windows 2000 includes a File Signature Verification tool (Sigverif.exe). Used in conjunction with troubleshooting procedures, only the files in the %Windir%\System32\Drivers folder need to be tested.

In this lab, you verified driver file signatures. By the end of this lab, you were able to

■ Use the Sigverif.exe utility.

■ Monitor and troubleshoot driver signing.

To monitor and troubleshoot driver signing on the file server, perform the following steps:

Step 1.   Click Start | Run and type **Sigverif.exe**.

The File Signature Verification utility window will open, as shown here.

Click the Advanced button. The Advanced File Signature Verification Settings window appears with an activated Search tab, as shown next.

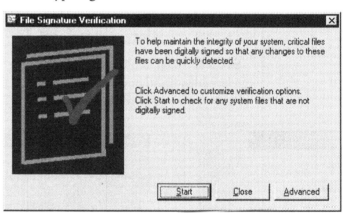

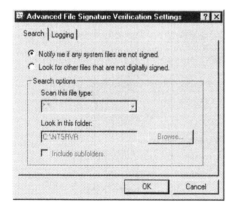

Step 2.   Keep the default setting, Notify Me if Any System Files Are Not Signed, selected. A log file named Sigverif.txt will be created in your Administrator home directory after the discovery process.

Click the Logging tab. The default setting saves the file signature verification to a log file named Sigverif.txt, as shown here.

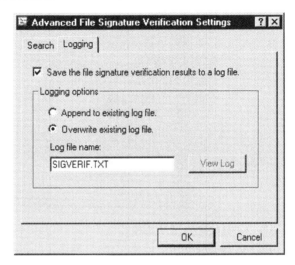

Step 3. Click OK to exit the Advanced window, and click Start. When the utility completes its discovery process, review the result list of files that are not signed by clicking the View Log button in the Logging window, as shown in Figure 17-4. A decision needs to be made as to whether to keep or remove the files. Unwanted files can be moved to a folder created to hold these unsigned files, as shown next. Click Close to exit the File Signature Verification utility.

```
SIGVERIF - Notepad
File  Edit  Format  Help
*****************************************

Microsoft Signature Verification

Log file generated on 5/3/2002 at 12:10 PM
OS Platform:  Windows 2000 (x86), Version:  5.0, Build: 2195, CSDVersion:
Scan Results:  Total Files: 643, Signed: 627, Unsigned: 0, Not Scanned: 16

File                    Modified        Version        Status          Cata
------------------     ------------    -----------     ------------    -------
[c:\]
ntdetect.com            12/7/1999       2:5.0           Signed          NT5.C
ntldr                   12/7/1999       2:5.0           Signed          NT5.C
[c:\ntsrvr]
explorer.exe            12/7/1999       2:5.0           Signed          NT5.C
explorer.scf            12/7/1999       2:5.0           Signed          NT5.C
regedit.exe             12/7/1999       2:5.0           Signed          NT5.C
taskman.exe             12/7/1999       2:5.0           Signed          NT5.C
```

lab
Warning   *Removing any digitally unsigned files may result in hardware problems. Only do this if you have installed hardware that is not working properly.*

FIGURE 17-4

Click the View
button to open
the log file in
Notepad.

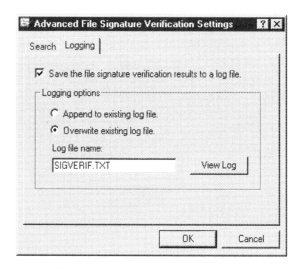

Lab Solution 17.04

Windows 2000 automatically detects and configures most hardware devices during
setup. When troubleshooting devices, it may be necessary to use the Add/Remove
Hardware Wizard to reactivate the device. If the device is not Plug and Play, you
may have to use the Add/Remove Hardware Wizard in Control Panel to tell
Windows 2000 what type of device you are installing. After the device is detected,
or you identify the device using the Add/Remove Hardware Wizard, Windows 2000
may ask you to insert the Windows 2000 CD-ROM or the manufacturer's floppy
disk so it can load the proper device drivers.

In this lab, you learned how to troubleshoot a non-PnP device. By the end of this
lab, you were able to

- Use the Add/Remove Hardware Wizard.
- Troubleshoot a network card.

To troubleshoot a nonfunctioning network card, perform the following steps:

Step 1.   Click Start | Settings | Control Panel and double-click Add/Remove
Hardware. Click Next.

Step 2.   In this window, you want to activate the utility's Troubleshooting
Wizard. Click the Add/Troubleshoot a Device radio button, as shown in Figure
17-5. Click Next. The wizard will check for any new hardware.

Step 3.   After the wizard checks for new hardware, a list of testable devices will
appear in the window, as shown in Figure 17-6. Double-click the nonfunctioning

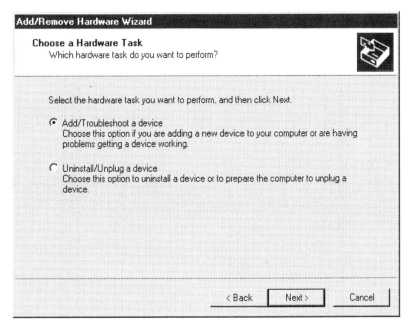

FIGURE 17-5

The wizard will help troubleshoot problem hardware components.

network card to troubleshoot. Take note of the results of this text. The screen informs you that the card has been disabled. Windows will enable the card. Click Next to do so. A resulting window will confirm that the card has been reactivated. Click Finish to exit the wizard.

FIGURE 17-6

The red X showing on the icon indicates that the card is not working.

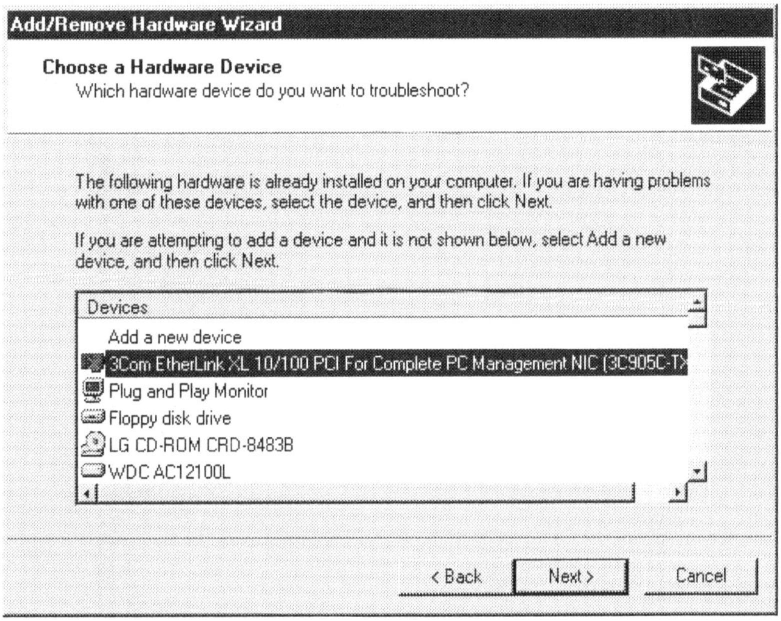

ANSWERS TO LAB ANALYSIS

1. Launch the Add/Remove Hardware Wizard and select the Uninstall/Unplug a Device task in the Choose a Hardware Task window.

2. A device driver enables a specific device to communicate with an operating system. Although a device is installed on your system, Windows 2000 cannot use it until the appropriate driver is installed.

3. By detecting new devices in a computer, installing device drivers for the piece of hardware, and configuring both the hardware and driver to use the same system resource.

4. The three options to configure driver signing settings are Ignore, which doesn't verify signatures and installs the drivers anyway; Warn, which means the system will check for signatures and alert you to make a decision if a signature doesn't exist; and Block, which blocks the installation of unsigned drivers.

5. Non-PnP devices are not detected by Windows 2000 and their requirements are unknown to the Device Manager. It is necessary to manually configure the device using the Add/Remove Hardware Wizard.

ANSWERS TO KEY TERM QUIZ

1. Digital signature

2. Plug and Play (PnP)

3. sigverif

4. Driver signing

5. Hardware compatibility list (HCL)

18

Troubleshooting Startup Problems

LAB EXERCISES

18.01   Create and Interpret a Startup
         Log File

18.02   Repair an Operating System by
         Using Various Startup Options

18.03   Repair an Operating System by
         Using the Recovery Console

18.04   Recover Data from a Hard Disk in
         the Event that the Operating System
         Will Not Start

18.05   Restore an Operating System and
         Data from Backup

■   Lab Analysis Test

■   Key Term Quiz

■   Lab Solutions

W ith its predecessor, fixing hardware problems was often a difficult, costly, and time-consuming process. Windows 2000 makes it easier to win the battle against the "blue screen of death."

Like Windows 9x, Windows 2000 allows you to boot the system into Safe mode after a failure. Safe mode usually prevents Windows 2000 from freezing at the blue screen by loading with a minimal set of drivers and services. You're limited in what you can do in Safe mode, but accessing the Windows interface gives you a leg up on solving problems from a command prompt.

Some hardware failures are so severe they prevent booting in Safe mode. In such a case, you can try using the Recovery Console, a command-line environment designed to help recover Windows 2000 after a catastrophic failure.

On a scale of 1 to 10, where 10 is the worst-case scenario, hardware and operating system failure and recovery rates somewhere in the middle. Although it may involve system downtime, eventually the system is repaired and back online. The most devastating event with any system is the loss of valuable data—this rates a 12 on our scale of 1 to 10! An administrator must take measures to back up this information on a daily basis, and maybe more if the information is time-critical. Then, when that information does get deleted, or overwritten, or becomes corrupted accidentally, it can easily be recovered from backup media.

In this chapter, we will look at what can go wrong and how to troubleshoot and recover from boot failures and operating system failures, and how to restore data loss. Additionally, we'll utilize some tools provided by Windows 2000 that can be used to troubleshoot problems that prevent a computer from booting properly.

CERTIFICATION OBJECTIVE 18.01

Create and Interpret a Startup Log File

10 Minutes

You've just finished building a Windows 2000 Server computer for a small-business customer. All the applications and hardware components that the customer has requested have been installed. Before you deliver the computer, you want to boot the system and create a boot log to verify that all necessary services and drivers have been initialized. How is this boot log created at boot-up?

Learning Objectives

In this lab, you'll create a baseline boot log. By the end of this lab, you'll be able to

- Create an Ntbtlog.txt file.
- Interpret a startup log file.

Lab Materials and Setup

For this lab exercise, you'll need

- A working computer
- Installed network card (NIC)
- Windows 2000 Server software (installed)
- TCP/IP installed

Getting Down to Business

To create a startup log file, perform the following steps:

Step 1.   In order to create a boot log in Windows 2000, press F8 during the initial part of the system boot. Choose Enable Boot Logging, and Windows 2000 will continue to boot as normal and log the results.

Step 2.   When the system has completed the boot sequence, you should find a file in the Winnt directory on your hard drive, named ntbtlog.txt. This is the file that was generated during the boot. Review the list of drivers that the system attempted to load, along with the status (Loaded Driver or Did Not Load Driver), and path to the driver (those without a full path are located in the winnt\system32\drivers folder). Determine whether there were drivers that need to be resolved.

CERTIFICATION OBJECTIVE 18.02

Repair an Operating System by Using Various Startup Options

15 Minutes

As a regular function of your job as network administrator, you search the Internet for updated drivers for your installed components. A new NIC driver update has been posted on the manufacturer's web site. You download and install the driver without paying attention to the read-me file that was part of the compressed files—a big "no no." After you install the driver and reboot, a message appears at the end of the reboot that at least one of the services did not start. You realize that something must have gone wrong when the NIC driver tried to initialize since the system was working fine prior to the NIC driver update. How can you revert back to a previous configuration and recover from the error?

Learning Objectives

In this lab, you'll troubleshoot a boot failure by using Last Known Good Configuration. By the end of this lab, you'll be able to

- Boot a Windows 2000 computer with Last Known Good configuration.

Lab Materials and Setup

For this lab exercise, you'll need

- A working computer
- Installed network card (NIC)
- Windows 2000 Server software (installed)
- TCP/IP installed

Getting Down to Business

To boot into Last Known Good configuration mode, perform the following steps:

Step 1. Restart your server. When you see the message Please Select the Operating System to Start, press F8.

Step 2. Select and invoke Last Known Good Configuration. Verify that all services and drivers were loaded.

CERTIFICATION OBJECTIVE 18.03

Repair an Operating System by Using the Recovery Console

15 Minutes

Lillian is a network administrator responsible for a Windows 2000 Server computer and four workstations at the Bright-Lite Lighting Store. The system is used for inventory of the 475 different lighting fixtures and accessories, and the 10,000 total unit inventory of the store. Always one to keep up with the Microsoft service packs, she installs the latest one on this particular Sunday afternoon, because the store is closed. After the update, the system will not boot. The screen displays an error message and a notice that the system will shut down in 30 seconds. Her numerous attempts to resolve the issue through the standard Safe mode options are fruitless. She determines that there is a problem with the master boot record of the operating system. Her last resort is to repair the operating system using the Recovery Console. How does Lillian go about running this utility and restoring her system?

Learning Objectives

In this lab, you'll learn how to use the Recovery Console. By the end of this lab, you'll be able to

- Troubleshoot a boot problem.
- Use Recovery Console.
- Perform recovery tasks.

cross
Reference

For further information, and available Recovery Console commands, refer to the recovery console section of Chapter 18 in "Managing a Microsoft Windows 2000 Network Environment Study Guide."

Lab Materials and Setup

For this lab exercise, you'll need

- A working computer
- Installed network card (NIC)
- Windows 2000 Server software (installed)
- TCP/IP installed
- The Windows 2000 Server distribution CD

Getting Down to Business

To start the Windows 2000 Recovery Console from the Windows 2000 CD and repair an installation, perform the following steps:

Step 1. Insert the Windows 2000 Server CD in the CD-ROM drive and reboot the computer. Type **R** to repair a Windows 2000 installation.

Step 2. Start the Recovery Console and log on to the system. At the C:\Winnt command prompt, change to the root folder. Type the command to repair the master boot record.

Step 3. Remove the CD from the drive, exit and reboot. The system will boot with a newly created master boot record.

CERTIFICATION OBJECTIVE 18.04

Recover Data from a Hard Disk in the Event that the Operating System Will Not Start

15 Minutes

You are the network administrator for the Millie-Due Accounting firm. The network contains 16 workstations and 1 Windows 2000 Server computer, which you are responsible for. Recently, a new Windows 2000 Server computer has been purchased and configured as a database server for the 1,250 clients the company serves. Before putting it online, you want to create an emergency repair disk (ERD) and perform a mock system restore with the disk. What steps are necessary to create a disk and perform the system restore with the ERD?

Learning Objectives

In this lab, you'll create and use the emergency repair disk. By the end of this lab, you'll be able to

- Create an ERD.
- Restore settings using the ERD.

Lab Materials and Setup

For this lab exercise, you'll need

- A working computer
- Installed network card (NIC)
- Windows 2000 Server software (installed)
- TCP/IP installed
- The Windows 2000 Server distribution cd
- A blank 1.44MB floppy disk

Getting Down to Business

To create an ERD and use it to restore a Windows 2000 system, perform the following steps:

Step 1. First, you need to create an emergency repair disk (ERD). Log on to your computer as Administrator. Launch the Backup utility. Create an emergency repair disk.

Step 2. Use a blank, formatted 1.44MB disk in drive A. When the process is complete, remove the disk and label it appropriately. You should re-create the ERD on a scheduled basis to reflect any changes made to the configuration of the computer.

Step 3.   Now, you want to put the ERD to the test. Start your computer with the Windows 2000 Server CD. After Setup copies files from the CD or disk, the system reboots and starts the operating system installation.

Step 4.   When you see the Welcome to Setup screen, select to repair or recover a Windows 2000 installation.

Step 5.   The Manual Repair option requests the ERD disk in drive A or attempts to locate Windows 2000 automatically. The Fast Repair option allows you to select the tasks to perform and then requests the ERD disk be inserted in drive A.

Step 6.   When the repair process completes, the computer automatically reboots and Windows 2000 loads. Missing or corrupted files are reloaded from the original media. This means that any changes made, software installed, or service packs applied will be lost.

lab

Warning   *When prompted to replace a new file with an older file, select No for all normally functioning files installed on your system.*

CERTIFICATION OBJECTIVE 18.05

Restore an Operating System and Data from Backup

15 Minutes

Jean is the network administrator for a small greeting card company. A new server has been added to the four other servers on the network. Knowing that critical data must be recoverable through daily backups, he wants to test the backup and restore function on the server before he puts the server online. What are the steps involved in the backup and restore process that he can confidently rely on for successful backups?

Learning Objectives

In this lab, you'll learn how to use the Backup Wizard and Restore Wizard. By the end of this lab, you'll be able to

- Create a backup job using the Backup Wizard.
- Restore files from a normal backup using the Restore Wizard.

Lab Materials and Setup

For this lab exercise, you'll need

- A working computer
- Installed network card (NIC)
- Windows 2000 Server software (installed)
- TCP/IP installed

Getting Down to Business

To use the Backup and Restore Wizards, perform the following steps:

Step 1.   First, you want to create a sample backup job. Launch the Backup utility from the Start menu. Add a job using the Schedule Job tab. Select sample data that you would like to back up.

Step 2.   Choose the media to save the files. Select a Normal type of backup to perform. You want to verify data after backup in order to check the backup's integrity.

Step 3.   Back up the data to a file. Provide Test backup as the Job name, and schedule the backup job to run five minutes ahead of the present time. Complete the schedule process.

Step 4.   Now, you want to restore the file from the backup job. Launch the Backup utility from the Start menu, if it is not open already. In the Restore window, select the backup set you would like to restore from and expand the file listings.

Step 5.   Restore the files to their original location. Start the Restore process. When the restore is complete, the Restore Progress window will allow you to view a report of the restore actions or close the utility.

LAB ANALYSIS TEST

1. As a Windows 2000 boot option, what function does Safe mode provide and why would you use it?

   _____

   _____

2. What is the Recovery Console and what is its purpose?

   _____

   _____

3. If you load a new device driver and your computer will not boot, which safe boot option would you use to recover?

   _____

   _____

4. How does the Recovery Console differ from Safe Mode with Command Prompt?

   _____

   _____

5. When is the Ntbtlog.txt file created, and if a previous boot log already exists, what happens to that information?

   _____

   _____

KEY TERM QUIZ

Use the following vocabulary terms to complete the sentences below. Not all of the terms will be used. Definitions for these terms can be found in "Managing a Microsoft Windows 2000 Network Environment Study Guide."

> Last Known Good configuration
>
> Emergency repair disk (ERD)
>
> Safe mode
>
> Media
>
> Boot log
>
> Recovery Console
>
> Catalog
>
> Backup log
>
> Backup

1. The _____ contains information about the current Windows system settings and can be used to rebuild the system if the file system becomes corrupt or the operating system will not start up.

2. _____ is the process of copying data as a precautionary measure in case the primary data becomes corrupt or is nonexistent.

3. A _____ contains backup log records created during a backup session.

4. _____ is a command-line console that you can use after starting the computer with the Setup CD.

5. _____ is a diagnostic tool for troubleshooting problems that can occur with starting and running Windows 2000.

LAB SOLUTIONS FOR CHAPTER 18

In this section, you'll find solutions to the lab exercises, Lab Analysis Test, and Key Term Quiz.

Lab Solution 18.01

In this lab exercise, you want to make sure that all system services and drivers are functioning properly. One of the ways to verify their status is to create a boot log, named Ntbtlog.txt, at boot-up. This is accomplished by pressing F8 during the initial part of the boot process.

When Boot Logging is enabled, it starts Windows 2000 while logging all the drivers and services that were loaded (or not loaded) by the system to a file. This file is called ntbtlog.txt, and it is located in the %windir% directory. When using Safe Mode, Safe Mode with Networking, and Safe Mode with Command Prompt, a boot log is automatically generated listing all the drivers and services that are loaded.

In this lab, you created a baseline boot log. By the end of this lab, you were able to

■ Create a Ntbtlog.txt file.

■ Interpret a startup log file.

To create a startup log file, perform the following steps:

Step 1. In order to create a boot log in Windows 2000, press F8 during the initial part of the system boot. This appears as an option when the screen is black, and there is a line of squares across the bottom. After pressing F8, a menu will appear offering several boot options, such as Safe Mode, Safe Mode with Networking, Safe Mode with Command Prompt, Enable Boot Logging, Enable VGA Mode, and more. Choose Enable Boot Logging, and Windows 2000 will continue to boot as normal and log the results.

Step 2. When the system has completed the boot sequence, you should find a file in the Winnt directory named ntbtlog.txt, as shown in Figure 18-1. This is the file that was generated during the boot.

FIGURE 18-1

Open the
ntbtlog.txt
from the
Winnt directory.

Step 3.   The Windows 2000 version and build number will be at the beginning of the current log, along with the current date and time. What follows is a list of drivers that the system attempted to load, along with the status (Loaded Driver or Did Not Load Driver), and path to the driver (those without a full path are located in the winnt\system32\drivers folder), as shown in Figure 18-2.

Lab Solution 18.02

You download and install a NIC update driver without paying attention to the attached read-me file. During the reboot, a message appears stating that at least one of the services did not start. You need to invoke the Last Known Good configuration to recover from this mishap.

   If you make a change to your system and want to be able to back out of it, you can do so by restarting your system and invoking the Last Known Good configuration. This configuration is automatically saved whenever a user successfully logs on to the computer. This state represents the last configuration settings that were able to support

FIGURE 18-2

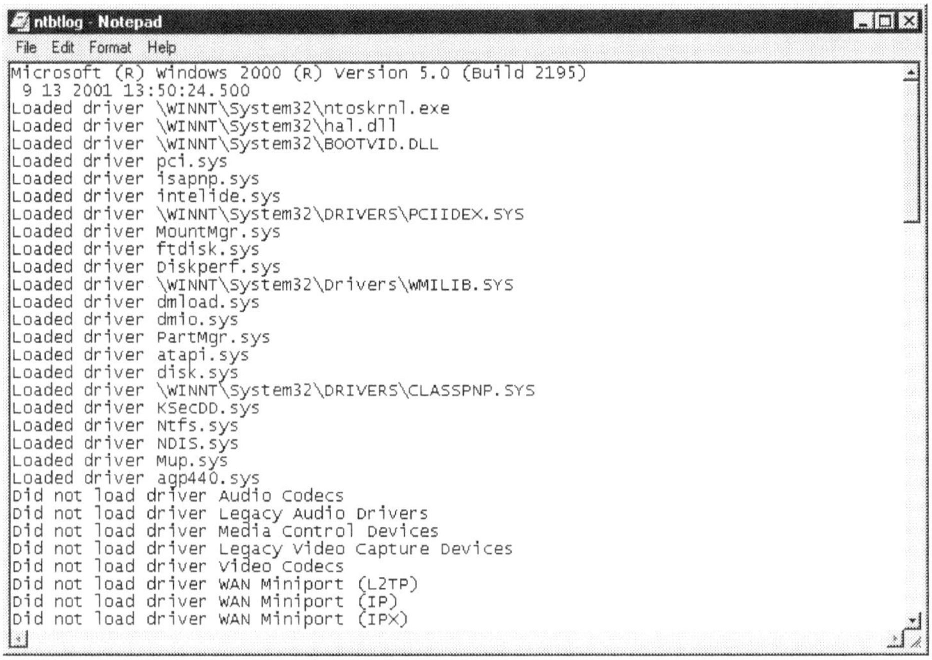

The ntbtlog.txt file contains driver status and location.

```
ntbtlog - Notepad
File  Edit  Format  Help
Microsoft (R) windows 2000 (R) version 5.0 (Build 2195)
 9 13 2001 13:50:24.500
Loaded driver \WINNT\System32\ntoskrnl.exe
Loaded driver \WINNT\System32\hal.dll
Loaded driver \WINNT\System32\BOOTVID.DLL
Loaded driver pci.sys
Loaded driver isapnp.sys
Loaded driver intelide.sys
Loaded driver \WINNT\System32\DRIVERS\PCIIDEX.SYS
Loaded driver MountMgr.sys
Loaded driver ftdisk.sys
Loaded driver Diskperf.sys
Loaded driver \WINNT\System32\Drivers\WMILIB.SYS
Loaded driver dmload.sys
Loaded driver dmio.sys
Loaded driver PartMgr.sys
Loaded driver atapi.sys
Loaded driver disk.sys
Loaded driver \WINNT\System32\DRIVERS\CLASSPNP.SYS
Loaded driver KSecDD.sys
Loaded driver Ntfs.sys
Loaded driver NDIS.sys
Loaded driver Mup.sys
Loaded driver agp440.sys
Did not load driver Audio Codecs
Did not load driver Legacy Audio Drivers
Did not load driver Media Control Devices
Did not load driver Legacy Video Capture Devices
Did not load driver video Codecs
Did not load driver WAN Miniport (L2TP)
Did not load driver WAN Miniport (IP)
Did not load driver WAN Miniport (IPX)
```

a logon. Boot problems are usually caused by hardware components, drivers, software, and even update files. As always, additions or deletions of any kind to the system should be done during off-hours, or when an offline situation will have the least impact on end users.

In this lab, your task was to troubleshoot a boot failure by using Last Known Good configuration. By the end of this lab, you were able to

■ Boot a Windows 2000 computer with Last Known Good configuration.

To boot into Last Known Good configuration mode, perform the following steps:

Step 1. Click Start to restart your server. When you see the message Please Select the Operating System to Start, press F8.

Step 2. Use the arrow keys to highlight Last Known Good Configuration, and then press ENTER. Verify that all services and drivers were loaded by checking the Ntbtlog.txt file.

Lab Solution 18.03

In this lab scenario, Lillian installs the latest service pack only to find that the system will not reboot. Her last resort is to repair the operating system using the Recovery Console. The Recovery Console provides a command line during startup from which you can make system changes when Windows 2000 doesn't start. The Recovery Console is particularly useful if you need to repair your system by copying a file from a floppy disk or CD-ROM to your hard drive or if you need to modify a service that prevents your computer from starting properly.

In this lab, you learned how to use the Recovery Console. By the end of this lab, you were able to

- Troubleshoot a boot problem.
- Perform recovery tasks.

For further information, refer to the "Recovery Console" section of Chapter 18 in "Managing a Microsoft Windows 2000 Network Environment Study Guide."

To start the Windows 2000 Recovery Console from the Windows 2000 CD and repair an installation, perform the following steps:

Step 1.   Insert the Windows 2000 Server CD in the CD-ROM drive and reboot the computer. Type **R** to repair a Windows 2000 installation. The Windows 2000 Repair Options screen appears.

Step 2.   Type C to start the Recovery Console. Select the appropriate OS if you have more than one, and then press ENTER. Type the Administrator password. At the C:\Winnt command prompt, change to the root folder.

Step 3.   Because it has been determined that there is a problem with the master boot record, you need to type the command to fix it. The command fixmbr [device_name] (that is, fixmbr c:) will create a new master boot record. Remove the CD from the drive, exit and reboot.

Lab Solution 18.04

Before putting a new server online, you want to create an emergency repair disk (ERD) and perform a mock system restore with the disk. This is just a trial run to ensure that in case you need to perform an actual emergency repair, you feel confident that the disk will work.

You can use the Windows 2000 emergency repair feature to fix problems that may be preventing you from starting your computer. This includes problems with your registry, system files, partition boot sector, and startup environment. In this lab, you created and used the emergency repair disk. By the end of this lab, you were able to

- Create an ERD.
- Restore settings using the ERD.

To create an ERD and use it to restore a Windows 2000 system, perform the following steps:

Step 1.   First, you need to create an emergency repair disk (ERD). Log on to your computer as Administrator. Click Start | Programs | Accessories |System Tools and select Backup. Select the Emergency Repair Disk icon or select the Tools menu item and click on the Emergency Repair Disk icon, as shown in Figure 18-3.

FIGURE 18-3

Select the Emergency Repair Disk icon to create a disk.

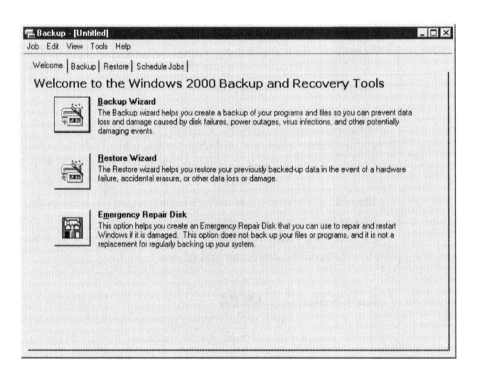

Step 2. Insert a blank, formatted 1.44MB disk in drive A and click OK. When the process is complete, remove the disk and label it appropriately. You should re-create the ERD on a scheduled basis to reflect any changes made to the configuration of the computer. Choosing to back up the registry will help you to recover your system if the registry becomes corrupt, as shown here.

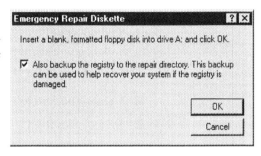

Step 3. Now, you want to perform your test run to make sure that you can perform a system restore using the ERD. Start your computer with the Windows 2000 Server CD. After Setup copies files from the CD or disk, the system reboots and starts the operating system installation.

Step 4. At the Welcome to Setup screen, select the R option to repair or recover a Windows 2000 installation. Select the R option to repair a damaged Windows 2000 installation. Select the Manual Repair option if you don't want to repair the registry and want to selectively repair the system files, partition boot sector, or startup environment.

Step 5. Select the Fast Repair option if you want to repair the system files, the boot sector, startup environment, and system registry. The Manual Repair option requests the ERD disk in drive A or attempts to locate Windows 2000 automatically. The Fast Repair option allows you to select the tasks to perform and then requests the ERD disk be inserted in drive A.

Step 6. If you have the Windows 2000 Server CD, you can choose to have Setup verify your installation against corruption. When the repair process completes, the computer automatically reboots and Windows 2000 loads. Missing or corrupted files are reloaded from the original media. This means that any changes made, software installed, or service packs applied will be lost.

Lab Solution 18.05

Jean wants to test the backup and restore function on the server before he puts the server online. Early in his networking career, he had blind confidence in the backup process, only to discover that when a file restore request was made, the file either was not backed up or was corrupted.

In this lab, you learned how to use the Backup Wizard and Restore Wizard. By the end of this lab, you were able to

■ Create a backup job using the Backup Wizard.

■ Restore files from a normal backup using the Restore Wizard.

To use the Backup and Restore Wizards, perform the following steps:

Step 1. First, you want to create a sample backup job. Click Start | Programs | Accessories | Select System Tools and select Backup. Select the Schedule Job tab and click Add Job in the bottom-right side of the calendar, as shown next. On the Backup Wizard window, click Next.

Step 2. Select the type of data you would like to back up, as shown here:

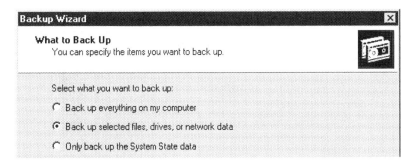

If you are backing up selected files, the Backup Wizard displays a tree diagram of the files on your computer, as you can see in Figure 18-4. Select a file or directory to mark it and anything below it for backup. Click Next.

Step 3.   Choose the media to save the files to (in this case, a floppy disk will do), as shown next. Click Next. Select the type of backup to perform (Normal in this

Backup Wizard

Items to Back Up
You can back up any combination of drives, folders, or files.

Click to select the check box next to any drive, folder, or file that you want to back up.

What to back up:

- My Computer
  - A:
  - C:
  - D:
  - System State
  - ch18
  - chapter 19
  - My Documents
  - My Network Places

Name	Comment
My Computer	
ch18	
chapter 19	
My Documents	
My Network Places	

< Back   Next >   Cancel

case) and click Next. Select Verify Data After Backup if you want to check the backup's integrity and hardware compression (if it is available). Click Next.

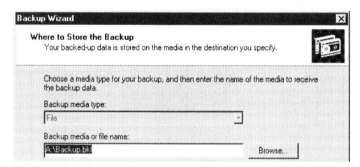

Step 4. Since you are using a floppy for test purposes, we want to replace the data. If you were using a tape storage unit, you would select to append the data. Click Next. Change the backup labels if you are following a particular standard. Click Next.

Step 5. Provide Test backup as the Job name and click Set Schedule. Select the schedule to run the backup job on—again, in our case, we want to schedule it five minutes ahead of the present time—and click OK, as shown next. Click Next. Click Finish to create the scheduled job.

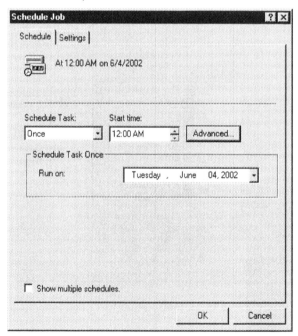

Step 6. Now, you want to restore the file from the backup job. Select the Restore tab in the Backup Wizard window. In the left frame, select the backup set you would like to restore from and expand the file listings, as shown in Figure 18-5.

Step 7. Use the Restore Files drop-down menu in the bottom-left part of the window to select the original location of the files. Click Start Restore. Change the path of the backup set if it has changed. We will be restoring files from the backup job on the floppy in drive A, as shown here. Proceed with the restore process.

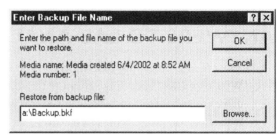

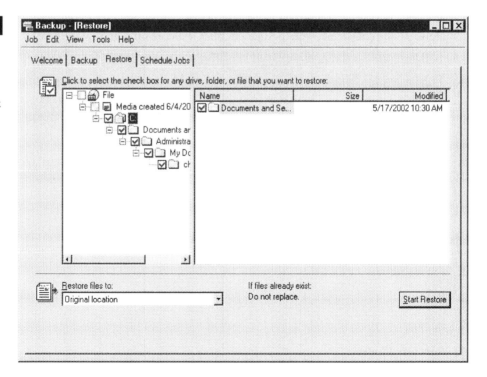

FIGURE 18-5

Select the drive, folder, or files you need to restore in the left window pane.

Step 8. When the restore is complete, as shown here, the Restore Progress window will allow you to view a report of the restore actions or close the utility.

ANSWERS TO LAB ANALYSIS

1. Safe mode is an option that allows you to load the Windows 2000 operating system with a basic set of drivers that provide access to the system, while bypassing the more advanced features that might be causing a boot problem.

2. The Recovery Console is a command-line interface that allows you to perform basic system maintenance and troubleshooting tasks without loading the Windows 2000 operating system.

3. The best option is to reboot the computer, press F8 during the boot process, and select the Last Known Good configuration. When a new driver is installed, a temporary change is made to the registry. The change becomes permanent after a successful reboot with the new driver. Rebooting with this option discards the addition to the registry and reverts to a working environment.

4. The Recovery Console does not rely on a bootable operating system as Safe mode does. The Recovery Console can be used even if the Windows 2000 operating system is not bootable through regular means. Conversely, Safe mode provides a full set of command-line commands, where the Recovery Console offers a limited set of commands.

5. A boot log file, Ntbtlog.txt, is automatically created every time the computer is started in Safe mode. If a boot log file using that name already exists, the new data is appended to the existing file.

ANSWERS TO KEY TERM QUIZ

1. Emergency repair disk (ERD)

2. Backup

3. catalog

4. Recovery Console

5. Safe mode

MICROSOFT CERTIFIED SYSTEMS ASSOCIATE

19

Monitoring and Troubleshooting Server Health and Performance

LAB EXERCISES

19.01   Monitoring and Interpreting Real-Time Performance by Using System Monitor

19.02   Configuring System Monitor Alerts and Logging

19.03   Diagnosing Server Health Problems with Event Viewer

19.04   Identifying and Disabling Unnecessary Services

   ■   Lab Analysis Test

   ■   Key Term Quiz

   ■   Lab Solutions

Periodic monitoring of your Windows 2000 Server is important to the process of optimization. By gathering current information and comparing it to established performance standards for your systems (a baseline), you can detect bottlenecks and identify those system components that are slowing down server performance, and fix them before they become a problem to your users.

A baseline is an established performance standard for the operation of your server as determined by normal load. This baseline can then be used as a basis of comparison for future performance to see whether repairable problems exist. As the configuration of your server changes, new baselines are established to reflect the new expected performance.

It is very important that a baseline be established before problems begin to occur. If users are already beginning to complain that the network is slow, it is too late to establish a baseline because the statistics gathered include whatever performance factors are contributing to the users' dissatisfaction.

The Performance Monitor allows you to watch various facets of your system. Whether you are looking for real-time graphical views or a log that you can peruse at your convenience, the Performance Monitor can provide the kind of data you need to evaluate performance and recommend any needed system modification.

Another tool that can help you maintain a healthy system is the Event Viewer. Tracking and viewing the three Windows 2000 events—system, security, and application—is a powerful method of ensuring that your systems are secure and running properly. Windows 2000 enables you to monitor most events on a system. As an administrator, you need to monitor events to track security, system performance, and application errors. Events are recorded in event logs. You can view and analyze event logs to determine whether or not security breaches are occurring or system services are failing, or to determine the nature of application errors.

In this chapter, we will look at topics related to the assessment of server performance and preventive maintenance. It includes a variety of monitoring and logging utilities found in Performance Console and Event Viewer.

CERTIFICATION OBJECTIVE 19.01

Monitoring and Interpreting Real-Time Performance by Using System Monitor

10 Minutes

You are the network administrator for the Correct Answer Testing Center in the state of Rhode Island. For the last two weeks, you've been getting complaints that users have had a longer than normal delay in saving and getting files from the server. Calls have been increasing since then, even though you have rebooted the server once thinking that it had something to do with RAM. You need to track the server Page File and Memory to see if there is a memory leak. The documentation suggests that you use System Monitor to track the Processor object—specifically, the Page Faults/Sec and Page File Bytes counters. What steps do you take to accomplish this task?

Learning Objectives

In this lab, you'll configure and monitor Processor Performance object counters in System Monitor to become familiar with monitoring and interpreting real-time information. By the end of this lab, you'll be able to

- Use System Monitor.
- Configure Processor Performance objects.
- Collect data using Performance Monitor.

Lab Materials and Setup

For this lab exercise, you'll need

- A working computer
- Installed network card (NIC)
- Windows 2000 Server software (installed)
- TCP/IP installed

Getting Down to Business

To add Processor Performance object counters and monitor their performance, perform the following steps:

Step 1.   Open the Performance application. In Performance, select System Monitor. Create an entry in System Monitor by clicking the Add (+) icon.

Step 2.   Select the Process Performance object. You will see the list of available counters. Select the two counters needed to track a potential memory leak: Page Faults/Sec and Page File Bytes. If you need to know what a counter means, select the counter and click the Explain button.

Step 3. When you have finished adding the counters you need to monitor, click Add. Click Close when you are finished. Your counters will now be graphed. The default size for page file bytes is equal to 1.5 times the amount of physical memory.

CERTIFICATION OBJECTIVE 19.02

Configuring System Monitor Alerts and Logging

15 Minutes

Brent is the network administrator of the Knot-for-Knot-Ting marine services company. He wants to determine whether or not his server is short of memory. Under light load, users get good response. However, as load increases, so does the lack of responsiveness. The Windows 2000 Server, which has 128MB of RAM, is supporting 15 users. He knows that the two counters he needs to track to see exactly what the memory situation is are Paging File %Usage and Peak, and the Memory Page Faults/Sec count. What tool would he use to track these two performance objects, and how would he set up the tracking process to create a counter log?

Learning Objectives

In this lab, you'll create a counter log for monitoring performance. By the end of this lab, you'll be able to

- Create a counter log.
- Monitor paging and Memory Performance objects.

Lab Materials and Setup

For this lab exercise, you'll need

- A working computer
- Installed network card (NIC)
- Windows 2000 Server software (installed)
- TCP/IP installed

Getting Down to Business

To configure a counter log for monitoring performance on paging and memory, perform the following steps:

Step 1.   Select Performance Monitor and open the Performance Console, then expand the section called Performance Logs and Alerts. Select the New Log Settings from the context menu of the Counter Logs object. When prompted, type a name describing the purpose of this log—**Memory Tracking**.

Step 2.   On the General property sheet, add the counters you want to log: select Paging File, select %Usage as the counter, and select _Total as the instance.

Step 3.   Select the object Paging File, select %Usage Peak as the counter, and select _Total as the instance. Lastly, select the object Memory, select Page Faults/Sec as the counter, and click Add. Close the window.

Step 4.   We want to track the instances at five-minute intervals. We also want to create the folder where the log will record its information.

Step 5.   To schedule the start of the tracking process, we need to click Counter Logs in the tree. Open the Properties window of Counter Logs and move to the Schedule tab.

Step 6.   In the Start log section, set the start time and date to match the current time and date. In the Stop log section, click After and set the period of time to track performance to eight hours. Select the Log Files tab and select the Record Option in a Text Format. Click OK to complete the process.

lab
(h)int   *For the purpose of this lab, you may want to reduce the period of time to track performance to a shorter span—maybe an hour or less.*

CERTIFICATION OBJECTIVE 19.03

Diagnosing Server Health Problems with Event Viewer

10 Minutes

The Common Solutions Group on the college campus is concerned about recent internal unauthorized access to the administrative side of the network. One of the members would like you to compile a report containing logon information that would help pinpoint at least the days and times that these intrusions are occurring.

What tool would you use to obtain this information, and how would you manipulate the information to extract only the logon sessions?

Learning Objectives

In this lab, you'll learn how to use the Event Viewer as a troubleshooting tool. By the end of this lab, you'll be able to

- Interpret Event Viewer information.
- Build a filter in Event Viewer.

Lab Materials and Setup

For this lab exercise, you'll need

- A working computer
- Installed network card (NIC)
- Windows 2000 Server software (installed)
- TCP/IP installed

Getting Down to Business

To use Event Viewer and configure a filter, perform the following steps:

Step 1.   Open the Event Viewer from the Start menu. Expand the Event Viewer object to display the three types of logs: System, Application, and Security.

Step 2.   You want to view the contents of the system log. The contents of the log will appear on the right side of the window. You'll notice various types of events: Error, Warning, Information, Success Audit, and Failure Audit. Not all of these events will be displayed—it depends on your system configuration.

Step 3.   You want to filter the events to focus on logon activity. To do so, you need to open the Properties of the system log. Move to the Filter tab. Click the list arrow in the Event Source box, scroll through the options, and select Netlogon. In the Event Types section, be sure that only the Error Event Types is checked off—all other types should be deactivated. Click OK to complete the process and display events focused only on failed logon events.

CERTIFICATION OBJECTIVE 19.04

Identifying and Disabling Unnecessary Services

10 Minutes

While directly logged on to a Windows 2000 server using Internet Explorer, you discover that the program is not responding to any keystrokes, including your attempts to close the program. The Office Word window you're also working with functions just fine. How can you close Internet Explorer without interrupting Word?

Learning Objectives

In this lab, you'll learn how to delete a process. By the end of this lab, you'll be able to

- Use Task Manager.
- Stop a running process.

Lab Materials and Setup

For this lab exercise, you'll need

- A working computer
- Installed network card (NIC)
- Windows 2000 Server software (installed)
- TCP/IP installed
- Internet Explorer (installed and opened)

Getting Down to Business

To stop a process using Task Manager, perform the following steps:

Step 1. Open the Task Manager. Select the Processes tab and locate the process you want to stop—in this case, Internet Explorer.

Step 2. Select Internet Explorer to either End Process (to stop just that specific process) or End Process Tree (to end that process and all the other processes it spawned in its lifetime).

Step 3. When the warning box appears, click Yes to end the process.

LAB ANALYSIS TEST

1. What are the two types of logs available in Performance Monitor, and how can you distinguish between the two?

   _____

   _____

2. What are the two methods for opening the Windows 2000 Task Manager?

   _____

   _____

3. In Event Viewer, which three logs does Windows 2000 display by default?

   _____

   _____

4. What is a baseline, and why is it important to establish one on your network?

   _____

   _____

5. What function does System Monitor provide and what kind of information can you measure and collect with it?

   _____

   _____

KEY TERM QUIZ

Use the following vocabulary terms to complete the sentences below. Not all of the terms will be used. Definitions for these terms can be found in "Managing a Microsoft Windows 2000 Network Environment Study Guide."

Benchmark

Performance Monitor

System Monitor

Event Viewer

Task Manager

Counter log

Security log

Application log

Error log

Thread

1. A tool used for monitoring and displaying statistics, server utilization, and data flow is named
   _____.

2. _____ is a utility that provides information about programs and processes running on the computer.

3. A _____ is a measurement standard for hardware and software. It is used to establish performance baselines under various usage loads and circumstances.

4. A collection of performance information, _____ records this information in a file for later review.

5. _____ maintains logs about application, security, and system events on a computer.

LAB SOLUTIONS FOR CHAPTER 19

In this section, you'll find solutions to the lab exercises, Lab Analysis Test, and Key Term Quiz.

Lab Solution 19.01

Your objective in this lab scenario is to track three DHCP counters to set down a benchmark standard for your system. The counters are Offers/Sec, Requests/Sec, and Releases/Sec. You use System Monitor to collect and view real-time performance data relating to the usage of hardware resources and the activity of system services on the DHCP server.

By the end of this lab, you configured and monitored a DHCP counter in System Monitor. By the end of this lab, you were able to

■ Use System Monitor.

■ Configure DHCP counter.

To add a DHCP counter and monitor its performance, perform the following steps:

Step 1. Choose Start | Programs | Administrative Tools and select Performance to open the Performance application. Here, select System Monitor to create an entry in System Monitor, then click the Add (+) icon. In the Add Counters window, click the Select Counters from Computer radio button to manually choose the objects you wish to track.

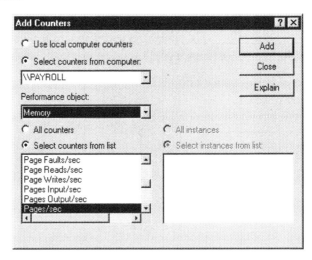

Step 2.   Select the Process Performance object. You will see the list of available counters. Select the two counters you need to create to track a potential memory leak: Page Faults/Sec and Page File Bytes. If you need to know what a counter means, select the counter and click the Explain button.

Step 3.   When you have finished adding the counters you need to monitor, click Add. Click Close when you are finished. Your counters will now be graphed.

Lab Solution 19.02

Brent knows that the two counters he needs to track to see exactly what the memory situation is are Paging File %Usage and Peak, and the Memory Page Faults/Sec count. Creating a counter log on these two performance objects will determine whether or not he needs to add more memory to the system. The system has 128MB of RAM installed.

With performance logs and alerts, you can collect performance data automatically from local or remote computers and view logged counter data using System Monitor, or export the data to spreadsheet programs or databases for analysis and report generation. A counter log takes the same information that is captured by the System Monitor and, instead of displaying it in a graph, records it in a file.

In this lab, you created a counter log for monitoring performance. By the end of this lab, you were able to

■   Create a counter log.

■   Monitor paging and memory performance objects.

To configure a counter log for monitoring performance on paging and memory, perform the following steps:

Step 1.   Click Start | Programs | Administrative Tools and select Performance Monitor. From the Performance Console, expand the section called Performance Logs and Alerts; then, right-click Counter Logs and choose New Log Settings from the menu, as shown in Figure 19-1. When prompted, type a name describing the purpose of this log, Memory Tracking.

FIGURE 19-1

The New Log
Settings option
creates a new
counter log
configuration.

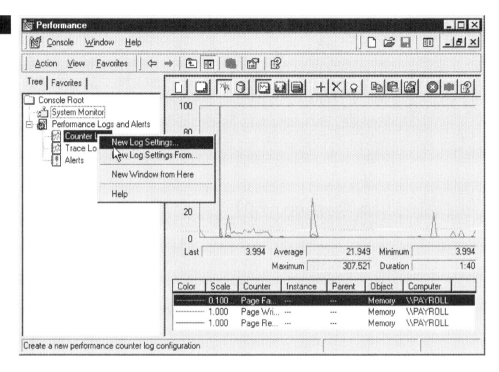

Step 2. On the General property sheet, add the counters you want to log. Select the performance object Paging File, select %Usage as the counter, and select _Total as the instance, as shown here. Click Add. This counter will monitor the number of page files in use.

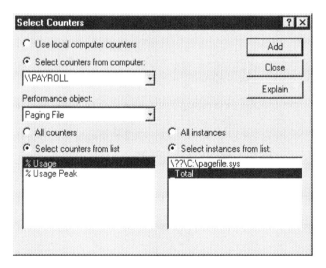

The sample data
will be collected
every five minutes.

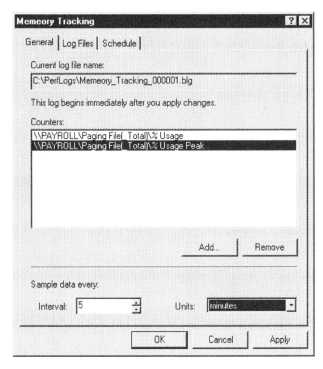

Step 3. Select the object Paging File, select %Usage Peak as the counter, and select _Total as the instance. Click Add. Lastly, select the object Memory, select Page Faults/Sec as the counter, and click Add. This will monitor the peak number of page files. Click Close.

Step 4. You want to track the instances at five-minute intervals by setting the Interval box to 5 and the Units box to minutes, as shown in Figure 19-2. Click OK. Click Yes to create the folder where the log will record its information.

Step 5. To schedule the start of the tracking process, we need to click Counter Logs in the tree. A Green Disk icon in front of the log name in the right-hand pane shows that the log is active. Right-click the log and select Properties, as shown next. Click the Schedule tab.

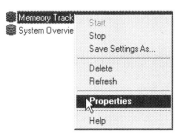

Step 6. In the Start Log section, set the start time and date to match the current time and date, as shown here:

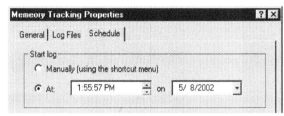

In the Stop Log section, Click After and set the period of time to track performance to eight hours. Select the Log Files tab and select the Record option in a text format. Click OK.

lab

⓵int *For the purpose of this lab, you may want to reduce the period of time to track performance to a shorter span—maybe an hour or less.*

Lab Solution 19.03

Logon information is contained in Event Viewer, and because you only need the failed attempts to log on to the administrative side of the network, we'll need to filter out everything but the failed attempts. The Security log records events that have to do with the security of the computer, such as logon and authentication, resource usage, and access.

In this lab, you learned how to use the Event Viewer as a troubleshooting tool. By the end of this lab, you were able to

- Interpret Event Viewer information.
- Build a filter in Event Viewer.

To use Event Viewer and configure a filter, perform the following steps:

Step 1. Click Start | Programs | Administrative Tools and select Event Viewer. Expand the Event Viewer object to display the three types of logs: System, Application, and Security, as shown here:

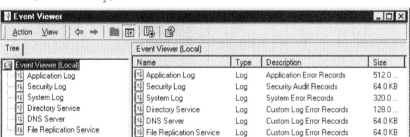

Step 2. If no logs appear in the tree, expand the tree by double-clicking Event Viewer. The contents of the log will appear on the right side of the window. You'll notice various types of events—Error, Warning, Information, Success Audit, and Failure Audit—as shown in Figure 19-3. Not all of these events will be displayed—it depends on your system configuration.

Step 3. You want to filter the events to focus on logon activity. Right-click System Log and select Properties from the context menu. Figure 19-4 displays the General tab window, containing information relative to the system log location, the size of the log, and what happens when the maximum size is reached.

Step 4. Select the Filter tab. Click the list arrow in the Event Source box, scroll through the options, and select Netlogon. Netlogon is associated with logon activity. Figure 19-5 displays the various filtering options. Be sure that only the Error type is checked; all other types should be deactivated. Click OK to complete the process and display events focused only on failed logon events.

FIGURE 19-3

Notice the various types of events displayed for the System Log: Warning, Error, and Information.

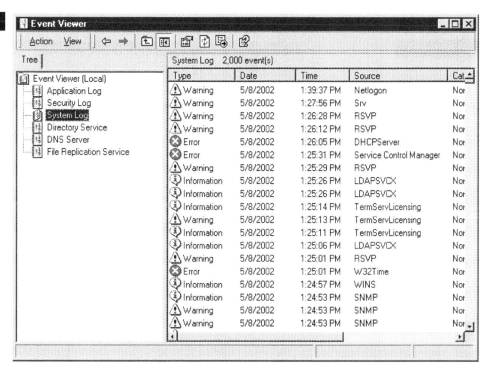

FIGURE 19-4

The General tab window contains information relative to the system log location, and the size of the log.

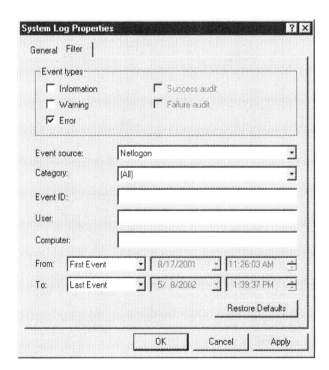

FIGURE 19-5

The Filter tab has options dealing with Event types, Event source, and the ability to configure the time range from which to extract the events.

Lab Solution 19.04

In this lab, you need to stop the nonresponding Internet Explorer, without interrupting other programs. The tool to use is Task Manager. When an application stops responding, you can try to close the application or you can use the Task Manager to manually stop the application.

In this lab, you'll learn how to delete a process associated with an application. By the end of this lab, you'll be able to

- Use Task Manager.
- Stop a running process.

To stop a process using Task Manager, perform the following steps:

Step 1. Open the Task Manager. You can either right-click the toolbar or press the CTRL-ALT-DEL keys. Click the Processes tab and locate the process you want to stop; in this case, it's Internet Explorer, as shown in Figure 19-6.

Step 2. Right-click the process that you want to end and choose either End Process (to stop just that specific process) or End Process Tree (to end that process and all the other processes it spawned in its lifetime).

FIGURE 19-6

Select the Internet Explorer process that you wish to halt.

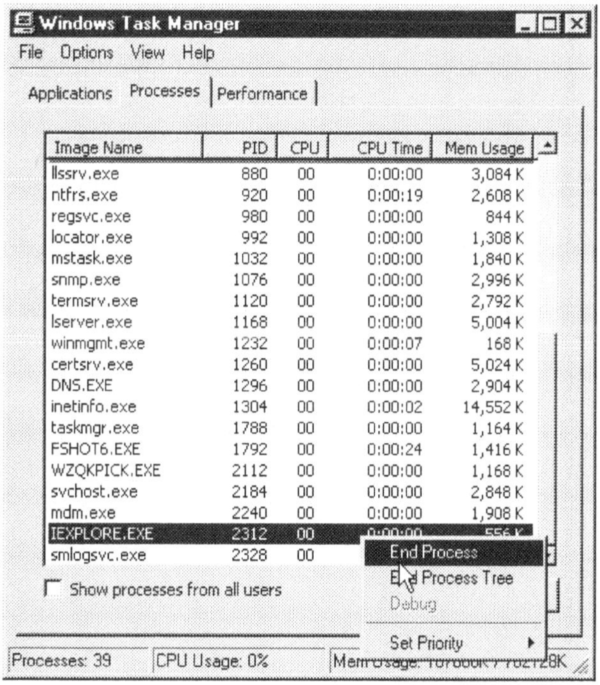

Step 3.   When the warning box appears, click Yes to end the process:

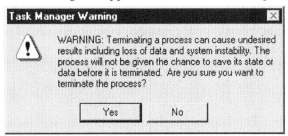

ANSWERS TO LAB ANALYSIS

1. The two kinds of logs are counter and tracer logs. The distinguishing feature is the collection trigger and how much control an administrator has over the collected information. The data collected in a counter log is controlled by time. The data collected in a trace log is controlled by events.

2. One way of opening the Task Manager is by pressing CTRL-ALT-DEL and selecting Task Manager in the Windows Security window. The other way is to right-click any empty space on the toolbar and select Task Manager from the context menu.

3. The three logs that are displayed by default in Event Viewer are system log, security log, and application log.

4. A baseline is an established performance standard for the operation of your server as determined by normal load. A baseline can then be used as a basis of comparison for future performance to see whether repairable problems exist. As the configuration of your server changes, new baselines are established to reflect the new expected performance.

5. With System Monitor, you can measure the performance of any computer on a network. You can collect and view real-time performance data; you can view data collected either currently or previously in a counter log; and you can view data in a printable graph, histogram, or report view.

ANSWERS TO KEY TERM QUIZ

1. Performance Monitor

2. Task Manager

3. Benchmark

4. Counter log

5. Event Viewer

20

Installing and Managing Software Updates

LAB EXERCISES

20.01   Using Slipstreaming to Update an Installation Source

20.02   Applying and Verifying a Service Pack Installation

20.03   Applying and Verifying a Hotfix Installation

20.04   Uninstalling a Hotfix and a Service Pack

■   Lab Analysis Test

■   Key Term Quiz

■   Lab Solutions

O ne of the many functions associated with a network administrator is the job of maintaining updated software on the computers. This especially applies to the operating system. This is a multifaceted process where the administrator needs to periodically visit Microsoft's support site, or subscribe to an industry-related newsletter, or receive e-mail updates as a member of the "'certified'" community. These updates are in one of two forms: service packs or hotfixes. Service packs are carefully planned and managed, and the goal is to deliver a well-tested, comprehensive set of fixes that is suitable for use on any customer's system. Hotfixes, also known as patches, are developed on an as-needed basis to combat specific, immediate threats to a system's security.

In this chapter we will look at the different aspects of service packs and hotfixes. We use a "tool" that lets us incorporate a service pack into a Windows 2000 folder, which affords us a way to deploy new Windows 2000 installations without the need to apply the service pack as a second step. We'll also look at applying and verifying a straight service pack installation, applying and verifying a hotfix installation, and the process of uninstalling a hotfix or service pack if the need arises.

CERTIFICATION OBJECTIVE 20.01

Using Slipstreaming to Update an Installation Source

20 Minutes

Pauline is the network administrator for a company with a twenty-computer LAN. Currently, her network has one Windows NT 4.0 domain controller, one Windows NT 4.0 member server, and eighteen Windows 98 client computers. She wants to upgrade her NT 4.0 servers to Windows 2000 Server. She has a distribution share for Windows 2000 Server named w2k. Today she received an e-mail that a Windows 2000 service pack is available for download. Pauline wants to update the two servers only once with the service pack included. Can she do that, and how would she go about integrating the service pack into the Windows 2000 distribution share?

Learning Objectives

Service pack slipstreaming allows you to install Windows 2000 from a distribution share automatically applying the service pack during the install. This process integrates, and mostly replaces, files from the service pack into the Windows 2000 installation files. This removes the need to reapply the service pack whenever a user adds components using the distribution share.

But first we need to download the service pack. There are two ways to install Windows 2000 SP2: Network installation and Express installation. The Network installation includes all of the Windows 2000 SP2 files needed for installing the service pack on Windows 2000 Professional, Server, or Advanced Server. This is the method of choice when multiple computers on a network need to be updated. A fast Internet connection—ISDN or cable modem—is strongly recommended. The Express installation detects your system components and installs only the updates that are necessary for your computer. This is good for a single-computer installation.

In this lab, you'll incorporate a server pack into a Windows 2000 distribution share. By the end of this lab, you'll be able to

- Download the service pack from the Microsoft web site.
- Extract the service pack files into a self-created directory, i386.
- Integrate the service pack into the distribution share.

Lab Materials and Setup

For this lab exercise, you'll need

- A working computer
- Installed network card (NIC)
- Windows 2000 Server software (installed)
- TCP/IP installed
- Active Directory (AD) installed
- Internet connection

lab

Warning *In order to successfully complete this lab, it is necessary to copy the i386 folder and its contents onto your hard drive.*

Getting Down to Business

To download Windows 2000 SP2 and use slipstreaming to update an installation distribution share, perform the following steps:

Step 1. Log on to Microsoft's web site by typing the following URL: **www.microsoft.com/Windows2000/downloads/servicepacks/sp2/download.asp**. Choose the SP2 Network Installation file (approximately 101MB in size). Follow the instructions to download the file onto your hard drive.

Step 2. Create a directory where the Windows 2000 SP2 file will be extracted. Extract the packed files into a directory, SP2, using a Command Prompt window.

lab

Hint *File extractions may also be performed using third-party software such as WinZip, PkZip, or WinAce.*

Step 3. Slipstream the Windows 2000 SP2 file into the Windows 2000 installation share using the Update.exe utility. Once the files have been integrated, the process is complete.

cross

Reference *For further information on slipstreaming syntax, refer to Chapter 20 of "Managing a Microsoft Windows 2000 Network Environment Study Guide."*

CERTIFICATION OBJECTIVE 20.02

25 Minutes

Applying and Verifying a Service Pack Installation

Angela is the new Windows 2000 network administrator at Marcus Aurelius trade school. She has been running three Windows 2000 servers for only six months when today she receives an e-mail informing her that the second Windows 2000 service pack is available for download. She needs to download the service pack and then be able to install the service pack on all three servers. How would she go about downloading and verifying the installation of the service pack, and what is the easiest way to provide installation files for the servers?

Learning Objectives

Service Pack 2 (any service pack for that matter) is a collection of updates for the Windows 2000 operating system. The service pack can be easily applied while Windows 2000 is running. Service Pack 2 also includes the updates contained in Service Pack 1. Service Pack 2 is a collection of updates for Windows 2000 that pertain to operating system reliability, application compatibility, Windows 2000 setup issues, and security issues. The service pack is a package of files that need to be extracted into an installation folder. It is a self-extracting executable.

Before you install this service pack, take a few precautionary measures. Close all debuggers and close all antivirus programs. To maximize recovery of the computer in the event of installation failure, you may want to update the system emergency repair disk. Perform a full backup of the computer, including the registry files, and check your computer's available disk space against the space requirements for the service pack. Additionally, you may need to disable antivirus checking in the BIOS.

At the completion of the installation, the service pack might prompt you to restart your system.

In this lab, you'll apply a Windows 2000 SP2 and verify its installation. By the end of this lab, you'll be able to

- Update a Windows 2000 Server computer.
- Verify a Windows 2000 SP2 installation.

Lab Materials and Setup

For this lab exercise, you will need

- A working computer
- Installed network card (NIC)
- Windows 2000 Server software (installed)
- TCP/IP installed

■ Active Directory (AD) installed

■ Internet connection

■ Windows 2000 SP2 downloaded from Microsoft web site

Getting Down to Business

To apply and verify a Windows 2000 SP2 installation, perform the following steps:

Step 1. Create a distribution folder, SP2, for the service pack on a network distribution share. Expand the service pack executable file to the network share.

Step 2. Run the service pack executable file from the distribution share to install the service pack on your Windows 2000 server.

Step 3. To verify the installation of the service pack, use the regedt32.exe utility. You'll need to browse to the CurrentVersion key of the Software/Microsoft/WindowsNT subhive.

CERTIFICATION OBJECTIVE 20.03

20 Minutes

Applying and Verifying a Hotfix Installation

Fred is the administrator of the Sentimental Greeting Company, which has a large Windows 2000–based network. He oversees the maintenance of 20 Windows 2000 servers. All his servers were installed from a network share. He has received an alert that a hotfix file for Windows 2000 is available for download. It is a critical patch to the operating system and he needs to install tonight. What does Fred need to do to download and apply this hotfix to each of the 20 Windows 2000 servers?

Learning Objectives

Hotfixes are small, problem-specific executables whose purpose is to correct a specific flaw or security issue in the operating system or other installed application.

These hotfixes usually result from the discovery of a weakness in the product. Applying the hotfix in a timely fashion is critical to ensure proper security or prevent degraded system performance.

In this lab, you'll apply and verify a hotfix installation downloaded from Microsoft. By the end of this lab, you'll be able to

- Discover and download a hotfix file.
- Apply the hotfix.
- Verify the hotfix installation.

Lab Materials and Setup

For this lab exercise, you will need

- A working computer
- Installed network card (NIC)
- Windows 2000 Server software (installed)
- TCP/IP installed
- Active Directory (AD) installed
- Internet connection

Getting Down to Business

To apply and verify a hotfix installation, perform the following steps:

Step 1.   Create a distribution folder (hotfix) for the hotfix file on a network distribution share. Download the hotfix file Q300845 from Microsoft's web site, http://www.microsoft.com/WINDOWS2000/downloads/critical/q300845/default.asp, into the distribution folder.

Step 2.   Install the hotfix from the distribution share. Verify the installation of the hotfix using the regedt32.exe utility. You'll need to browse to the CurrentVersion key of the Software/Microsoft/Updates subhive. The hotfix update is identified by its Q300845 number that appears on the subhive folder.

CERTIFICATION OBJECTIVE 20.04

Uninstalling a Hotfix and a Service Pack

15 Minutes

Greg is the system administrator in a Microsoft Certified Technical Education Center. He manages 90 Intel-based PCs that students use for both application and technical training. He notices that, since a service pack and hotfix install, one particular server is having software issues. The configuration of these machines is all the same, but he wonders why this one particular machine is having an issue, and it started after the updates. In troubleshooting the problem, he needs to determine which of the two updates—service pack or hotfix—is at fault. Greg, therefore, needs to uninstall the hotfix and the service pack and return the Windows 2000 server to its original condition. Then he can attempt to pinpoint the problem. How would Greg uninstall the service pack and the hotfix, and in which order?

Learning Objectives

A service pack and a hotfix contain an uninstall feature that you can use to restore your computer to its previous state. It's important to note that you cannot uninstall a service pack that you installed by using an integrated installation. If you install any programs or services that require the service pack, uninstalling the service pack can adversely affect those programs. If you installed any applications after the service pack was installed, you should not uninstall the service pack. The service pack does not contain system updates—such as file format, database format, and registry format changes—that Setup cannot uninstall. Lastly, if you turn off the automatic backup option for Update.exe, you cannot use the uninstall Service Pack 2 mechanism and, therefore, cannot uninstall the Service Pack 2.

In this lab, you'll uninstall a hotfix and Service Pack 2. By the end of this lab, you'll be able to

- Uninstall a hotfix installation.
- Uninstall a service pack.

Lab Materials and Setup

For this lab exercise, you will need

- A working computer
- Installed network card (NIC)
- Windows 2000 Server software (installed)
- TCP/IP installed
- Active Directory (AD) installed

Getting Down to Business

To uninstall a hotfix file and a service pack, perform the following steps:

Step I. First, let's remove the Windows 2000 hotfix. Access the Add/Remove Programs utility from your Control Panel. Select the Q300845 hotfix file. Follow the screen directions to remove the hotfix.

Step 2. Next, let's remove the Windows 2000 Service Pack 2. Access the Add/Remove Programs utility from your Control Panel. Select the Windows 2000 Service Pack 2. Follow the screen directions to remove the service pack.

LAB ANALYSIS TEST

1. A Windows 2000 service pack contains a collection of updates for the operating system. Which elements of Windows 2000 do the updates pertain to?

_____

_____

2. What are the download options for a Windows 2000 service pack?

_____

_____

3. What is the procedure for uninstalling a Windows 2000 service pack?

_____

_____

4. Why is it necessary to install a hotfix even though a service pack has already been applied?

_____

_____

5. When would it be necessary to uninstall a service pack or hotfix file?

_____

_____

KEY TERM QUIZ

Use the following vocabulary terms to complete the sentences below. Not all of the terms will be used. Definitions for these terms can be found in "Managing a Microsoft Windows 2000 Network Environment Study Guide."

Registry hive

Debuggers

Registry

CurrentVersion key

Express installation

Network installation

Hotfix

Slipstream

Slipstreaming

Service pack

1. The process of adding a service pack directly into the operating system's distribution share during extraction is known as _____.

2. A _____ is a collection of updates for Windows 2000 that pertain to an operating system's reliability, application compatibility, and security issues.

3. _____ is the ideal download method of a service pack from Microsoft's web site in order to use a network share for distribution.

4. A _____ is a collection of one or more files that can be applied to the operating system to correct a system or security problem.

5. A database used by Windows to store configuration information is known as a _____.

LAB SOLUTIONS FOR CHAPTER 20

In this section, you'll find solutions to the lab exercises, Lab Analysis Test, and Key Term Quiz.

Lab Solution 20.01

Slipstreaming ensures that a network share containing the Windows 2000 Server installation files is updated with the fixes that a service pack provides. This ensures that changes made to a Windows 2000 Server that require the installation files will automatically install the updated versions of files, provided that they come from an updated network share. In addition, this also ensures that new installations will automatically end up with the fixed files installed.

To download Windows 2000 SP2 and use slipstreaming to update an installation distribution share, perform the following steps:

Step 1. Launch a Web browser and log on to Microsoft's web site by typing the following URL:
www.microsoft.com/Windows2000/downloads/servicepacks/sp2/download.asp.
You'll be asked to choose a language—select English and click GO. This web page has information about the service pack and the available download options. Because we want to provide a distribution share on our network, choose the SP2 Network Installation file option. Follow the instructions to download the file.

lab
Hint *Personally, I suggest placing the file on the desktop for easier access when you're ready to extract the service pack.*

Step 2. Create a directory, SP2, where the Windows 2000 SP2 file will be extracted (this is a matter of personal preference). Extract the packed files into the directory using a Command Prompt window using the command w2ksp2 –x, as shown next.

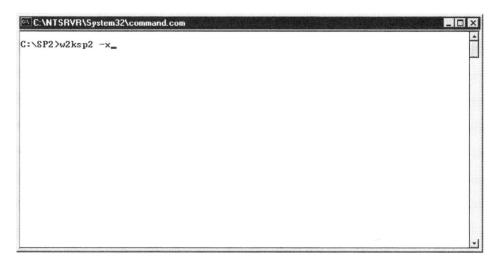

Or type the command in the Windows Run option. To slipstream the file into your Windows 2000 distribution folder and use the Command Prompt window, change to your distribution share folder (win2K) and type the following at the prompt:

```
c:\sp2\i386\update\update.exe /s:c:\w2k.
```

This will extract the contents of the directory and subdirectories in the w2k folder. A GUI will pop up and show the update progress until it is complete, as shown next. You will be prompted to reboot your system.

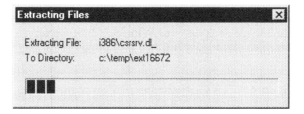

For further information on slipstreaming syntax, refer to Chapter 20 of "Managing a Microsoft Windows 2000 Network Environment Study Guide."

Lab Solution 20.02

The best thing about a service pack is that it contains all the necessary updates in one executable file. It doesn't require several steps to apply different components, one after the other. Once the service pack is installed, you can verify its existence by viewing the CurrentVersion key in the Registry database.

To apply and verify a Windows 2000 SP2 installation, perform the following steps:

Step 1.   Launch a web browser and log on to Microsoft's web site by typing the following url: **www.microsoft.com/Windows2000/downloads/servicepacks/sp2/download.asp**. You'll be asked to choose a language—select English and click GO. This web page has information about the service pack and the available download options. Because we want to provide a distribution share on our network, choose the SP2 Network Installation file option. Follow the instructions to download the file.

lab
Hint   *Personally, I suggest placing the file on the desktop for easier access when you're ready to extract the service pack.*

Step 2.   Create a directory, SP2, on a network distribution share where the Windows 2000 SP2 file will be extracted (this is a matter of personal preference). Extract the packed files into the directory using a Command Prompt window with the command w2ksp2 –x or type the command in Windows Run option.

Step 3.   Run the service pack executable file from the distribution share to install the service pack on your Windows 2000 server using the Install icon, as shown in Figure 20-1. You will be prompted to reboot your system.

Step 4.   To verify the installation of the service pack, use the regedt32.exe utility. Click Start | Run, and type **regedt32** in the text box. The Registry Editor window will open. Expand the HKEY_LOCAL_MACHINE folder down to the CurrentVersion key. The path will be HKEY_LOCAL_MACHINE /Software/Microsoft/WindowsNT/ CurrentVersion. The values on the right side of the window will display the addition of the service pack, as shown in Figure 20-2. Exit the Registry Editor when you've verified the existence of the service pack.

FIGURE 20-1

Click the Install
button to
execute the
service pack.

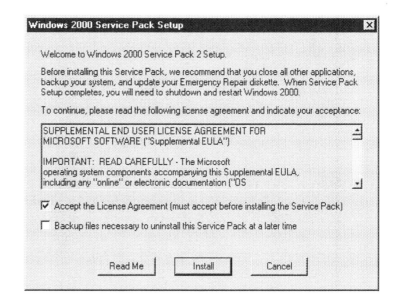

FIGURE 20-2

The service pack
update is
displayed in the
CurrentVersion
folder in the
Local Machine
hive.

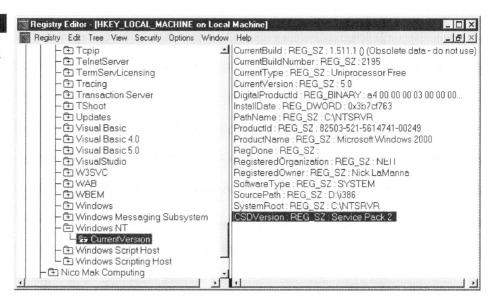

Lab Solution 20.03

Problems relating to a computer's operating system or security will arise between service pack releases. To address these problems, Microsoft will periodically issue hotfixes. These are specific patches that address specific issues dealing with Windows 2000, whether it is related to the operating system or security. It may even apply to an application incompatibility issue.

To apply and verify a hotfix installation, perform the following steps:

Step 1. Create a distribution folder (hotfix) for the hotfix file on a network distribution share. Download the hotfix file Q300845 titled Security Update, March 4, 2002 from Microsoft's web site at http://www.microsoft.com/windows2000/downloads/critical/q300845/default.asp into the distribution folder. Follow the instructions on the web page and select the Microsoft VM build 3805 for Microsoft Windows 2000 (Hotfix) item.

lab
Hint *Additional hotfix files and bulletins can be viewed and obtained from this Microsoft web site: http://www.microsoft.com/technet/treeview/default.asp?url=/technet/security/current.asp.*

Step 2. Install the hotfix, Q300845.exe, from the distribution share. Verify the installation of the hotfix using the regedt32.exe utility.

Step 3. To verify the installation of the hotfix, use the regedt32.exe utility. Click Start | Run, and type **regedt32** in the text box. The Registry Editor window will open. You'll need to browse to the CurrentVersion key of the Software/Microsoft/Updates subhive. The path will be HKEY_LOCAL_MACHINE /Software/Microsoft/WindowsNT/Updates. The values on the right side of the window will display the addition of the hotfix, which is identified by its Q300845 number that appears on the subhive folder. Exit the Registry Editor when you've verified the existence of the service pack.

Lab Solution 20.04

Once in a while a situation occurs when the hotfix or service pack will result in a new and undocumented problem with either Windows 2000 or an application installed on that computer. This situation now turns into a troubleshooting process:

the need to trace your steps, what new hardware or software product was introduced to the system, when was it introduced, and what is causing the conflict. It's up to the network administrator to unapply and reapply each new element, one at a time, and test out the system to either rule in, or rule out, in our case, the service pack or hotfix.

To uninstall a hotfix file and a service pack, perform the following steps:

Step 1. First, let's remove the Windows 2000 hotfix. Click Start | Settings | Control Panel, and then click the Add/Remove Programs icon. Scroll through the items in this window and select the Q300845 hotfix file. Click Remove and follow the screen directions to remove the hotfix.

Step 2. Next, let's remove the Windows 2000 Service Pack 2. If you're not in the Add or Remove Programs window, click Start | Settings | Control Panel, and then click the Add/Remove Programs icon. Scroll through the items in the window and select the Windows 2000 Service Pack 2, as shown in Figure 20-3. Click Remove and follow the screen directions to remove the service pack. Exit out of the Add or Remove Programs window and the Control Panel window.

FIGURE 20-3

Uninstall Service Pack 2 using the Add or Remove Programs utility.

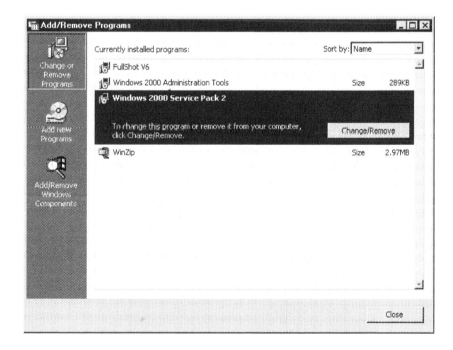

ANSWERS TO LAB ANALYSIS

1. A Windows 2000 Service Pack 2 provides the latest updates to the Windows 2000 operating systems. These updates are a collection of fixes that address the following areas: application compatibility, operating system reliability, security, and setup.

2. There are two available options. The Network installation will download the complete Windows 2000 service pack files to a computer. This will give a network administrator the ability to deploy the service pack through the use of a distribution share on the network. The Express installation is a faster method that detects a system's components and installs only those updates that are necessary for the system. This method is recommended for end users who want to quickly update their system with the latest updates to Windows 2000.

3. A service pack contains an uninstall feature that you can use to restore a computer to its previous state. When you run the Update.exe program to install the service pack, a subfolder named $ntservicepackuninstall$ is created in the administrator's %windir% folder. You can uninstall the service pack by using Add/Remove Programs in Control Panel or by running the Uninstall program from the command prompt.

4. Hotfixes are problem-specific executable files whose purpose is to correct a specific flaw or security issue in a Windows operating system or application. These hotfixes are a direct result from the discovery of a weakness in a Windows product. The timely application of a hotfix is critical to the operating system.

5. There may be an instance when the installation of a service pack or hotfix will interact unfavorably with a Windows 2000 application or security component. In this situation, it may be necessary to uninstall the service pack or hotfix in order to troubleshoot the problem. If both a service pack and hotfix have been installed, uninstall the hotfix first and the service pack second. In between the removals, evaluate the issue and attempt to identify what is generating the problem.

ANSWERS TO KEY TERM QUIZ

1. Slipstreaming
2. Service pack
3. Network installation
4. Hotfix
5. Registry

INDEX

A

(A) Host, 54
Access Control Settings window, 158-159
Action menu, 118
Active Directory
    Active Directory-integrated zones, 50-53, 62-68
    IAS servers, 312
Active Directory, managing/troubleshooting
    global catalog servers, 203-204, 213
    key term quiz, 208, 216
    lab analysis test, 207, 215-216
    objects, 200-202, 209-212
    replication, 204-206, 214-215
Active Directory, publishing resources, 161-178
    key term quiz, 169, 178
    lab analysis test, 168, 177-178
    network services, 165-167, 174-177
    shared folders, 162-163, 170-173
    shared printers, 164-165, 173-174
    software, 180
Active Directory, users/groups
    delegating administrative control, 113-114,
        130-132
    domain user accounts, 104-107, 117-121
    Global Groups, 109-111, 124-126
    key term quiz, 116, 133
    lab analysis test, 115, 133
    organizational units, 111-113, 126-130
    overview of, 104
    user profiles, 107-109, 121-124
Active Directory Sites and Services
    global catalog servers, 204, 213
    replication, 206, 214-215

Active Directory Users and Computers
    application categories, 187
    default user profiles, 122
    delegation of control, 114, 131
    domain user accounts, 106, 118-121
    Global Groups, 110-111, 125-126
    group policies. *See* group policies
    OUs, 112-113, 128-130, 202, 209-212
    publishing shared folders, 163, 171-173
    publishing shared printers, 174
Add A New Category dialog box, 195
Add Exclusions window, 95
Add Network Components
    DNS, 63
    WINS, 40
Add Printer Wizard, 165
Add/Remove Hardware wizard, 362, 370-371
Add/Remove Programs utility
    DHCP server, 80
    DNS Server, 63
    hotfixes/service packs, 421, 429
    IAS, 302, 310
    IIS, 241-242, 249
    software categories, 184
    Terminal Services Licensing, 116
    WINS, 30
administration
    Active Directory, 113-114, 130-132
    delegating authority of OU, 142-143, 153-155
    remote, 323-324, 331-333
Administrator account
    creating default user profiles, 122-123
    creating Global Groups, 125-127

creating OUs, 128-130
creating user accounts, 120
delegating control, 131-132
Advanced Attributes dialog box, 232-233
Advanced Security Configuration window, 269-270
Advanced Security settings dialog window, 157
Advanced TCP/IP Settings dialog box, 43, 44-45
alerts, System Monitor, 398-399, 405-408
application categories, 184-185, 193-196
Audit Entry dialog window, 157-158
audit policies, 139-141, 150-152
auditing
    configuring, 260-262, 269-271
    overview of, 260
Auditing window, 145
authentication
    overview of, 240
    RAS and, 283-285, 295-296
    Web/FTP sites, 244-245, 254-255
authentication protocols
    dial-up servers and, 303-305, 315-316
    remote access and, 285-286, 296-297
authorization, DHCP server, 80-81, 92-93

Certificate Services, 166-167, 174-177
clients
    DHCP, 84-86, 98-100
    DNS, 56-57, 72-73
    TCP/IP, 2-4, 13
    WINS, configuring, 31, 41-42
    WINS, troubleshooting, 31-33, 46-47
CNAME records, DNS
    creating/configuring, 54-55, 68-70
    defined, 54
Command Prompt window
    compacting DHCP database, 87,
        100-102
    route configuration, 7, 19
    slipstreaming and, 416, 424-425
    troubleshooting with IPconfig, 21-22
    troubleshooting with PING, 22-23
    troubleshooting with TRACERT, 23-24
computer configuration settings, 136
Configure Device dialog box, 294-295
Configure DHCP Options window, 96
Configure DNS Server Wizard, 52-53, 65
Create a New Dfs Link window, 236
Create Scope Wizard, DHCP, 82, 94
Create Volume Wizard, 229-230

B-node (broadcast node), NetBIOS, 36-38
Backup/Restore Configuration utility, IIS, 255-256
Backup Wizard, 380-381, 390-394
backups
    OS/data, 380-381, 389-394
    web site data, 246, 255-256
baselines, 396
boot logs, 375
bridgehead servers, 206, 214-215
broadcast node (B-node), NetBIOS, 36-38

DACL (discretionary access control list), 140
Data Encryption Standard (DES), 304
data storage
    Dfs, 223-224, 233-237
    disk quotas, 220-221, 231-232
    disks/volumes, 218-220, 227-230
    EFS, 222, 232-233
    key term quiz, 226, 237
    lab analysis test, 225, 237
DDNS (dynamic DNS), 55-56, 71-72
Delegate Control utility, OUs, 143
delegating authority, group policies, 142-143,
    153-155

Categories dialog window, 185, 194-195
Categories option, software, 184-185, 193-196

Delegation of Control Wizard
  delegating control to administrator, 155
  delegating control to user, 201-202, 211-212
  delegating control to users/groups, 114, 130-132
demand-dial routers, 303-305, 315-317
Deploy Software dialog window, Group Policy,
  183, 193
DES (Data Encryption Standard), 304
Dfs (Distributed File System)
  implementing/managing, 223-224, 233-237
  overview of, 218
  publishing Dfs folders, 162-163, 170-173
DHCP (Dynamic Host Configuration Protocol)
  client configuration, 84-86, 98-100
  DNS integration and, 83-84, 97
  dynamic DNS and, 55-56
  key term quiz, 89, 102
  lab analysis test, 88, 102
  overview of, 78
  scopes, 81-82, 92-96
  server installation/authorization, 78-81, 90-92
  troubleshooting, 86-87, 100-102
  WINS clients, configuring, 31, 44-45
  WINS, troubleshooting, 32-33
Dial-up Connection Properties window, ICS,
  343, 349
digital signatures, 360-361, 368-370
discretionary access control list (DACL), 140
Disk Management
  configuring disks/volumes, 218-220, 227-230
  overview of, 218
disk quotas, 220-221, 231-232
disks
  configuring, 218-220, 227-230
  quotas, 220-221, 231-232
  recovering data, 378-380, 387-389
Disks to Upgrade dialog box, Disk Management, 219,
  227-228
Display Properties dialog box, user profiles, 123-125
Distributed File System. *See* Dfs (Distributed File
  System)

DNS (Domain Name System)
  Active Directory-integrated zone, 50-53,
    62-68
  client computers and, 56-57, 72-73
  database records, 53-55, 68-70
  DDNS, 55-56, 71-72
  DHCP Servers, integrating with, 83-84, 97
  installing Windows 2000, 52-53, 62-64
  key term quiz, 61, 76
  lab analysis test, 60, 75
  overview of, 50
  troubleshooting, 58-59, 73-74
DNS monitoring snap-in, 58
domain user accounts, Active Directory, 104-107,
  117-121
DOS sessions
  FTP sites and, 244, 253-254
  troubleshooting with IPconfig, 21-22
double quotes ("."), 39
driver signing options
  configuring, 359-360, 367
  monitoring/troubleshooting, 360-361
Driver Signing Options dialog box, 367
dynamic DNS (DDNS), 55-56, 71-72
Dynamic Host Configuration Protocol. *See* DHCP
  (Dynamic Host Configuration Protocol)

E

EAP (Extensible Authentication Protocol), 304
Edit Alias dialog box, 242, 250-251
EFS (Encrypting File System)
  implementing, 222, 232-233
  overview of, 218
emergency repair disks (ERDs), creating, 379-380,
  387-389
Encryption dialog window, 316-317
encryption protocols
  applying, 303-305, 315-317
  configuring remote access security, 328,
    336-338

Remote Desktop Protocol, 322
verifying for remote access, 289, 296-297
ERDs (emergency repair disks), creating, 379-380, 387-389
error messages
Event Viewer checking for NAT, 352
jetpack program, 101
Event Viewer
checking for NAT error warnings, 352
defined, 396
diagnosing server health/performance, 399-400, 408-410
Excluded Address Range window, DHCP scopes, 95
Execute application permission, sharing web folders, 251
Express installation, Windows 2000 SP2, 415
Extensible Authentication Protocol (EAP), 304

F

Filter tab, Event Viewer, 409-410
filters, building, 400, 408-410
Folder Properties dialog box, 250
folders
encrypting, 222, 232-233
publishing shared, 162-163, 170-173
sharing web, 240-242, 249-252
Forward Lookup Zone window, 65
Forward Lookup Zones folder, 69-70
FQDNs (fully qualified domain names), 55
FTP sites
creating, 242-244, 252-253
securing, 244-245, 254-255
fully qualified domain names (FQDNs), 55

G

General tab, Event Viewer, 410
global catalog servers, 203-204, 213
Global Groups, Active Directory, 109-111, 124-126

GPOs (Group Policy Objects)
defined, 182
deploying software with, 181-184, 190-193
group policies, security policies
audit policies, 139-141, 150-152
delegating authority, 142-143, 153-155
key term quiz, 147, 159
lab analysis test, 146, 158-159
overview of, 136-137
security settings, 137-139, 148-150
troubleshooting, 144-145, 156-158
group policies, software deployment, 179-198
application categories, 184-185, 193-196
deploying software, 181-183
key term quiz, 189, 198
lab analysis test, 188, 198
lab solutions, 190-196
overview of, 180-181
removing software, 186-187, 196-197
Group Policy Objects (GPOs)
defined, 182
deploying software, 181-184, 190-193
groups. See Active Directory, users/groups

H

H-node (hybrid node), NetBIOS, 37
hard disks, recovering data from, 378-380, 387-389. See also disks
hardware compatibility list (hcl), 358
hardware, server/client, 357-372
compatibility, 358-359, 365-366
digitally signed, 360-361, 368-370
driver signing options, 359-360, 367
key term quiz, 364, 372
lab analysis test, 363, 372
legacy hardware, 361-362, 370-371
hcl (hardware compatibility list), defined, 358
hotfixes
applying/verifying, 418-419, 428
defined, 414

overview of, 418-419
uninstalling, 420-421, 428-429
hybrid node (H-node), NetBIOS, 37

I

i386 folder, 416
IAS (Internet Authentication Service), 301-303,
310-315
ICS (Internet Connection Sharing), 341-355
installing and configuring, 342-343, 349-350
key term quiz, 348, 355
lab analysis test, 347, 355
overview of, 342
troubleshooting, 344-345, 350-351
IIS dialog box, installing IIS, 241-242, 249-250
IIS (Internet Information Services), 239-258
FTP sites, 242-244, 252-253
installing, 241-242
key term quiz, 248, 257
lab analysis test, 247, 257
maintaining/troubleshooting, 245-246,
255-257
overview of, 240
securing Web/FTP sites, 244-245, 254-255
Web sites, 240-242, 249-252
Import Policy dialog window, security templates, 139,
149-150
.INF extension, 263
Internet Authentication Service (IAS), 301-303,
310-315
Internet Information Services console, 244-245,
254-255
Internet Protocol Security (IPSec), 304
Internet Protocol (TCP/IP) Properties dialog box
DHCP client configuration, 85, 98-100
DNS client configuration, 72-73
TCP/IP configuration, 4, 13-15
WINS client configuration, 44-46
WINS server, configuring as WINS client, 42-44

Internet Services Manager
backing up/restoring IIS configuration, 246,
255-256
creating FTP sites, 243-244, 252-253
securing Web/FTP sites, 245, 254-255
IP addresses
DHCP scopes, 93-96
NAT interface, 354
NetBIOS and, 27
subnet masks, 6, 16-18
TCP/IP configuration and, 3-4, 13-16
Windows 2000 DNS Server configuration,
52-53
WINS configuration, 31
IPconfig utility
DNS, 58
ICS, 344-345, 350-351
TCP/IP, 9, 21-22
WINS, 32-33, 46-47
IPSec (Internet Protocol Security), 304

J

jetpack program, 87, 100-102

K

key term quizzes
Active Directory, managing/troubleshooting,
208, 216
Active Directory, publishing resources,
169, 178
Active Directory, users/groups, 116, 133
data storage, 226, 237
DHCP, 89, 102
DNS, 61, 76
hardware, 364, 372
ICS, 348, 355
IIS, 248, 257
name resolution, 35, 48

NAT, 348, 355
remote access connections, 288, 298
security, 268, 276
security policies, implementing, 147, 159
security policies, remote access, 309, 320
server performance, 403, 412
software deployment, 189, 198
software updates, 423, 430
startup, 383, 394
TCP/IP, 12, 24
Terminal Services, 330, 340
VPN connections, 288, 298
KKC (knowledge consistency checker), 203

L

lab analysis tests
Active Directory, managing/troubleshooting, 207, 215-216
Active Directory, publishing resources, 168, 177-178
Active Directory, users/groups, 115, 133
data storage, 225, 237
DHCP, 88, 102
DNS, 60, 75
hardware, 363, 372
ICS, 347, 355
IIS, 247, 257
name resolution, 34, 48
NAT, 347, 355
remote access connections, 287, 298
security, 267, 276
security policies, implementing, 146, 158-159
security policies, remote access, 308, 320
server performance, 402, 412
software deployment, 188, 198
software updates, 422, 430
startup, 382, 394
TCP/IP, 11, 24

Terminal Services, 329, 339
VPN connections, 287, 298
Last Known Good configuration mode, 376-377, 385-386
Lease Duration window, DHCP scopes, 96
legacy hardware, 361-362, 370-371
licenses, 115-117, 324-326
LMHOSTS file, 28-29, 38-39
Local Area Connection Properties dialog box
DNS client, 57, 72-73
TCP/IP servers/clients, 3-4, 13, 16
WINS client, 44-46
WINS server as client, 42-44
log files, 374-375, 384-385
logging, System Monitor, 398-399, 405-408

M

M-node (modified node), NetBIOS, 37
MAC (media access control) addresses, 26
mail exchangers (MX records), DNS, 54
mapping, 144, 159
media access control (MAC) addresses, 26
Microsoft Challenge Handshake Authentication Protocol (MS-CHAP v2), 304
Microsoft Distributed File System. *See* Dfs (Distributed File System)
Microsoft Management Console, 264-266
Microsoft Windows Update web site, 358-359, 365-366
modified node (M-node), NetBIOS, 37
Move dialog box, 130
MS-CHAP v2 (Microsoft Challenge Handshake Authentication Protocol), 304
.msi files, 180, 183
MX records (mail exchangers), DNS, 54
My Network Places
deploying software with, 183
installing/configuring ICS, 343, 349

N

name resolution
 DNS, 56-57, 72-73
 key term quiz, 35, 48
 lab analysis test, 34, 48
 NetBIOS, 28-29, 37-39
 overview of, 26-28, 36-37
 troubleshooting DNS, 58-59, 73-74
 troubleshooting WINS, 31-33, 46-47
 WINS, 29-31, 40-46
Name Server (NS), DNS, 54
NAT (Network Address Translation)
 configuring, 345-346, 351-354
 key term quiz, 348, 355
NetBIOS (Network Basic Input/Output System)
 configuring, 28-29, 37-39
 name resolution, 26-28
 node types, 36-38
 overview of, 26
NetDiag utility, 58
Network Address Translation. *See* NAT (Network Address Translation)
Network and Dial-up Connections window
 DHCP client configuration, 85, 98-99
 DHCP server installation, 90
 DNS client configuration, 57, 72
 ICS configuration, 349
 TCP/IP configuration, 3-4, 13-14
 WINS configuration, 31, 40
network cards, 22
network services, publishing, 165-167, 174-177
Networking Services
 configuring WINS, 41
 installing DHCP server, 80, 90-92
 installing IAS, 310-311
 installing WINS, 31
New Dfs Root Wizard, 223-224, 233-236
New Interface for NAT dialog box, 353-354
New Object - Group dialog box, 125-126
New Object - Shared Folder dialog window, 172

New Object - User dialog box, 118-119, 128
New Resource Record dialog box, 54-55, 70
New User Account Parameters window, 106
New Zone Wizard, 52, 67-68
node types, NetBIOS, 36-38, 46-47
NS (Name Server), DNS, 54
Nslookup utility, 58
ntbtlog.txt file, 384
NTDS Settings object, 204, 213
NTFS
 security auditing, 261-262, 269-271
 shared web folder permissions, 242, 251-252
 upgrading to dynamic storage, 219-220

O

operating systems. *See* OS (operating systems)
Optional Windows Networking Components Wizard dialog box, 41
organizational units. *See* OUs (organizational units)
OS (operating systems)
 legacy hardware support, 361-362, 370-371
 recovering hard disk data, 378-380, 387-389
 repairing with Recovery Console, 377-378, 387
 repairing with startup options, 376-377, 385-386
 restoring from backup, 380-381, 389-394
OUs (organizational units)
 creating/managing, 111-113, 126-130
 delegating control of, 114, 130-132
 delegating control to administrator, 142-143, 153-155
 delegating control to user, 200-202, 209-212
 security settings for, 137
Override/Forcing Group Policy, 159

P

P-node (point-to-point node), NetBIOS, 37
PAP (Password Authentication Protocol), 304
passwords
  IAS, 313-315
  user account, 119
Performance Logs and Alerts, 399, 405-406
Performance Monitor
  configuring alerts/logging, 398-399, 405-406
  defined, 396
  monitoring real-time performance, 397-398
permissions
  OUs, 129-130
  remote access, 328
PING utility
  lab exercise on, 9-10
  troubleshooting ICS, 344-345, 350-351
  troubleshooting with, 22-23
PnP (Plug and Play) utility, 358
point-to-point node (P-node), NetBIOS, 37
Point-to-Point Tunneling Protocol. See PPTP
  (Point-to-Point Tunneling Protocol)
Pointer (PTR), DNS, 54
Ports Properties dialog box, 294
PPTP (Point-to-Point Tunneling Protocol)
  overview of, 283-284
  server-to-server, 283-285, 295-296
  VPN configuration, 282-283, 293-295
#PRE, 38-39
printers, shared, 164-165, 173-174
Processor Performance object counters, 397-398
PTR (Pointer), DNS, 54
publishing resources. See Active Directory, publishing
  resources

Q

Quota Entries for Local Disk dialog box, 221, 232
quotas, disk, 220-221, 231-232

R

RADIUS (Remote Authentication Dial-In User
  Service)
  configuring IAS, 302-303, 310-315
  IAS as, 301-302
  overview of, 301
RAS (Remote Access Security)
  configuring, 326-328, 336-338
  server-to-server PPTP connections, 283-285,
    295-296
RDP (Remote Desktop Protocol)
  defined, 322
  remote access security and, 327-328, 336-338
records, DNS database, 53-55, 68-70
Recovery Console
  commands, 377
  defined, 374
  repairing OS with, 377-378, 387
recursive queries, DNS, 74
regedt32.exe utility
  hotfix installations, 428
  service pack installations, 426
/release command switch, IPconfig, 22
remote access. See also security policies; Terminal
  Services
  key term quiz, 288, 298
  lab analysis test, 287, 298
  policies, 280-282, 291-293
  RRAS VPN servers, 278-280, 289-291
  server-to-server PPTP connections, 283-285,
    295-296
  troubleshooting, 305-307, 317-319
  VPN security and, 285-286, 296-297
  VPNs using PPTP connections, 282-283,
    293-295
Remote Access Security. See RAS (Remote Access
  Security)
Remote Administration, Terminal Services,
  323-324, 331-333

Remote Authentication Dial-In User Service. *See* RADIUS (Remote Authentication Dial-In User Service)
Remote Desktop Protocol. *See* RDP (Remote Desktop Protocol)
/renew command switch, IPconfig, 22
replication, Active Directory, 204-206, 214-215
Restore Wizard, 380-381, 390-394
Reverse Lookup Zone window, 66-68
ROUTE command, 6-8, 18-20
router, defined, 6
routes, configuring, 6-8, 18-20
Routing and Remote Access console
    authentication protocols, 305, 316
      NAT, 346, 352-353
      PPTP-based VPN connections, 318-319
      remote access policies, 281-282, 291-293, 307
      Remote Access Security, 285, 295-296
      RRAS VPN server, 279-280, 289-291
Routing and Remote Access Server Setup Wizard, 279-280, 289-291
RRAS (Routing and Remote Access Service)
    IAS and, 301-303, 310-315
    NAT and, 345-346, 351-354
    VPN servers and, 278-280, 289-291
RRAS VPN server, 278-280, 289-291
Run option, Start menu, 101

S

SACL (system access control list), 140
Safe mode, 374
Scope Name window, DHCP, 94
scopes
    defined, 93-94
    DHCP, 81-82, 92-96
security, 259-276
    configuring/auditing, 260-262, 269-271
    key term quiz, 268, 276
    lab analysis test, 267, 276

    settings, 264-266, 273-276
    templates, 262-264, 271-273
    Terminal Services, 326-328, 336-338
    Web/FTP sites and, 244-245, 254-255
Security Configuration and Analysis MMC snap-in, 264-266, 271-276
security policies
    audit policies, 139-141, 150-152
    defining, 137-138
    delegating group policy authority, 142-143, 153-155
    demand-dial routers, 303-305, 315-317
    group policy settings, 137-139, 148-150
    key term quiz, 147, 159, 309, 320
    lab analysis test, 146, 158-159, 308, 320
    overview of, 136-137, 300
    RRAS, configuring to use IAS, 301-303, 310-315
    troubleshooting group policies, 144-145, 156-158
    troubleshooting remote access policy, 305-307, 317-319
Security Settings for Computer Configurations, 149-150
Security Settings snap-in, 136, 158
Security Templates MMC snap-in, 263-264, 271-273
Select User, Computers, or Groups window, 131-132
server performance, 395-412
    alerts/logging, 398-399, 405-408
    disabling services, 401, 411-412
    Event Viewer, 399-400, 408-410
    key term quiz, 403, 412
    lab analysis test, 402, 412
    System Monitor, 396-398, 404-405
servers, TCP/IP on, 2-4, 13
service packs
    applying/verifying, 416, 426-427
    defined, 414

slipstreaming, 414-416, 424-425
uninstalling, 420-421, 428-429
Setting Definition dialog window, 151-152
shared folders, 162-163, 170-173
shared printers, 164-165, 173-174
Shiva Password Authentication Protocol (SPAP), 304
Sigverif.exe utility, 360-361, 368-370
slipstreaming, 414-416, 424-425
small office/home office (SOHO) environments, 342
software deployment. *See* group policies, software
  deployment
Software Installation Properties window, 185
Software Installation snap-in, 180-181
software, thin clients, 322
software updates, 413-430
    hotfixes, installing, 418-419, 428
    hotfixes, uninstalling, 420-421, 428-429
    key term quiz, 423, 430
    lab analysis test, 422, 430
    overview of, 414
    service packs, installing, 416, 426-427
    service packs, uninstalling, 420-421, 428-429
    slipstreaming, 414-416, 424-425
SOHO (small office/home office) environments, 342
SPAP (Shiva Password Authentication Protocol), 304
startup problems
    key term quiz, 383, 394
    lab analysis test, 382, 394
    log files, 374-375, 384-385
    overview of, 374
    recovering hard disk data, 378-380, 387-389
    repairing OS with Recovery Console,
      377-378, 387
    repairing OS with startup options, 376-377,
      385-386
    restoring OS/data from backup, 380-381,
      389-394
storage. *See* data storage
subnet masks
    custom, 4-6, 16-18
    DHCP scopes and, 95

system access control list (SACL), 140
System Monitor
    alerts/logging, 398-399, 405-408
    performance monitoring, 396-398, 404-405
Systems Settings Change dialog box, 220, 229

T

Task Manager, 401, 411-412
Tasks to Delegate dialog box, 114, 131
TCP/IP Properties dialog box, 31
TCP/IP (Transmission Control Protocol/Internet
  Protocol)
    custom subnet masks, 4-6, 16-18
    key term quiz, 12, 24
    lab analysis, 11, 24
    NetBIOS names, 37
    routes, 6-8, 18-20
    servers/clients, 2-4, 13
    troubleshooting, 8-10, 20-24
templates, security
    administering, 262-264, 271-273
    importing/applying, 138-139, 148-150
    overview of, 159
templates, user profiles, 108-109, 122-123
Terminal Server User group, 337
Terminal Services, 321-340
    key term quiz, 330, 340
    lab analysis test, 329, 339
    overview of, 322-323
    Remote Access Security, 326-328, 336-338
    Remote Administration, 323-324, 331-333
    Terminal Services Licensing Server, 324-326,
      333-335
Terminal Services Configuration program,
  336-338
Terminal Services Licensing Server, 324-326,
  333-335
Terminal Services Setup window, 331-332
terminology. *See* key term quiz
thin client software, 322

Time to Live (TTL) field, 23
TRACERT utility, 10, 23-24
Transmission Control Protocol/Internet Protocol. *See*
  TCP/IP (Transmission Control Protocol/Internet
  Protocol)
Transmission Security, implementing, 327-328,
  336-338
Triple DES (3DES), 304
troubleshooting. *See also* startup, troubleshooting
    Active Directory replication, 204-206, 214-215
    DHCP, 86-87, 100-102
    DNS name resolution, 58-59, 73-74
    driver signing, 361
    group policies, 144-145, 156-158
    hotfixes/service packs, 420-421, 428-429
    ICS, 344-345, 350-351
    IIS, 245-246, 255-257
    remote access policy, 305-307, 317-319
    TCP/IP, 8-10, 20-24
    WINS client, 31-33, 46-47
Troubleshooting Wizard, 362, 370-371
Trusting Domains window, Dfs, 234
TTL (Time to Live) field, 23
.txt extension, 39

UNC (Universal Naming Convention), 163, 172
Update.exe utility, 416
updates, 358-359, 365-366. *See also* software updates
Upgrade Disks dialog box, 228
upgrades, dynamic disks, 219
user configuration settings, 136
users. *See also* Active Directory, users/groups
    default user profiles, 107-109, 121-124
    deploying software for, 183-184
    publishing software for, 180
    user accounts, 104-107, 117-121

virtual directories, 249
Virtual Private Network. *See* VPN (Virtual Private
  Network)
volumes, 218-220
VPN (Virtual Private Network)
    overview of, 279
    PPTP connections, 282-283, 293-295
    RRAS VPN servers, 278-280, 289-291
    verifying connection security, 285-286,
      296-297

Web Sharing service, 242, 250
Web sites
    creating, 240-242, 249-252
    securing, 244-245, 254-255
Windows 2000 DNS server, 52-53, 62-64
Windows 2000 SP2
    downloading, 424
    installing, 415-416
Windows Components dialog box
    configuring IIS, 249
    installing DHCP server, 90
Windows Components Wizard
    configuring Terminal Services, 324,
      331-333
    enabling Terminal Services Licensing,
      116-117
    installing DHCP server, 80
    installing IAS, 310-311
    installing IIS, 249
Windows Explorer, 262, 269-270
Windows Installer, 181
Windows Internet Naming Service. *See* WINS
  (Windows Internet Naming Service)

Windows Optional Networking Components Wizard
    configuring WINS, 30-31, 40-41
    installing DHCP server, 80, 90-91
    installing Windows 2000 DNS Server, 52-53, 63
Windows Update web site, 358-359, 365-366
WINS (Windows Internet Naming Service)
    implementing/configuring, 29-31, 40-46
    node types and, 37
    overview of, 26
    troubleshooting, 31-33, 46-47

Z

.zap files, 180
Zone Name dialog box, 66
Zone Properties window, DNS, 71-72
Zone Type dialog box, 66-67

INTERNATIONAL CONTACT INFORMATION

AUSTRALIA
McGraw-Hill Book Company Australia Pty. Ltd.
TEL +61-2-9415-9899
FAX +61-2-9415-5687
http://www.mcgraw-hill.com.au
books-it_sydney@mcgraw-hill.com

CANADA
McGraw-Hill Ryerson Ltd.
TEL +905-430-5000
FAX +905-430-5020
http://www.mcgrawhill.ca

GREECE, MIDDLE EAST,
NORTHERN AFRICA
McGraw-Hill Hellas
TEL +30-1-656-0990-3-4
FAX +30-1-654-5525

MEXICO (Also serving Latin America)
McGraw-Hill Interamericana Editores S.A. de C.V.
TEL +525-117-1583
FAX +525-117-1589
http://www.mcgraw-hill.com.mx
fernando_castellanos@mcgraw-hill.com

SINGAPORE (Serving Asia)
McGraw-Hill Book Company
TEL +65-863-1580
FAX +65-862-3354
http://www.mcgraw-hill.com.sg
mghasia@mcgraw-hill.com

SOUTH AFRICA
McGraw-Hill South Africa
TEL +27-11-622-7512
FAX +27-11-622-9045
robyn_swanepoel@mcgraw-hill.com

UNITED KINGDOM & EUROPE
(Excluding Southern Europe)
McGraw-Hill Education Europe
TEL +44-1-628-502500
FAX +44-1-628-770224
http://www.mcgraw-hill.co.uk
computing_neurope@mcgraw-hill.com

ALL OTHER INQUIRIES Contact:
Osborne/McGraw-Hill
TEL +1-510-549-6600
FAX +1-510-883-7600
http://www.osborne.com
omg_international@mcgraw-hill.com

www.ingramcontent.com/pod-product-compliance
Lightning Source LLC
Chambersburg PA
CBHW080136060326

40689CB00018B/3803